To Have and to Hold

Larry E. Hudson Jr.

To Have and to Hold

SLAVE WORK AND FAMILY LIFE IN

ANTEBELLUM SOUTH CAROLINA

THE UNIVERSITY OF GEORGIA PRESS

ATHENS AND LONDON

© 1997 by the University of Georgia Press
Athens, Georgia 30602
All rights reserved
Designed by Betty Palmer McDaniel
Set in 10/14 Janson Text by G&S Typesetters, Inc.
Printed and bound by Braun-Brumfield, Inc.
The paper in this book meets the guidelines for
permanence and durability of the Committee on
Production Guidelines for Book Longevity of the
Council on Library Resources.

Printed in the United States of America
01 00 99 98 97   c   5 4 3 2 1

Library of Congress Cataloging in Publication Data
Hudson, Larry E., Jr., 1952–
     To have and to hold : slave work and family life
in antebellum South Carolina / Larry E. Hudson, Jr.
        p.   cm.
     Includes bibliographical references and index.
     ISBN 0-8203-1830-2 (alk. paper)
     1. Slaves—South Carolina—Social conditions.
     2. Slaves—South Carolina—Family relationships.
     3. Plantation life—South Carolina—History—19th century.
     4. South Carolina—History—1775–1865.
     I. Title.
     E445.S7H83   1997
     305.5'67'09757—dc20   96-13711

British Library Cataloging in Publication Data available

In loving memory of Dorothy

The work of the day being over, I sat down upon my
doorstep, pipe in hand, to rest awhile in
the cool of the evening.

—*To Have and to Hold* by Mary Johnston

Contents

Genealogical Charts

Preface

Writing in 1908, W. E. B. Du Bois complained about the difficulty in arriving at some "clear picture of the family relations of slaves between the Southern apologist and his picture of cabin life, with idyllic devotion and careless toil, and that of the abolitionist, with his tales of family disruption and cruelty and illegitimate mulattoes." He warned that "between these pictures the student must steer clear to find a reasonable statement of the average truth."[1] *To Have and to Hold: Slave Work and Family Life in Antebellum South Carolina* is an attempt to walk a line between these two extremes. If it has a bias, it is against so heavy an emphasis on the brutality of the institution that it obscures the humanity, endeavor, and creativity of the enslaved. Slavery was a brutal institution deserving of all the condemnation heaped upon it; but all too often, our indictment of the system leads to the implicit indictment of those who were its unwilling victims.

In *To Have and to Hold*, rather than focusing on the institution of slavery, I examine two focal areas in the lives of slaves: work and family. Slave owners used slaves as their property, for their own benefit. Whatever relationships developed between master and slave, the economic factor remained fundamental. Few masters purchased slaves merely for the pleasure of their company or as objects for their sadism. The basic ethos behind plantation management was "dictated by a desire for profit maximization and the need to reduce losses."[2] The political economy of the South echoed as loudly in the public world of the slave owner's farm and plantation as their economic imperatives did in the private world of the slaves. Slave owners wanted their slaves to work hard and, when possible, to reproduce themselves, whereas slaves wanted as much control over their lives as they could wrest from their owners.

The interests of masters and the hopes of slaves converged in the area of work and family. Antebellum slave owners and their slaves knew that the stability of the economic and social institutions in both worlds depended upon the slaves' productivity in the work arena and reproductivity in the quarters. Slaves also were aware that their work efforts for their owners and for themselves facilitated the development and maintenance of important institutions in the slave quarters, although their efforts could not guarantee stability in their private world. Slaves were not passive victims. Few ever became what their owners wished them to be: hardworking but docile, enterprising but obedient. The slaves' domestic economy—the production and marketing of goods by, for, and largely among themselves—was made possible by a system under which masters encouraged the slaves to work first for their owners in the fields and then in gardens of their own. The forms of these labor arrangements were never determined wholly by slave owners individually or as a group; on every farm and plantation slaves endeavored to influence the nature of their work experience and take advantage of available opportunities. An ability (and willingness) to execute their work assignments in the public world efficiently gained the slaves more time to spend working their gardens and increased their "living space." The success of these efforts was reflected in a growing level of mutual trust that reduced the slave owners' need for vigilance and increased the slaves' autonomy.

Within the relative privacy of the slave quarters, the slaves' work efforts resulted in such accumulation of property and wealth that clear social and economic differences emerged among slave families. The slaves' internal economy facilitated the exchange of goods beyond the slave quarters and gave those with the necessary means access to goods and services otherwise available only through their owner, if at all. Those slaves who were organized in productive family units were best placed to exploit their gardens, accumulate property, and provide much needed extras for themselves. Rather than relying on their owners, these slaves endeavored to provide for their own. At the same time, their productivity, stability, and influence in the slave quarters made them increasingly indispensable to their owners.

The more slave owners relied on and trusted their slaves to remain hardworking, productive, and family centered, the more social and cultural space they conceded to the slaves. For their part, the slaves used this space to control important areas of their lives. Nowhere was this clearer than in their efforts to organize themselves into families and to work to protect the integrity of those families. A close reading of the available evidence on slave life—from both those who were slaves and those who owned slaves, as well as the statistical evidence from census data and birth records—reveals the importance slaves placed on their families as a source of emotional comfort and solace and as a major means to even the conditions in which they struggled against the demands of what was, ultimately, a pernicious and debilitating institution. In *To Have and to Hold* I use this evidence to examine the decisions slaves made about their lives. I show that, more often than not, given their options, slaves made good decisions—particularly those that affected the most important institution in the slaves' world: their families.

I try to present the slaves as the multidimensional individuals they were as they responded in intelligent and understandable ways to the world around them. They thus appear neither as passive objects of victimization nor as revolutionaries lacking only a suitable leader. This approach reflects my starting point: the belief that whether enslaved or free, African Americans produced and contributed a great deal to American life and culture; that the slave past has much to teach us about ourselves; and that the available sources must be mined to provide the fullest and most accurate story of that past.

Because slaves were property, they could neither legally own property nor marry; that they managed to do both was the reality of slavery. Antebellum slaves could and did act as if they were legal owners of land and other property, and slave owners, if not the courts, recognized them as property holders, which influenced the slaves' behavior.[3] Although slave owners could not (and many did not seek to) protect their slaves from marital separation through sale, slaves tried to render their marriages as binding as possible. The weight of community sanction of the slave marriage is evidenced in their courting and marriage rituals and the efforts slave quarter communities made to ensure that once married, partners remained faithful to each other.

All too often the law of slavery intruded upon the private world of the slaves but did not dominate their values. Nor did the slaves accept the legal impediments the public world placed upon their property ownership and family life. As slaves, African Americans had to adjust to the reality of their situation and the ever-present possibility of sale and family disruption. Their efforts to protect themselves against forced separation, for example, are evidenced in such cultural practices as naming patterns that tried to maintain a recognizable link between family members separated by sale or death.[4]

The enslaved claimed numerous rights and privileges even though unsanctioned by law. Among these were the right to "own" property and the privilege of marrying and establishing a family. Without legal protection, slaves had to use less formal methods to protect the results of their hard-earned efforts.

This book is about the slaves' endeavor to influence crucial areas of their lives, to exploit a small piece of land and produce surplus provisions that led to significant property accumulation in the slave quarters. Property holding improved the slaves' ability "to have and to hold" that which was most dear—a family.

For the slave to have and to hold anything of value under slavery demanded a constant struggle over terrain that was forever shifting and always uneven. The primacy of work in their lives remained constant: hard work promised the opportunity to produce necessary goods and services for themselves and some hope of family stability. By working together as a family unit enslaved men and women accumulated the financial and emotional resources that provided a buffer against the most debilitating evils of a cruel institution. Although they could not look to the law to protect what was most dear to them, there was much that they were able to have and to hold.

Acknowledgments

This study began in 1984 at the University of Keele as a Masters Thesis in United States History. Since my advisor Mary Ellison, Martin Crawford, Steve Mills, and David Adams guided me through the rigors of the Keele graduate program, I have incurred many debts and not a few friends.

The kind assistance and courtesy extended to me during my field trip to Washington, D.C., and North and South Carolina confirmed in me the wisdom of my choice of profession. I would like to thank Philip Morgan and John Blassingame who directed me toward the most pertinent libraries and archives, and David Moltke-Hansen and Allen Stokes who led me to important sources that might otherwise have been overlooked.

Edward Countryman was the first to read extracts from the dissertation and offered much needed encouragement and advice, as did Gad Heuman at Warwick University, and Howard Temperley at the University of East Anglia.

In Fall 1990, at the University of Rochester, I sat in on Eugene Genovese's final class at the school and, along with a number of very gifted students, found out that Genovese, the teacher, is as potent a force as Genovese, the scholar.

My colleagues at Rochester provided for me an atmosphere in which I could develop my teaching skills while preparing my manuscript for publication. As chair, the late Christopher Lasch, assisted by the then departmental secretary, Jean De Groat, went out of his way to ensure that I quickly settled into my new position, and had the time and funds for research trips, and the opportunity to present papers and discuss my ideas at conferences, workshops and seminars.

I presented versions of chapters at the Social Science History Association, Southern Historical Association, The Johns Hopkins University, and The College of William and Mary, as well as the University of Rochester. The book is much improved thanks to comments on my work from Jack Greene, Robert Gross, Charles Joyner, Franklin Knight, Roderick McDonald, Anne Patton Malone, Robert Olwell, Robert Paquette, James Roark, and Loren Schweninger.

I am especially grateful to those who read all or parts of the manuscript and offered helpful criticism, including: Richard Blackett, Daniel Littlefield, August Mieir, Phillip Morgan, Norrece Jones, Charles Joyner, Joseph Riedy, Deborah Gray White, and Mary Young. Throughout the seemingly unending process of rewrites and resubmissions to editors Stanley Engerman always willing to read and comment on the latest and finally the last version.

Of course, the assistance of friends and colleagues does not diminish my final responsibility for the ideas expressed in *To Have and To Hold*.

The inspiration for this study was kindled and continually nurtured by my dear friends from Pawleys Island, South Carolina: Patrick O'Rear, his late wife, Dorothy—to whose memory this book is dedicated—and their daughter, Noel O'Rear Morton.

Last but not least, my own sustenance has stemmed from an ever growing faith and a strong family. My mother, father and four siblings, each in their own way, has helped to make my life free from the burdens that so often hinder the completion of a project dear to one's heart. I love them, and thank them.

Introduction

The last fifteen years or so have witnessed a marked shift in the approach to the study of slave life and culture. The new focus on the slaves' domestic production and their internal economy has raised questions and moved attention away from what the masters did for the slaves to what the slaves were able to do for themselves.[1]

A close examination of work practices and their influence on behavior in the slave quarters suggests a clear relationship between the slaves' economic activities and family life: the work system was an important determinant of slave family structure. Because work was central in the lives of slaves, this book examines the work systems that slave owners operated in rural South Carolina. Antebellum slave owners applied work systems they hoped would produce slaves who were industrious, efficient, manageable, and contented. For their part, slaves aspired to the twin goals of some control over their working life and the ability to create and maintain social institutions of their own making. As was so often the case under slavery, neither master nor slave was ever completely satisfied with the resulting arrangement.

A major point of intersection in the aspirations of both masters and slaves, however, was the slave family. Although slaveholders tended to view the slave family as little more than a means of controlling and reproducing their slave labor force, the slaves cherished the opportunity to organize their lives around the family unit and made it the primary institution in the slave quarters. The quality of life former slaves recalled having experienced under slavery was consistently informed by the nature of their interaction with family members. Slaves reached for any opportunity to take control of this important area of their lives, and the work and garden systems under which they worked provided a small window of opportunity. Because slave owners wanted hardworking and well-behaved slaves and slaves equally desired the economic and social space that might improve their ability to protect themselves and their families against the rigors of slavery, the links between work and slave family structure were clear to both antagonists.[2] Although South Carolina slave owners tried to use their advantageous position to realize their goals without making any concession to their slaves, they had to accede to the slaves' demands for some control over their private life. If masters were to realize any of the gains they expected from innovative work systems, they had to give the slaves some incentive to fulfill their part.

By looking at the state not as a whole but, whenever possible, as three distinct regions (low, middle, and up-country), I identify and examine the work practices of each region and assess their influence on slave family structure. The evidence suggests that work systems facilitated the creation of some economic and social space between the slaves and their world and the owners and their world that permitted the slaves some control over their family life. Working for themselves, slaves throughout the state managed to provide more than a modicum of their needs. The production of surplus goods, made possible by laboring under work and garden systems, resulted in considerable property accumulation and social differences among slaves. Another result was the development of a dynamic commercial arena among slaves.

The variations in wealth among slave families reflected the differences among families, not only in size but more in performance. How well an individual executed his or her work obligations was important; how a group of individuals organized in a mutually supportive and productive economic unit was more important as hardworking and productive families established for themselves a position from which they could better protect their immediate interests. For most, this was the integrity of the family.

How slaves worked, therefore, is a major concern of this book because the satisfactory execution of work assignments for their owners directly contributed to the slave family's ability to create a living space between the public world of the master and the more private world of the slaves. The more sophisticated the work system under which the slaves labored, the more likely they were to accumulate the property that could affect their life chances under slavery. The slaves' ability to find suitable partners, marry, start families, and provide some protection against external attacks was dependent on their ability to function well in the work arena. South Carolina's slaves gave themselves some edge against the violent attacks on their persons and their families that were an ever-present characteristic of slavery by organizing themselves into productive, mutually supportive family units. At their most successful, slave families could hope to have some control over important areas of their lives—even to begin to carve out lives of their own.

The aim of this volume, however, is not simply to show that the slave family was strong and vibrant, equipped with the adaptive abilities required to survive the harshness and brutality of slavery in the American South. It attempts to present a more satisfactory way of looking at the family and assessing its strengths and weaknesses and to present an explanation for slaves organizing in stable and productive families that goes beyond the "natural tendency" or "African retentions" arguments.[3] To demonstrate that the slaves had or did not have strong stable families, then, is only part of the exercise. More relevant is an appreciation of what the family meant to the slaves, the numerous benefits it provided, and the disadvantages for those who, for whatever reason, found themselves without a supportive family group.

As far as possible, this study draws on sources that give voice to the slaves and those who knew them best or those closest to them. Whenever possible, I let the slaves and former slaves tell of their lives. In this way a little more light might shine on their intimate world: how they worked, loved, played, and viewed their world in an attempt, as Charles Joyner terms it, to recreate the "emotional texture" of slave family life.[4]

This book is divided into two parts. The first seeks to explain why slaves worked so hard at the risky business of organizing themselves in stable families. Work and the provision of extra goods and services for family members are considered to be major organizing principles of stable family formation. The opportunity to reap material benefits from working within a family unit provided a solid framework for the slave family, which, in turn, determined the contours of the community's social structure. Within that structure, the best-organized families dominated the slave quarter community. The stronger the families, the better able they were to provide the goods and services that sometimes made the difference between surviving the rigors of slavery and becoming one of the many casualties of an often cruel and brutal institution. The second section examines the primary obstacles that lay in the slaves' path toward the fulfillment of their desire to find partners, marry, and raise families. Finally, an attempt is made to assess South Carolina slaves' success in constructing and maintaining stable families.

To provide a general model that might serve for the wider slave South, for purposes of analysis, the state is divided into three regions—low country, middle country, and up-country—that by virtue of their topography, climate, and length of settlement approximate conditions to be found throughout the antebellum South. Whenever possible and pertinent, I will point out any advantage slaves might have enjoyed depending on which of the state's three regions was their home and how the different conditions might have influenced their life chances, particularly as they pertain to family stability. I hope that this approach will provide a useful method for examining the quality of life experienced by slaves throughout the antebellum South.

҂I҂

For Better for Worse:
The Slaves' World of Work

Until recently, popular pictures of slavery have identified a class-based construct of slave life in which the slaves who lived and worked within the world of the master received from him the benefits and rewards that determined their economic and social well-being. These "fortunate" few occupied the upper echelons of the slave hierarchy, while the vast majority of slaves, whose working life was spent in the fields, struggled to rise above their lowly status and move into the ranks of the slave elite.[1] The primary means by which slaves were able to gain status in the private world of the slave quarters, however, was not necessarily related to their physical or social proximity to their masters but depended far more on their ability and willingness to work hard for themselves.

Slaves had to perform well in the public arena working for their masters, but how they used their time outside the master's world profoundly affected their economic and social life. Therefore, unskilled field slaves, who had little or no positive contact with white masters and infrequently were recipients of white largesse, could still accumulate the material wherewithal to place themselves high up in the social hierarchy of the slave quarters.[2]

How they used the time available after completing the work assigned by the master primarily determined the economic and social benefits that accrued to the slaves, their families, and the slave quarter community. The rewards that resulted from these "extra-work" activities structured

I

significant institutions in the slave quarters, particularly slave family life. Of course, the nature and quantity of "extra" time the slave enjoyed depended on the disposition of the master, his financial situation, the location of the plantation, the amount of land available for cultivation, the staples produced, and the size of the slave labor force. These were the factors that not only made slavery viable in some areas and less so in others but also gave the institution its perplexing variety, examples of which were all present in antebellum South Carolina.[3]

By the late eighteenth century a system whereby slaves were assigned a measured amount of work to be completed within a given period of time, usually a working day, had taken root in low-country plantations.[4] Low-country slaves were thus permitted some control over the length of their working day. The agricultural standard workday of "from sunup to sundown" was not forced on all low-country slaves, whether they labored in the rice or the cotton fields. Furthermore, as the practice of tasking spread to a wider variety of labor activities on the plantation, it also moved beyond South Carolina's tidewater regions.

Although the task system did not automatically shorten the slaves' workday, this remained a consistent result and may have been intended. In most cases the length of the working day would have depended on the size of the task combined with the slave's ability, desire, and willingness to work at a pace that would complete the task within the allotted time. Writing in 1858, Sandy Island planter James R. Sparkman recorded that the "ordinary plantation task is easily accomplished during the winter months in 8 to 9 hours and in the summer, my people seldom exceed 10 hours labor per day." As the necessary incentive, "whenever the daily task is finished the balance of the day is appropriated to their own purposes."[5] For Sparkman the system clearly operated as an incentive for his slaves to work hard and complete their task as quickly as they could.

Some masters introduced an additional feature to the task system by making the slaves responsible for the working of a particular area of a field throughout the seasons' full cycle of ground preparation, planting, weeding, and harvesting. These planters hoped their slaves would develop an attachment to the land that might produce in them a sense of pride and responsibility.[6] One such planter, writing in 1833 in the *Southern Agriculturalist*, advocated this beneficial aspect of the task system: "Whatever tasks a negro commences with," he wrote, "are considered his throughout the working of the crop." Allowing that sickness and other unforeseen events were likely to produce a "little variation in this plan," the planter explained that "where a negro knows that the task he is working is to be worked by him the next time he goes over the field, he is induced, in order to render the next working as light as possible, to work it well at first."[7]

Where custom and experience had not already established the size of tasks, planters had to be careful with their allocations, for increasing a task once set, regardless of how quickly slaves completed their work, ran the risk of seriously disrupting the plantation routine.[8] J. R. Sparkman used a simple but popular formula for calculating and assigning tasks to his work-ers. Rather than gearing the work requirement to the best, the average, or the worst worker, as was sometimes done, Sparkman allocated tasks to each slave in proportion to the crucial variables of physical ability, age, and state of health. The Sparkman slaves were rated as quarter, half, three-quarters, or full task hands. In this way, allowances could be made for the individual and the proportion of a task he or she could be expected to ac-complish in a given period of time while the size of the task itself would remain fixed. For example, female slaves, who might normally have been considered full or three-quarter hands and assigned the corresponding task, would have had their work status reduced to quarter or half hand dur-ing a pregnancy and while they recovered from childbirth. Thus the old and the very young could be brought together as various fractions of a hand to work a full task. With such mixed groups, adult slaves could mind slave children not yet ready to go into the fields as working hands, instruct those about ready to take on more demanding field work, and keep an eye on those recovering from a pregnancy or an illness.[9] The classification of slaves into full hands and part hands soon became fixed as the arrangement "hardened into custom, backed by strong sentiment that many masters found it good policy to respect."[10]

In their recollections, former slaves from the low country viewed task-ing in much the same light as planters such as Sparkman. Born a slave on Waddalaw Island, Prince Smith recalled the workings of the task system on his plantation. There the slaves were categorized into three groups. The "whole hands," a "person in his prime," was given two tasks for his day's work. When slaves worked in cotton fields, a task would be from twenty-four to twenty-five rows, a row being thirty-five feet long by twenty-five feet wide. The three-quarter hand would be given a task of twelve rows. The working children were expected to manage a task of twelve rows, while the "old slaves" did a half task for a day's work. During the cotton-picking season, "de three forth hand had to pick thirty pound' an' de half han' twenty fur dere day's wurk." Characteristically, full hands were provided additional incentives to perform to their maximum rather than being set a minimum target. Smith also revealed that some of his fellows were tasked by the week, and those who failed to complete their assignments were obliged to work on Sunday.[11]

Other former slaves threw additional light on the workings and the widening use and significance of tasking. "Ebery slabe," recalled Sam Polite, born a slave on St. Helena Island, "hab tas' to do. Sometime one task sometime two tas' and sometime t'ree." As the demands of the plantation and the seasons changed, so would the slave's obligations. The bottom line was, as Polite pointed out, "You haf for wuk 'til tas' t'ru'. W'en cotton done mek, you hab odder tas'."[12] Failing to do one's task could have dire consequences, as Gabe Lance, a Sandy Island slave, recalled: "Didn't done task put 'em in barn and least cut they give 'em (with lash) been twenty-five to fifty."[13]

At its most successful the task system resulted in a degree of trust and mutual responsibility on the part of both master and slave. Masters were encouraged to maintain their part of the bargain. "Should any owner increase the work beyond what is customary," wrote one South Carolina planter, "he subjects himself to the reproach of his neighbors and to such discontent among his slaves to make them of but little use to him."[14] The slaves, in their turn, were expected to complete their assignments in an acceptable time, manner, and level of efficiency. Treating them as individuals and giving them responsibility for a particular piece of land, the task system did not require the close supervision usually associated with forced labor. Tasked slaves were expected not only to do their jobs but to do them well. Having satisfactorily accomplished their side of the bargain, masters were obliged to respect the slaves "nonwork" time—indeed, this time "became sacrosanct," and the slaves' right to use it as they saw fit (within certain parameters) was acknowledged by low-country planters.[15]

By the early nineteenth century, the tasking requirements were well established in all Sea Island operations.[16] The popularity of tasking in rice-

and cotton-producing areas—with all the material and spiritual rewards the slaves could reap from the system—soon spread to other related tasks, to other staples, and to other regions of the state. The preference of low-country planters and their slaves for the task system was not restricted to the coastal rice- and long-staple cotton-producing regions of South Carolina.

The cotton-producing regions of the middle country were no stranger to the task system of labor organization. John M. DeSaussure, owner of plantations in Kershaw and Sumter districts, organized his workers under the task system in producing both short-staple cotton and corn. The slaves would work a full acre of forty-two rows at five feet distance apart as a task when working cotton. Here time and experience had added a certain sophistication to the setting of tasks whereby masters could make allowance for special circumstances. DeSaussure instructed his overseer: "In shaving down, or trimming and the land [is] hard, [you] may give five rows less, but give five rows over acre at next working." [17]

Orangeburg District was typical of the middle country. Its population of some 16,224 slaves and 8,108 white inhabitants in 1860 reflected the extensive slaveholding and large plantations that characterized the antebellum period. Its average slaveholding was about 16 shared among some 1,044 masters. In her study of Orangeburg County, Jayne Morris-Crowther concentrates on those slaveholders who "had the greatest interest in the system," namely, those owning more than 15 slaves. Of these, the average holding was 36 slaves, and a few planters owned as many as 169 and 184 slaves.[18]

Orangeburg District planter Michael Gramling used a sophisticated system of tasking on his middle-country plantation. He assigned his slaves the same area of ground for their task throughout the growing season, a practice that probably reflected his desire to create in his slaves a sense of responsibility as well as a greater attachment to the plantation. Gramling divided up his fields into cotton tasks of "three quarters of an acre large." Furthermore, although he mainly produced cotton and corn, Gramling did not hesitate to use the task system with nonagricultural pursuits, as when he commenced a lucrative barrel-making operation in 1847.[19]

Middle-country former slaves recalled their positive and negative experiences with the task system. Marion District's John Glover, born late in slavery on Eliza Gerson's plantation, recalled that when "dey ring dem bells en blow dem horns in de mornin', dat mean you better get up en go about your task fer dat day." Fellow Marion District resident Louisa Gause reported that her overseer would "give yu a task to do en you had to do it, if you never want your neck broke." Agnes James recalled that her "old Massa," Hector Cameron, "would give her [Mamma] task to pick cotton en hoe cotton en peas." Jake McLeod, a Sumter District former slave, grew up on his master's farm in Lynchburg. He remembered the consequences of not doing the assigned work. They "give us task to do en if you didn't do it, dey put de little thing to you . . . some kind of whip."[20]

Of course, the task system did not suit all slaves or all masters. Edgefield District's James H. Hammond, for example, expended a great deal of time and energy in a vain attempt to break his slaves of their habit of working under the task system. He feared the independence the task system gave the slaves, "both in the field, where they were free to determine the pace of their work, and during the unsupervised hours after their tasks were completed." Eventually, Hammond and his slaves "reached a truce that permitted a level of production acceptable to Hammond and a level of endeavor tolerable to the slaves": the Hammond slaves continued to work under the task system and Hammond continued to complain about slaves who were free to leave the fields by mid-afternoon.[21]

Despite the obvious benefits to slaves of tasking, some preferred alternatives to this highly individualized system of labor. Clarendon District's Gabe Lockier had struggled in the fields. "I was so slow," he recalled, "dat when de rest knock off dey make me work on . . . my hands look like dey put on wrong." Lockier may sometimes have enjoyed the assistance of his fellow slaves, someone in the mold of Richard Mack of Orangeburg District, a slave to Cherry and Bebo Mack. As he explained, "Had task I done my task and I help others with their task so they wouldn't get whipped."[22] Mack could enjoy helping his fellow slaves and reaping whatever rewards came his way, be they spiritual or earthly, because the task system allowed this slave the opportunity to develop his physical and technical abilities and the occasion to demonstrate his individuality, as well as his sense of community responsibility.

Sylvia Cannon, born a slave on Bill Gregg's Florence District plantation, described one of the numerous and perhaps unmeasurable benefits slaves obtained from a work system that permitted them a measure of au-

6

tonomy and encouraged the development of pride and personal satisfaction in the crucial arena of work. As she explained, the "overseer didn' have to be right behind to see that you work." On the Gregg plantation all the fields were named and the overseer "just had to call en de horn en tell you what field to go work in dat day." On Saturday "evening" the overseer would come "to see what you done." And if your work proved to be unsatisfactory, "he put de nigger dog on you en he run you all night till he find you [and whip you]."[23] Although less prevalent in the literature on the middle regions of the state, the task system was clearly not uncommon in the middle country. There as elsewhere, some jobs were less suitable for tasking, and the system operated best with a large and diverse labor force.

From the earliest days the South Carolina up-country differed from the rest of the state, yet, even here, the practice of tasking was not uncommon. The up-country had been settled largely by migrants from the frontiers of Pennsylvania, Virginia, and North Carolina about the time of the Revolution. Before 1795, the area remained cut off from the rest of the state because transportation was so difficult. It was no easier to travel to the coast than it was to reach Philadelphia.[24] One result of the region's inaccessibility was that self-sufficient farming characterized the region. The cash crops that were most commonly produced were cereals, wheat, flour, and tobacco, with only very small amounts of cotton. But the spread of short-staple cotton to the up-country after 1795 quickly displaced tobacco as both farmers and planters turned to the new crop.

High cotton prices converted grain and tobacco farmers to cotton production and turned many small farmers into slaveholders and some into planters. Up-country slaveholders could have done no worse than to look to more experienced middle- and low-country cotton producers for guidance in organizing the business of cotton production.

Despite its sparse population and smaller production units with fewer slaves, the up-country quickly took on many of the characteristics of the other cotton-producing regions. In 1760, less than one-tenth of the colony's slaves resided outside the low country; by 1810 almost one-half lived in the South Carolina hinterland. Between 1820 and 1850, the up-country slave population grew from 56,529 to 118,474. The average slave-holding was approximately 11 divided among some 5,560 slaveholders. By 1860, the 1,210 farms and plantations of the up-country averaged

142 acres of improved land and 242 acres of unimproved land. Of course, the amount and quality of land masters had to share with their slaves had a profound impact on the slaves' world. Furthermore, with cotton now its main staple, the region's corn, wheat, rice, oats, peas, beans, and livestock were grown primarily for home consumption.[25]

William J. Connors, of Lancaster District, was in many ways a typical up-country planter. With two or three slave families consisting of probably no more than eight to ten working hands, Connors and his two sons worked his plantation, producing cotton as its main cash crop. Whenever possible, Connors used the task system. An entry for July 3, 1841, reveals that he tasked his plow hands. Jim and Elvira, plow hands, were able to complete their tasks by noon, "after which they worked for themselves." An entry four days later reads: "Plows finished the 19 acre field by mid-afternoon after which they worked for themselves." The hoe hands constituted the majority of the workers and could have expected a longer day in the field. The following entry suggests that they too were tasked: "The hoe hands drew up cotton in the 30 acre field, but about 11 o'clock, before they got through their tasks we were blest with a good heavy storm." Two weeks later, Connors complained that the female hands hoeing slips had not completed their tasks and that they would have done so "had it not been for Emma that was somewhat behind . . . all of the others [having] finished their tasks." That these slaves were accustomed to completing their assignments efficiently is further suggested by an entry in Connors's journal. Emma's slowness and the group's inability to complete its task was probably caused by Emma who, two days later, was listed as "sick."[26]

Up-country former slaves left a mixed picture of their working life. Isiah Jefferies was born a slave in Cherokee District in 1849. He did not confirm the prevalence of the task system there, but he did recall that although "de whole plantation was allus up at sun up . . . we did not work very late." William Pratt lived in Chester District and had belonged to Robert K. Kennedy. He recalled having to get up before day, going to work, and working until sundown. In addition, he had to work all day Saturday. Another Chester District resident, Benjamin Russell, born in 1849, recalled that as a boy, he plowed from "sun to sun" with only one hour for a break. But Victoria Adams, born in 1847, a Fairfield District slave, told a different tale. Adams's workday was both broken up and considerably shorter than that of her Chester counterpart. She worked from "light til noon, with dinner 'til 2 pm, then work 'til dark." Adams also noted that the slaves "don't do much work at night after they gets home." For Laurens District slaves, however, work could go on into the night if they failed to complete their tasks. George Fleming recalled that when slaves came from the field "deir day's work was done. Fact is everybody's work was done 'cept maybe some of the spinners or weavers dat didn't quite finish deir task." But Fleming adds, "dey was the onliest ones dat had to ever work after dark, and dat not often." Where planters were willing to experiment with arrangements that came closest to satisfying both master and slaves, the task system was likely to be used in one form or another. Sometimes used in combination with the gang system, variations of the task system developed to suit particular conditions.[27]

The situation in the up-country, like that of the middle country, appears to be one of variety and experimentation with labor systems.[28] Once again, the Connors plantation might be used as an example of the region and its likely work systems. Because up-country plantations tended to be much smaller than those in the other regions of the state and with markedly fewer hands, it would not always have been possible to set tasks and expect they would be completed in an easily measured period of time. It was probably more common for assigned tasks to be put aside temporarily to attend to more immediate plantation work, forever carrying over the tasks to the next day. These work assignments—much of their distinction as task work lost—would deny the slaves some of the more obvious benefits of the system. A correlation probably existed between a small work force, low level of job specialization with little or no division of labor, and a low occurrence of tasking. This should not automatically eliminate the possibility that tasking was used by up-country masters when it was convenient and practicable. But where the task system was used, slaves could enjoy certain material and psychological benefits not available to those working a tight regimen of from "sun to sun" under an inflexible gang system.

Given the statewide variations in the practice of tasking, the location of South Carolina's slaves would have produced markedly different attitudes toward their work and the world around them. The level of autonomy, pride, and personal esteem slaves could experience hinged to a large extent on which part of the state they lived in. Slaves on large rice and cotton plantations in the low country were far more likely than their up-country counterparts to have worked under a sophisticated system of tasking, while slaves on middle-country plantations, could have expected to perform most of their work requirements under a task system if the size of the labor force permitted it. Where tasking was not in evidence, a work system that incorporated elements, and some of the benefits, of tasking developed. Complementing these work arrangements was the opportunity for the slaves to work a small piece of land for their own use. This privilege was one of the major planks on which the task system was successfully built.

When the task system, with its promise of time to work for oneself, was combined with access to a small garden, the benefits slaves could obtain under a task and garden system (and other work arrangements that produced similar results) rendered the slaves' regional experience less varied. Although the slaves' location in the state, on larger or smaller farms or plantations in the low, middle, or up-country, could have had a profound effect on their material, social, and spiritual well-being, the significant variable was the ability successfully to exploit their opportunities.

By the 1820s, the practice of slaves working a small area of land for their own use was common throughout the state. Some planters used coercion to encourage their slaves to develop what they considered to be a very good habit. In an 1828 edition of the *Southern Agriculturalist*, the Butler estate overseer, Roswell King, describing conditions on the plantation, advised that "every means be used to encourage [the slaves] and impress on their minds the advantage of holding property and the disgrace of idleness." If slaves could be taught the value of industry and enterprise through the management of their own "piece of land," so the argument went, these qualities would be reflected in the work they did for the master and in their feelings both for him and for the "home place." Two years later, the journal printed a letter in which the author, B. M. McBride, a large planter, made the same point even more forcefully. "All my slaves," he announced, "are to be supplied with sufficient land on which [the overseer will] encourage and even compel them to plant and cultivate a crop." As to the destiny of this crop McBride was unequivocal: it would be purchased from the slaves "at a fair price."[29]

In encouraging the practice of slaves' use of land for their own purposes, masters seemed to have had in mind a curious mixture of duty, discipline, and a desire to extend their sphere of control. They stood to benefit greatly from any labor arrangement based on a work and garden system because it promised to instill in the slave a sense of industry; encouraging the slave literally to "grab a stake in slavery," the master was likely to get the best out of workers who felt some attachment to the home place, and, by extension, to the master. Masters thus could expect that the values of industry and economic success which characterized the public world of the white South would permeate the more private world of the quarters.[30]

When slave owners combined elements of the task system with the opportunity for their slaves to cultivate a piece of land, they anticipated an increase in the slaves' identification with the plantation and with the economic and moral concerns of the master.[31] On McBride's plantation the slaves would be tasked and their own crops would be tended "during their idle hour after task work is done," which, as McBride was convinced, might otherwise "be spent in the perpetration of some act that would subject them to severe punishment." In South Carolina as elsewhere, masters tended to agree that slaves ought to be kept as busy as possible working and, consequently, out of mischief. The apogee of this relationship was summed up neatly by the overseer Roswell King in 1828. "No Negro," the experienced King asserted, "with a well stocked poultry house, a small crop advancing, a canoe partly finished, or a few cubs unsold, all of which he calculates soon to enjoy, will ever run away."[32] Encouraging an economic "busyness" in their slaves, masters, of course, gained a formidable method of controlling and disciplining slaves who relied increasingly upon work done in their gardens to augment their daily or weekly allowance and improve their standard of living.

Low-country planters endeavored to reap the benefits of a work and garden system that encouraged their slaves to work quickly and efficiently. Beaufort District's Oliver P. Bostick appeared before the Southern Claims Commission (SCC), established in 1871, to hear claims for financial reimbursement from Southerners loyal to the Union whose property had been commandeered by Union troops during the Civil War. He testified that he had allowed his slaves "to own and have their own property and have little crops of their own, for it encouraged them to do well and be satisfied at home."[33] Eliza Goethe, also of Beaufort District, testified that she and her husband "allowed our slaves some land to plant some provisions in their spare time."[34] Osland Bailey owned a plantation on Wadalaw Island in Charleston County, where Prince Smith recalled that all the slaves "could plant as much as we could for our own use. We could raise fowls and could raise hogs." Sam Mitchell, who had been raised a slave on John Chaplin's Ladies Island plantation, reported, "De slave had 'bout two task ob land to cultivate for se'f in w'at call nigger field." St. Helena Island's Sam Polite recalled that he and his fellow slaves might "hab two or t'ree tas' ob land," work on which would be done "w'en you knock off work." Dr. Arthur Gordon Rose had plantations on Big Island and Coals Island, where his slaves were tasked, and "when you finished your task you could quit." Henry Brown, who had belonged to Rose, recalled one of the many variations on the task and garden system. On Rose's plantation, work began at 4 A.M. when the "people went in the garden." This garden consisted of some three acres planted by the master and worked by the slaves for their own use. The crops from the garden were distributed to the slaves and provided a fresh and fairly constant stock of fruit and vegetables. At about 8 or 9 A.M. the slaves would finish their work in the garden and go into the fields. Even with this late start, some of the slaves were able to "finnish their tas' by twelve," though others might have to "work 'til seven but had the tas' to finnish."[35] Such variations on the task and garden system were not peculiar to the low country, and their very success may well have encouraged imitation elsewhere. Moreover, work and garden systems would have traveled with low-country residents seeking new and less expensive land in the interior.

In the middle country, planters such as J. B. Miller of Sumter County were probably not typical, but Miller's ideas on plantation management spread far beyond his own plantation. An estate manager and commissioner in equity, Miller had a great deal of influence on the many slaveholders who called on him for help and advice. In 1855, he recorded that his slaves "all have land to plant—very inclusive and very near to them." He gave them time and made "them manure and plant their crop as I do my own."[36] Jake McLeod's master may well have been one such planter influenced by the system used successfully by Miller. McLeod recalled that slaves on his Lynchburg plantation were given a "garden en extra patches of we own dat we work on Saturday evenings." Jake was one of about twenty-five slaves who were members of some three or four families on a plantation of about six hundred acres.[37]

Middle-country slaves commonly worked a piece of land for their own use, but the amount of the land at their disposal varied widely. Priscilla Prince, who had belonged to Peter Odom of Marlboro District, enjoyed the use of "a small garden around my house," and her husband, Carolina Prince, "had just such a garden at his 'quarter.'"[38] The Princes' small gardens did not compare to the amount of land made available to Silas Cook. A senior man on Thomas Cook's Marlboro District plantation, Silas had been Cook's blacksmith and foreman and had been "allowed to cultivate four acres for my own benefit."[39]

No automatic correlation existed between status in the public world of the master and size of land given for slaves' use. Like Cook, Pompey Lewis was a blacksmith, but his allotment of land was substantially smaller. Lewis testified before the SCC that he cultivated no land of his own because he had "less than a quarter acre around my dwelling."[40] Low status in the public world did not deny slaves the chance to control sizable pieces of land. Marion District's Agnes James benefited from her master Hector Cameron's policy of allowing "all de people . . . [to] make dey own garden." Hector Smith's master also "low em all to have a garden of dey own [which] dey work . . . by de moonshine en fore light good in de mornin' cause dey had to turn dey hand to dey master work when day light come." Where Genia Woodberry worked as a slave near Bretton Neck in Marlboro District, her master Jim Stevenson "gi'e he colored peoples mos' ev'thing dey hab en den he 'low every family to hab en acre uv land uv dey own to plant." This land was worked at night.[41] Middle-country slaves, then, could have boasted the use of some land, if only a small patch around or near their dwelling.

The work and garden system, though perhaps not as widespread and sophisticated in the middle country as in the low country, was, nonetheless, fairly common. The peculiar features of the up-country, however, would have denied many slaves there as full a participation in the work and garden system because agricultural units were both more numerous and smaller than in the lower regions of the state.[42]

It was far more typical in the up-country for the master or mistress to plant a large garden of some three, four, or five acres from which the slaves were supplied with fresh vegetables as part of their regular food allowance. The Reverend Thomas Harper, who had been a slave on John Stanley's Broad River plantation in Fairfield District, recalled that the slaves "didn't have any garden," but Stanley "had a big plantation, lots of slaves and worked a garden for himself." John Davenport of Newberry District reported a similar situation on Pierce Lake's farm; Lake had a big garden, "but he didn't let his slaves have any garden of their own." Lake ran a small to medium-sized operation with the labor of about two families of slaves. Albert Oxner and his fellow slaves fared little better living in a much larger slave quarters. Their owner, Chesley Davies, farmed near Indian Creek with some seventy-five to one hundred slaves. Despite the material and social benefits that might have accrued to Davies from the work and garden system, his slaves "never had any of our own" but obtained their fresh vegetables "from de white folks' garden."[43]

In the up-country and elsewhere, however, even when masters operated communal gardens, slave gardens sometimes also existed. On Ivey Suber's Dutch Fork plantation in Newberry District, Lila Rutherford had the benefit of both the "white folks' big garden and patches on which the slaves could raise corn and vegetables." These Suber slaves worked their "patches of ground" on Saturday afternoons. And Emoline Glasgow's master, Pettus Gillian of Indian Creek, planted a big garden for his twenty-nine slaves but also allowed them "a small patch of about half acre for us to raise cotton or anything we wanted." And Union District's Nellie Loyd lived on her master George Buchanan's place near Goshen Hill, where the slaves did not have their own gardens but had "small watermelon patches."[44]

An additional benefit to masters of the work and garden system was that it allowed them to control the distribution and the division of land to "deserving" slaves. In the up-country, where cleared land was at a premium, masters were more discriminating in their distribution of available land. Mary Jane Kelly's master, Bill Jeter, for example, was most particular as to who received a piece of land on his Santuc plantation. Only "sometimes" would he allow his slaves to have a piece of land and then only to a family unit "to plant watermelons in." On William Brice's Fairfield District plantation there were "seventy-two slaves," one of whom was Andy Marion, who recalled that only married slaves were "encouraged to have their own garden."[45]

Access to a garden, of course, was no guarantee that up-country slaves would "busy" themselves like their fellows in other parts of the state. Henry Jefferies, for one, may have had some difficulty getting his slaves to enter into the reciprocal arrangement of a work and garden system that required them to take on extra work. A former slave on his plantation, Isiah Jefferies, recalled that "all de slaves had dere gardens." His master "made dem do it, and dey liked it."[46] Few slaves were likely to rush willingly into such working relationships without some confidence that they would indeed benefit. No doubt, like laborers everywhere, some slaves would have required an element of coercion to perform what they may have viewed initially as additional demands upon their time and energy without any assurance of receiving the promised rewards. Because their basic subsistence was provided through daily or weekly allowances, slaves disinclined to make the extra effort to produce provisions or cash crops for their own use may have been pressured to do so by family and friends keen to take advantage of this opportunity to reduce their dependency on the master and create for themselves a modicum of independence. Writing of the slaves she had encountered on the Sea Islands, one visitor remarked that the best of them "have carried their own crops well, and their example is beneficial in stimulating the larger ones to exertion. There is a good deal of emulation among them, they will not sit quietly and see another earning all the money."[47]

Throughout the state, masters used a task system to a greater or lesser degree, and, whenever possible, they allowed their slaves a small piece of land to plant for their own use. Seldom smaller than a quarter acre, these plots were sometimes as large as twelve or fifteen acres. Where the task system was not widely used, slaves were given set times—usually a Saturday afternoon—to work for themselves. Masters often allowed their slaves whole days to work on their crops. With Sunday free, most slaves would have been able to work their land then, although some masters and neighborhoods frowned upon any such work being done on the Sabbath. Mary Scott of Florence District told her interviewer about her uncle, who "when white people come by going to church [and] he hoeing his rice. Dey didn't want him work on Sunday." Their mistress, Elizabeth Gamble, "tell dem he gwine to chop his rice on Sunday."[48] When this extra time was either not allowed or proved insufficient, slaves were obliged to work by moonlight or with the assistance of torches made from fat burned in a frying pan. Sometimes a little work could be squeezed in during work breaks, which could be as long as two or three hours for lunch during the summer months.[49] However slaves came by the time to devote to working for themselves, most managed to produce provisions laboring under some form of a work and garden system that allowed them to control some of the more important areas of their lives. Although the location of the farm or plantation where the slaves lived and worked made a significant difference in the quality of life, the work and garden system facilitated the development of the slaves' internal economy largely of their own making. The private economy of the slaves—driven in large part by the production of goods and services that the work and garden system stimulated—broke out of the confines of individual slave quarters and into the wider slave community, literally broadening the slaves' world and influencing their worldview. Exploitation of the work and garden system and successful participation in the internal economy placed an additional premium on the productive family unit.

The effort to identify the moving forces behind the establishment of the work and garden system and its prevalence throughout the state has focused, necessarily, on the men and women who owned and managed slaves rather than on the slaves, who were, more often than not, obliged to respond to their masters' initiatives. The long-term success of any work system, however, required reciprocity on the part of both master and slave. At their most successful, the work and garden systems represented the acceptance by master and slave of a level of trust and mutual responsibility. This reciprocal arrangement enabled both parties to withdraw more and more into their own "worlds." Having improved the slaves' chances of achieving some personal satisfaction—materially and spiritually—the master significantly increased his own ability to control and discipline the slaves. The benefits to the master were substantial, numerous, and straightforward. Those accruing to the slaves, though also substantial and numerous, were far more complex.

A work system that permitted slaves to control the length of their workday and to spend any free time laboring for themselves provided a basis for some economic independence among the slaves. In South Carolina, not unlike the British Caribbean, Spanish America, and Brazil, slaves' economic activities contradicted their legal status as propertyless chattels.[50]

Throughout the Americas slaves learned to value their gardens and were generally prepared to take the opportunity to work for themselves. Only in some cases, however, most notably Jamaica and Brazil, were they openly permitted to learn how to "defend and expand their interests in vigorous market place competition."[51]

By and large, South Carolina slaves had to be satisfied with the creation and maintenance of a private rather than public commercial arena. Separate but inextricably linked to the public world, this commercial activity was nonetheless a crucial aspect of the slaves' life because it conditioned their value system, reflected important aspects of their worldview, and had a significant bearing on the development and organization of their family life.[52]

There is little evidence to suggest that the development of the slaves' economy was an anticipated and welcomed outcome of the work and garden system so popular with slave masters throughout the state. Given that masters were successful in encouraging their slaves to improve their work habits and that slaves took advantage of available opportunities to improve their standard of living, it is not surprising that they produced surplus provisions, which they hoped to sell or trade for money or other goods. But slaves trading their goods to all and sundry was disconcerting to masters, who endeavored to control these commercial activities. One planter writing in the *Southern Cultivator* in 1850 summed up the opposition to this form of slave enterprise. Noting that many slaveholders allowed their slaves to work some land and cultivate a small crop of their own, this planter considered the plan a "bad one." Among his reasons was that it was "impossible to keep them from working their crops on the Sabbath. They labor nights when they should be at rest." And perhaps of most concern to him, "they will pilfer to add to what corn or cotton they may have made." For this planter, slave initiative was tantamount to temptation, and he considered it "best to place temptation out of their reach."[53]

Not all planters with reservations about the work and garden system attempted to deny the slaves all initiative. Some were more agitated about the risks to themselves in case of a direct clash of interests than they were about the cause of the problem: the work and garden system itself. One concerned slaveholder addressed the cotton planters of the "Upper Country" on the question of how the moral condition of the slave would be benefited "if slaves were prohibited from planting cotton." He advised his up-country readers that every indulgence should be extended to the slaves "at work as far as it is for their own benefit, exacting from them no more than a reasonable day's work, and that by task work as far as it is practicably, [after which time] there should be no calls on them." He nonetheless revealed his concern that, given the opportunity, the slaves would neglect their own crops "knowing where to make up the deficiency."[54] He voiced no objections to the slaves being allowed to plant other crops, but clearly this temptation had to be denied them. Even Edgefield's James H. Hammond, who attacked the slaves' use of the task system in his attempt to "destroy the autonomy of the slave community and bring its members under his direct and total domination," did not deny his slaves the right to produce and trade their goods, albeit with certain stipulations. Although he permitted his slaves to continue working their patches "for gardens to cultivate in their own time," Hammond would not go so far as to allow them "to cultivate, gather in [their] own time any crop similar to the main crop of [their] master." This, he felt, was "too strong a temptation to unlimited stealing and trading."[55]

There were, of course, other ways of controlling this aspect of slave life. More typical of South Carolina planters was the contributor to a southern journal who, in 1833, revealed that he "never restrict[s] [his slaves] in any acts of industry but reward[s] them punctually for their exertions by taking from them at a fair price whatever they justly have to offer."[56] For reasons of securing their property, the ever-present desire to control their slaves, and the legal prohibitions against slaves owning property and trading in goods, most masters considered it good sense, if not their duty, to make some attempt to control the commercial activity of their slaves. One popular method was to deny them access to the wider market. In this significant respect, slaves in the American South differed from their counterparts elsewhere in the Americas.[57]

Although by the eighteenth century Jamaican planters had conceded the right of slaves to trade in a wide if not exhaustive range of their own produce,[58] South Carolina's slaveholders and the legislature were fighting a determined but losing battle to control this area of slave activity.[59] As the work and garden system with its surplus-producing potential made it necessary for slaves to sell some of their products, the master's response was circumscribed: he could permit the practice or control it by becoming the slaves' only retail outlet. One experienced overseer writing in 1836 advised that a planter "have upon his place a store of such articles as his slaves usually purchased elsewhere." These items could then be "dealt out to them for their corn and such things as they have to sell." In this way, your "negroes will be better and more cheaply provided and be put out of the way of the temptation of roguery."[60] Furthermore, some slaveholders, fearing the temptation for slaves to trade illicitly with unscrupulous poor white southerners, were obliged to make the price they paid to slaves attractive, thereby putting the slave in a good position to bargain with his master.[61] James H. Hammond, for example, allowed his slaves to plant crops and to keep fowls with the proviso that he would purchase the eggs and chickens "at the highest market price and never allow any other purchaser unless with the most specific permit."[62]

The sums of money involved in the trade masters were so keen to curtail or control were by no means trivial. Masters had good reason for wanting to know how much, for what, and with whom their slaves were trading goods. The same planter who advised against allowing slaves to plant cotton wrote of a neighbor who "has never suffered his negroes to plant cotton." He had, however, "realized from their corn and fodder from thirty dollars each according to their ability." James Sparkman, who encouraged his slaves to produce their own crops and to keep livestock, purchased all they had to sell, including provisions saved from their allowance. Writing in March 1858, Sparkman calculated the value of the goods he had purchased from his slaves during the past year. In cash money, the sum was "upwards of $130," and in luxuries such as "sugar, molasses, flour, coffee, handkerchiefs, aprons, homespun, and calico, pavilion gause [mosquito nets]," and necessities such as "tin buckets, hats, pocket knives, and sieves, another $110 could be added." Two men were credited with $27 and $25 each; both had made the money from selling Sparkman "hogs of their own raising."[63]

While attempting to retain an important measure of control, masters generally felt justified (even obliged) to extend to their slaves the opportunity to increase their commitment to a system essentially at odds with their interests: creating "a happy coalition of interests between the master and the slave" through the cultivation and marketing of their own crops.[64]

Serving the master, however, this arrangement also served the slave. As Sparkman wrote in 1858, the point established "is that by reasonable industry and ordinary providence, our people [the slaves] all have it in their power to add materially to their comforts and indulgences, and that their owners very wisely and humanely offer every encouragement to this effort."[65] The more slaves were able to associate these "indulgences" with their own efforts, the more likely they were to identify with the home place and their masters. Paradoxically, the more the slaves associated their own time and energies with the ability to provide much needed goods and services for themselves and their families, the more of a burden giving up to their masters a disproportionate amount of their time would become. In theory, by exposing their slaves to the heady experience of free market relations that could make them more dissatisfied with their position as chattel, masters were introducing a disturbing and potentially subversive element into the slave community.[66] In practice, however, productive and economically active slaves endeavored to make a life of their own, largely separate from and somewhat independent of the public world of their masters. Hence the slaves' increasing economic independence facilitated the development of a real "space" between their world and that of the masters wherein they could enjoy a level of cultural autonomy.[67]

Some slaves were better situated than others to take advantage of the opportunities that came their way. To be successful—to raise their material condition above a level that all too often proved inadequate for their needs—slaves had to be willing to work harder and longer than was required to fulfill their responsibilities in the public world. Some slaves, of course, would have lacked the desire, energy, or physical ability to perform the basic plantation tasks and also do extra labor to supplement their basic allowance. Some might choose other activities that were not materially rewarding. Others, of course, were not given the land to work, the stock to raise, or the opportunity to work a few extra hours to add to their income. These last were a minority, for the vast majority of South Carolina's slaves worked hard to exploit their opportunities.[68]

Evidence from slaves and former slaves who enjoyed some economic success under slavery in South Carolina reveals a common theme—a tale of a little good fortune and a lot of hard work. Records from the districts of Beaufort in the low country and from Marlboro in the middle country provide evidence of antebellum slaves exploiting available opportunities. Eliza Goethe, who had lived and farmed in Beaufort District, lost her husband some years before the Civil War. In 1877, appearing before the SCC, she testified that she had "always allowed [her] slaves to own and accumulate personal property," as did her husband, Washington Goethe. They had given their slaves "some land to plant some provisions in their spare time." Two beneficiaries of this practice were Rose Goethe and Ann Goethe. Rose, born in 1803, became a midwife and was thus able to make "money before and during the war." Rose also made money "by cropping in my own time." Ann Goethe was married in 1863 to Abraham, who had also belonged to the Goethes. As well as having the privilege of planting some land, Abraham was permitted to "own property such as a horse, hogs and poultry," paying for the horse from the money he made working in the blacksmith's shop.[69]

Another Beaufort resident, Oliver P. Bostick, allowed his slaves to "own property and have little crops of their own." Andrew Jackson, formerly a slave on the Bostick place, had his master as well as other witnesses support his claim of having five head of cattle (including a fine bull), seven hogs, and ten fowls lost to Union troops during the Civil War.[70] Andrew Guarin, born about 1835, was another Bostick slave permitted to "work out in my spare time." From his efforts he accumulated sufficient funds to purchase a cow from which he raised the remainder of the nine cattle he claimed before the SCC. Jackson's "fine bull" probably played some part in the rapid increase of Guarin's herd because the two men were "half-brother[s]." Living on the same place, Jackson had witnessed the Union troops taking the cattle, Guarin's "as well as my own." Bostick's neighbors did not seem unduly concerned about the extent of property owning undertaken by these slaves. James W. Dupees testified that Bostick allowed Guarin "as well as his other slaves to own cattle and other personal property." This neighbor described Bostick as a "good master and very indulgent to his slaves." Obviously, the Bosticks had a good relationship with their slaves, whom they considered "faithful and industrious servants."[71] And their slaves, in turn, took advantage of the opportunities available to them.

Elsewhere in the low country slaves worked hard to take charge of their economic fortunes in an attempt to make a life of their own under slavery.

During his master's long illness and following his death, David Harvey had "control of the farm" in Beaufort District. Similarly, during the Civil War while his young master, David Harvey, was fighting with the Confederates, David continued to manage the farm. He was "allowed to own property and plant a small crop for himself." Part of Harvey's claim before the SCC was for reimbursement for a horse, a saddle, and a bridle. He explained to the commission that he had purchased the horse from his master's brother C. J. Harvey and acquired the provisions by "working in my own time." David's former master testified that David had always had a good deal of provisions and poultry which "he and his family had raised." While David was riding his horse a mile or so from home, a foraging party of Union troops had taken his horse. The troops had invited him to go along with them. He turned down the invitation explaining that he "would not leave his family," which consisted of his wife, Mary, aged fifty, and his son Colon, aged twenty-five. They had lived together on the farm and were present when the troops returned later that day to relieve them of their provisions.[72]

Testimony from former slaves before the SCC suggests that property holding was fairly widespread, at least among Beaufort County slaves, and sheds additional light on the ways slaves managed to accumulate substantial amounts of property. If slaves were to provide a financial cushion for themselves and their families, they had to go beyond mere exploitation of their gardens for seasonal produce; they had to look to the future. Of course, the reality for many slaves was that they could expect only to provide much needed extras. Other slaves, however, aimed for self-sufficiency and more. Henry Newton was such a slave, and his story provides a revealing glimpse into the financial world of some slaves. Allowed to farm for himself "long before the war," Newton was able by working in his spare time to purchase a horse in the spring of 1864. He was in a position to pay the necessary $500 "rebel money" as well as some "state money." In addition, he used the $30 in silver and gold he had been "saving for years" before he finally became the owner of the horse. Newton had also owned cattle and hogs, and he filed a claim for the loss of sixty fowls along with the horse, bridle, and saddle taken by Union troops. By any stretch of the imagination, Newton, described by his former master as "very good and intelligent," had been willing and able to take advantage of the opportunities that had come his way under slavery despite the restrictions placed upon him and his family.[73]

Pompey Smith, another Beaufort slave, had the privilege of planting some land and raising a crop which he worked "in all the spare time I had." He testified that the property he had lost had been acquired by "hard work" from which he had "made money and bought it." The horse included in his claim before the commission had been purchased from K. S. Smith (probably a relative of Pompey's master) at a cost of $200. His former master's son testified that Pompey had "always planted ten to fifteen acres," which he had worked with the help of his horse. Smith had accumulated sufficient money that he was even able to loan money at interest.[74] As headman, Pompey Smith was in a favored position that allowed him to help himself and his family. The role of the horse in aiding Smith to amass his wealth is noteworthy. If the Smith family and others controlling large areas of land were to take full advantage of their opportunities, a mule or a horse would have been invaluable.

Benjamin Platts was another former slave who acquired a horse and further improved his earning potential. Like Smith's owner, John Platts had ample land on which his slaves could plant. Benjamin and his fellow slaves were allowed "as much land as they could work in their own time." Taking advantage of this opportunity, Benjamin planted "from seven to eight acres" which he worked with the help of his horse. Also in his claim before the commission were six hogs, four hundred pounds of bacon, twelve chickens, and six bushels of corn.[75] Platts had used the money accumulated through the sale of his cotton to purchase his horse.

The horse, then, was of crucial importance in the calculation of how much land a slave could reasonably manage in his or her free time. Although other factors also had to be considered, it seems that those who owned a horse were more likely to have planted larger pieces of land. Of course, to purchase a horse a slave probably first needed the income that could only have been obtained from the produce of a sizable piece of land or from some "profession," skill, or special talent. That they could make the huge financial commitment of a horse or mule provides an indication of the determination of these slaves to exploit the land available and perhaps to increase the amount of land under their control. Furthermore, in an agricultural community a horse would have served several important purposes. Working in the fields may have been a primary function, but the horse would also have been useful for transport to and from their place of work and to social events such as slave "frolics" on Saturday nights, to church on Sundays, and to visit family scattered about the community. If some slaves valued a horse primarily as a status symbol rather than as an essential work aid, others may have seen it as a much desired end in itself—a means to help overcome the obstacles imposed by slavery. Ownership of a mule or a horse, then, might offer a crude means of gauging the amount of land worked by particular slaves and provide some clue to their lifestyle and worldview.

Even slaves who lacked sizable amounts of cash could accumulate substantial property. Robert Bryant, born and raised on J. J. Chisholm's plantation in Black Creek, Beaufort District, had little success in acquiring "cash money." He was able, nonetheless, to purchase a mule for $167. Bryant had been allowed to raise hogs and poultry as well as to plant some "corn and other provisions." His master's son V. A. Chisholm testified that his father had purchased meat hogs from Bryant. Bryant did not grow cotton so had no ready source of a sizable cash income that might have enabled him to purchase a horse or a mule. Bryant testified that it had taken him "about two years to pay for the mule," which he had paid for in what he termed "laborments." As Bryant explained, "The colored population had the privilege of working overtime and raising stock, hogs, and such as that I call cotton, pork and such as I call laborments."[76] Bryant's "laborments" may have involved a system whereby he received the mule and then worked off the cost by "selling" goods to his master, doing extra work, and even supplying his master with the occasional hog. Such an arrangement, though not punishing slaves who had no access to cash money, might have actually placed them in a much more secure position than slaves who first had quietly and cautiously to hoard their cash.

The experience of Beaufort District's Peter Reid provides a reminder of the precarious nature of the rights of slaves to their own property and the difficulties some slaves may have had in maintaining the rewards of their hard work and endeavor. A former slave on Julia Speakes's plantation, Reid had enjoyed what Speakes considered "a good many privileges" which she made available to her slaves. She "gave them land to plant and allowed them to make something for themselves in their spare time." She also allowed them to raise hogs and poultry. Speakes described Reid as "such a trustworthy man that I left my farm altogether to his management after my husband's death in 1862." Reid, then, was in a position to work for himself, which he did, "and made money." About a year before the outbreak of war he purchased a mule, which he traded for a horse. Perhaps this was the route followed by the ambitious and upwardly socially mobile among South Carolina's slaves, from a mule, essentially a dray animal, to the more expensive but multipurpose horse. With the outbreak of war, however, his mistress's son Clarence, who lacked a horse to ride in the Confederate army, traded Reid his horse for a mule. Reid seems to have had little choice about trading his horse for a mule, nor was there any mention of money or goods to make up any discrepancies in the value of the two animals. Reid simply testified that Clarence "gave me the mule for my horse." [77]

Benjamin Tyson, born in 1817, was another Speakes slave. He held a job often associated with superannuated members of the slave force. Benjamin was Speakes's stock minder. Although he was old and perhaps infirm or suffering some disability, he managed to work hard and had made money under slavery. He too had enjoyed the assistance of a horse, one that was valued at $200. Also included in his claim were a saddle, five hundred pounds of bacon, and a hog. Speakes testified that she "believed Benjamin must have paid about $125 for his horse." Nero Williams was a slave on Pierson Peeples's plantation in Beaufort District. Born around 1815, Williams was well into middle age before the end of slavery. Perhaps as a result of his seniority on the Peeples place, he had acquired some special skill because he was able to expand his property ownership beyond the "average" to include a horse valued at $150. Williams, like most slaves, had made the property in his "spare time" and had purchased the horse from a member of his white family, in this case his owner. [78]

Property ownership among antebellum slaves was not restricted to the older, skilled, talented men, or the fortunate few who managed to catch the master's eye, or those who basked in his largesse. Often, young, female, and quite "ordinary" slaves were able to accumulate substantial amounts of property. Harriet Smith of Beaufort was one example. Born in 1826, Harriet had control of some land, two acres of which she planted in corn and "made at least 20 bushels to the acre." She had worked hard and made plenty of provisions and raised hogs and poultry. Included in her claim for eight hundred pounds of bacon, twenty bushels of potatoes, ten pounds of rice, and thirty pounds of sugar was part of the twelve bushels of corn she had received from her mistress as her corn rations for the year, some of which had been used for "fattening my hogs and some for living on."[79]

Pierson Peeples allowed Mooney Sinclair and his other slaves "to work for themselves and to own personal property." There is nothing to suggest that Sinclair and Harriet Smith were skilled or held responsible positions on the plantation. Born around 1840, Mooney was in his early twenties at the outbreak of war. Peeples described him as "an industrious man [who] made provisions in his own time." Owning neither mule nor horse, Mooney may have worked a piece of land not exceeding an acre or two, yet his claim included two hundred pounds of bacon, two hogs, ten bushels of rice, and twenty bushels of corn.[80]

James Ruth was another slave not as well situated as some of his Beaufort District fellows who climbed above the ordinary and took some control over important areas of their lives. His mistress, Nath Ruth's widow, allowed him to own personal property and to work for himself in his spare time. James also "worked out among neighbors and made money." One such neighbor, Joseph Rozier, testified that James made money for himself "working for me and my neighbor, Abner Ginn . . . and split rails for us both." Neither a foreman nor a skilled slave, James had little more than hard labor to sell, yet his claim for corn meal, fourteen chickens, five hogs, and two saddles should have also included a horse that was omitted from the official claim because it had not been filed in time. Thus, without any particular skill or special advantages except a willingness to work hard, James—as perhaps many like him for whom records are not available— was able to accumulate substantial property.[81]

A survey of claimants from Marlboro District in the middle country indicates that opportunities, although perhaps reduced, were available in the interior of the state. One variable may have been the relative unavailability of land to offer slaves for their own use. Moreover, the interior districts were farther from the rice and cotton plantations where some of the largest slave and land owners in the state lived. In 1850, for example, Beaufort District contained 842 farms with an average holding of 1,084 acres, 268 in improved land and 816 in unimproved land. Its slaveholders in 1860 numbered about 1,070 with an average holding of 30 slaves. For Marlboro District the average holding for the 612 farms was 466 acres, of which only 137 were improved land, and an average of some 13 slaves among its 540 or so slaveholders.[82] With more slaves and more land on which to house them, Beaufort District planters would have found it easier to "indulge" their slaves with sizable grants of land for their own use.

Middle-country slaves like Jacob Allman were less fortunate. Born a slave about 1827 and originally owned by Marlboro District's Nathaniel Allman, who died about six years before the outbreak of the war, Allman was then purchased by William Ellerbe, upon whose death, around 1860, he was inherited by Lawrence D. Prince. Perhaps because of Jacob's frequent change of abode he does not seem to have acquired any land or property up to this point. A carpenter by trade, Allman was permitted to hire out part of his time from his master, and he "would thus make a little profit and in addition would do extra jobs and make a little money." His good fortune, however, did not begin until he received the assistance of Alexander Quick, his wife's owner. Quick allowed Jacob and his wife "about five acres on his land" to tend, in addition to which Jacob "rented two acres from Peter T. Smith." On the five acres he planted corn and peas in 1864, and the year before he produced some seventy-five bushels of corn and peas. From the two-acre plot he made a bale of cotton weighing four hundred pounds. In 1863 he was sufficiently well off to purchase a mule that was later valued at $125. The mule, along with one thousand pounds of bacon, fifty bushels of corn, and six head of cattle, made up only part of Allman's considerable claim before the SCC. Appearing as a witness in support of the claim, Mrs. Allman's former master, Quick, described Jacob as a "shifty, smart fellow" who "saved all he earned. He made it and saved it. He was an honest, hard working fellow."[83] With his training as a carpenter, Allman would probably have fared well under slavery; his real success, however, was largely owing to the largesse of his wife's owner, who no doubt had good reasons for his generosity.

Silas Cook was another who acquired a skill under slavery. Born in 1813, Silas became foreman and blacksmith on Thomas Cook's Bennettsville plantation. Allowed to cultivate "nearly four acres," he raised crops "for many years before the war." Despite his skill, Silas never hired out his time but often worked for other people in "overtime" at night and made some money that way. He also sold his cotton every year. There were some seventy slaves on the Cook place and at least one free Negro who made it his home. Silas's daughter Emily had married a free man, William Bass. Although Emily's husband worked on another farm, her father "had use of about three acres of land which he and his children worked on in overtime." The whole family, including the son-in-law, lived under the same roof.[84]

The Cook plantation provides an example of the economic differences that could exist between slaves living in the same quarters. With almost four acres already gone to one of his top hands, Thomas Cook may have been hard-pressed to be as generous to less qualified slaves such as William Cook. William made no mention of having owned any land. A field hand "by occupation," whose wife and children lived on another plantation about a mile away, William seems to have been more concerned about his twice weekly conjugal visits. He did, however, find time away from Maria, his wife, and their children to earn money in "overtime" at night "splitting rails and other work." His claim for provisions included 434 pounds of bacon, 50 pounds of flour, and twenty-five chickens. Part of this property, Cook informed the commission, had been given to him by his wife's master, J. Covington, "for the support of herself and children during the year." After General William T. Sherman's troops passed through Marlboro District, William Cook, his wife, and their nine children were left destitute.[85] Because Cook lacked a sizable piece of land and had no special skill, his property holding was fragile and vulnerable to such vagaries.

Pompey Lewis also acquired property without working a sizable piece of land. Lewis was a blacksmith on the plantation of his master, Charles Earby, and did "extra time" at night. He claimed property of 540 pounds of bacon and assorted items that he had bought and raised. He told the commission that he had cultivated no land "on my own account and had less than a quarter acre around my dwelling."[86] Pompey, like Cook and his family, found themselves in serious difficulties when they lost their property to Union troops. Both these men, whose only resource was the garden around their cabins, had been able to accumulate sufficient property to assist in the upkeep of their families and to provide something for their immediate future. Without a sizable piece of land at their disposal, however, these slaves were particularly vulnerable to the vagaries of life under slavery. If nothing else, a piece of land gave the least skilled slaves an opportunity to fend for themselves, to hold their own against the more talented and highly skilled slaves, and to provide a buffer between themselves, their families, and the many uncertainties of life under slavery.

Slaves who were fortunate enough to have access to a sizable piece of land had to be willing to work very hard to exploit their opportunities. As long as they were willing to work longer and harder than they would otherwise have done, even the less talented slaves could hope to create some economic security for themselves and their families. The Princes are a case in point. Priscilla Prince worked as the cook on Peter Odom's plantation. She had no land for her own use "except a small garden around my house." Her husband, Carolina Prince, who lived on a plantation some nine miles away, also had "just such a garden at his quarters." Between them, they raised the three hogs and ten chickens that constituted the bulk of their claim. Priscilla had raised two hogs, and her husband raised one hog, the bacon from which he had brought to his wife's house, where Priscilla had raised the chickens. She had also "earned money working in overtime." [87]

Although Marlboro slaves were less likely to have enjoyed the use of large tracts of land, they often were given some land to tend for their own use. Even if this land was no more than a small area around their cabins, slaves like Priscilla and Carolina Prince and William Cook were able to put it to good use and accumulate personal property. Through extra work raising hogs and chickens and other livestock, the vast majority of South Carolina slaves would have been able to increase their personal income and perhaps influence the course of their lives.

In light of the evidence attesting to the prevalence of slave gardens, the income earned from them, and the accumulation of private property by slaves, the interviews of former slaves in the 1930s deserve closer inspection, particularly those statements that refer to work routines, slave gardens, money, and slaves' purchasing power. [88] For example, Henry Ryan of Edgefield District recalled that his master, Judge Pickens Butler, allowed the slaves "extra patches of ground to work for ourselves." Born in 1854,

Henry was a young boy under slavery. His recollection that the judge "used to give us a little money . . . for our work" raises the question, How much land did these slaves work, and how much money did adult slaves on the Butler place earn for their goods and services? Ryan recalled that they "bought clothes and things we had to have." This suggests a crucial distinction between weighty oppression and slaves being in a position to make certain life choices. For example, Sylvia Cannon and her family had some "3 acres of land . . . to plant for dey garden," the products from which her family had been able to use for themselves. Her account fails to provide any details of the economic rewards except her statement, the import of which has been often dismissed, that "peoples would have found we colored people rich wid de money we made on de extra crop."[89]

Former slaves from the up-country have left less conclusive records of their opportunities, efforts, and achievements, but they did provide powerful clues about the character of slave life in the region. Benjamin Russell, a teenager before the end of slavery, had lived on the farm of Rebecca Nance in Chester District, where the average farm size would have been around 390 acres of which more than 200 was improved land. He recalled that they were "permitted to have a fowl house for chickens" and also that he occasionally received small amounts of money from "white folks and visitors." However small these "gifts" might have been, Benjamin had used them to purchase "extra clothing for Sundays and fire crackers and candy at Christmas." For this young slave, a fowl house, a willingness to work hard, and encouragement to earn money may have been just the start he needed.[90]

Richard Jones of Union District perhaps had a better start than did Russell, but his enterprise and level of industry were different. Born on Jim Gist's plantation, Richard received his quarter acre when he was about seventeen or eighteen years of age. The first year, he planted potatoes, tobacco, and watermelons, while some of the other boys planted "pinders, canteloups, and matises (tomatoes) in their quarter acre." These young men seem to have eased their way into their first season as full task hands because the following year they "made corn and sold it to our master fer whatever he give us fer it."[91]

It is likely that slaves such as Richard Jones and Benjamin Russell in the up-country, Priscilla Prince and her husband, Carolina, in the middle country, and James Ruth and Mooney Sinclair in the low country— ordinary slaves by any measure—were typical of South Carolina's slaves.

Where the opportunity, willingness, and ability to work for themselves existed, slaves—of all classes—could improve their lives materially and spiritually and eke out a modicum of independence from their masters and the white world. Furthermore, industrious, property-owning slaves were among the most influential and well-respected members of the slave quarters. Their property accumulation alone would have enabled them to obtain and maintain positions of power and influence on the plantation, both in the public world of the master and in the private world of the quarters. However humble their beginnings, industrious slaves, be they skilled or unskilled, house or field, young or old, male or female, could, if they desired, aspire to positions of power and influence in the slave quarters. Few slaves, however, could expect to succeed without the assistance and protection of a hardworking and supportive family. Given the many advantages that forever remained with the masters, the only way for the vast majority of slaves to begin to balance the power of the master was to organize themselves into economically productive family units.

2

For Richer for Poorer: The Family as an Economic Unit

The work and garden system was a primary stimulus to collective family labor and provided both an organizing principle and a rationale for stable slave families. But slaves had probably always sought the added protection that group activity promised. Unable to provide all their individual needs, they combined their efforts in the world of the slave quarters much as they were called upon to do in the public world of the master. Thus the practice of slaves working as a family developed partly out of necessity and partly out of habit, but, as shown in Chapter 1, there was also an element of co-ercion on the part of masters. Although a work and garden system that ac-centuated the productive and social functions of the slave family provided an effective means for masters to obtain material and social benefits from their slaves, they were always ready and willing to resort to brute force when peaceable means proved unsuccessful.[1]

To exploit the opportunities available under a work and garden system and thus gain a modicum of control of their working life, slaves endeav-ored to surround themselves with those whose lives were most closely tied to their own and upon whom they could most readily rely—their imme-diate and extended families. Young or old, able-bodied or disabled, each member could contribute to the family's domestic productivity. The phys-ical exertion and the time required to perform satisfactorily for their owners and then to cultivate their own gardens placed a high premium on cooperative work practices. Without assistance from family members,

32

individual slaves would have struggled fully to exploit the land they tilled
and other means of reducing their dependency. Throughout the state
slaves worked in family groups and pooled their efforts. David Harvey, formerly a slave in low-country Beaufort District, appeared before the Southern Claims Commission in 1874. His former master testified on David's
behalf, recalling that the former slave had "always had a good deal of provisions and poultry which he and his family made and raised." The extent
to which David and his family formed an economic as well as a social unit
was perhaps part of the reason why he lost his horse to Union troops. Invited by the soldiers to go along with them, he had refused, explaining that
he "would not leave my family." Not even the prospect of immediate freedom or the desire to protect a highly valued possession could convince him
to leave his family.[2]

Emily Bass, from the middle country, assisted in the claim of her father,
Silas Cook, before the commission. Emily recalled living at her father's
house on Thomas Cook's Bennetsville plantation in Marlboro District.
Emily's family had lived together and worked together. The four acres of
land given to them by their master was tilled by Cook "and his children,"
who "worked on [it] in overtime"—that is, during the time they were not
working for their master. In this way Cook and his family were able to
"raise crops for many years before the war," and Cook cultivated his cotton, which he sold "every year."[3]

Family members were expected to contribute to the household economy. Even the youngest child might be called upon to perform some service in the family interest. It was not uncommon, for example, for young
children to work with the family group long before their owners sent them
into the fields as a fraction of a working hand. Margaret Hughes, born a
slave on Daniel Finley's Columbia plantation, was "too young to work" in
the fields, but she was old enough to have "helped work de gardens" with
her family. Hughes remembered working in the garden with her father.
Jessie Williams recalled having worked with his parents, Henry and Maria,
before he was old enough to "shoulder my poke and go to de field." A
former slave from the up-country, Henry Gladney of Fairfield District,
pointed out that although he "wasn't a very big boy in slavery time" he did
"'member choppin cotton and pickin cotton and peas 'lon 'side mammy in
de field."[4]

33

The work slaves did together for the family group was not restricted to their gardens. Their domestic labor could be both an additional source of income and an opportunity to produce essential goods for domestic consumption: clothing, bedding, cooking utensils, and furniture. Working for the family in the home confirmed the economic good sense of their joint enterprise there and elsewhere and strengthened noneconomic bonds between family members. After their task was completed and on Saturday evenings, slaves such as those in Sylvia Cannon's family regularly continued their work in the home. Cannon recalled how "when night came on en we go back to de quarters, we cook bread in de ashes en pick seed from de cotton en my mamma sit dere en sew heap of de time." Peter Stanton, who had been born on Sandy Stanton's plantation in Marlboro District, testified before the SCC, claiming a large quantity of bacon, lard, meal, and numerous household items including blankets, quilts, and sheets. He explained that he had purchased the blankets and "had got the leather and had the shoes made." His family, however, had "made the bed quilts and the sheets."[5]

Not until slaves worked together in family units and pooled their resources did they truly position themselves to take advantage of the opportunities for property accumulation available under the work and garden system. As an oppressed group, it would be expected that South Carolina's slaves, wherever they were located, were characterized by few of the usual variables that so often produced social distinctions among people. The work and garden system, however, created and highlighted numerous economic and social differences among slaves. As Charles Ball observed, "In our society, although we were all slaves, and all nominally in a condition of the most perfect equality, yet there was in fact a very great difference in the manner of [our] living, in the several families."[6] A close look at a moment in the productive and economic life of two groups of slaves reveals some of the numerous ways in which these differences developed and functioned on farms and plantations.

Working alongside family members in the public world of the master was not unfamiliar to South Carolina's slaves. On J. O. Willson's low-country Goose Creek plantation in Charleston District slaves often worked with family members when laboring for their owners. Though this practice was inevitable on farms and small plantations, where the slave force

consisted of only one or two families, it was less common on larger plantations, where slave managers used physical and technical criteria to allocate
work assignments. Yet among large labor forces, if slaves from the same
family demonstrated similar abilities, it would be expected that they would
qualify for the same grade and be assigned their work responsibilities
(tasked) accordingly. In 1844, Willson listed 124 slaves, among whom 29
were divided into several small work groups, ranging from two to five
members, under the headings "Hands Prime," "Half Hands," and "Plows."
The prime hands were divided into five groups, two of three hands and
three of four hands. In the first group were Peggy, Bill, and York. Peggy,
the thirty-eight-year-old mother of ten, was grouped with her twenty-
one-year-old son Bill and her sixteen-year-old nephew York. The second
group included Yanny, Andrew, Nell, and Edy. Twenty-four-year-old
Yanny was York's brother, and he is listed as working with his cousins,
Edy, aged twenty-eight, and Nell, aged twenty-four, two of Peggy's three
daughters. Only twenty-six-year-old Andrew was not direct blood kin, and
he was married to Nell. A third group was made up of Isaac, Yanty, Rachel,
and Bess. Both in their thirties, Isaac and Bess were brother and sister.
Yanty, at twenty-seven years of age, a younger brother, was married to the
last member of this group, Rachel, who had been purchased onto the plantation. Lucy, aged fifty, and Nancey, aged thirty-five, mother and daughter, and Hector and his thirty-eight-year-old wife, Charlotte, formed the
fourth group. Charlotte and Hector's daughter Sumitra, aged twenty-one,
was teamed not with her parents but with seventeen-year-old Betsey, and
a Peter whose identity is not clear because there were three Peters on
the place (aged fourteen, twenty-four, and fifty-six), any of whom could
conceivably have qualified for this group. But because the average age of
Willson's prime hands was thirty-one, it is likely that the twenty-four-
year-old Peter was a prime hand.

The makeup of the "half hands" was far more mixed and characteristic
of "trash gangs." Included in the largest group was Nelly, who might have
been the Nell listed above. She would have qualified (temporarily) for the
half hand status at this time for, like twenty-three-year-old Binah, the second member of the group, she had at least two very young children. Nelly
had given birth to her third child in June 1842 and to her fourth in August
1844. When these lists were made up, she would have been about five

months pregnant and may have just been reclassified from prime hand to half hand. Also in this group was forty-year-old Guy, who is elsewhere described as "not sound." A second group of half hands consisted of African-born Sylvia, aged about fifty, her twenty-four-year-old son Adam, sixteen-year-old Lucy, and eighteen-year-old Caesar. Lucy and Caesar would begin their own family in the spring of 1847. The last group in this category included Doublin, forty-four years old, and one of the two women named Phillis on the plantation: either the forty-one-year-old mother of six or the forty-nine-year-old Phillis. This last group consisted of the older hands and those past the average age for prime hands.

The third category listed was the plantation's "plows." These six hands were the plantation's laboring elite. All males, they were drawn (perhaps deliberately) from at least five different families and were named Solomon, Jacky, John, Nero, George, and York. Overall, the Willson records show that close family members with comparable abilities did work together, and the consistency of this pattern also suggests that the slaves might have had some say in the arrangement.[7]

Not all slaves were teamed with family members while working for their owners. Those who were may well have considered it the norm and gone directly from working in their owners' fields to working in their own. This practice was accepted by some slaves as an organizing principle in the public world of the master; others had their own good reasons to organize their efforts in a similar manner. By whatever route it was arrived at, family group working became an institutional norm in the slave quarters, and sanctions were applied for noncompliance. Edgefield District's Henry Ryan recalled that his master used to allow them Saturday afternoons to "work our own little patches or do some other work we had to do." The emphasis here seems to be on doing the work that had to be done in order to provide needed extras. Ryan does not sound too pleased when recalling that not everyone did what "had to be done"; rather, "some would frolic then wash up for Sunday, or set around."[8] Ryan and his fellow slaves had to make some choices about their short- and medium-term concerns, choices that did not always prove beneficial in the long term. Of course, there were less able slaves—the sick and those so tired by Saturday afternoon that they had little choice but to "frolic," "rest," or just "set around." South Carolina slave masters were fairly consistent in providing food and clothing for their slaves and did not reduce the allowance for slaves who produced extras for themselves. Thus "setting around" remained an option. As Charles Ball indicates, however, there were exceptions. Ball's master expected his slaves to clothe themselves from their "extra earnings." For these slaves, living on a plantation near Columbia in the middle country, working for themselves was less a matter of choice as of necessity. Despite the added inducement to provide for themselves, Ball recalled that some of these slaves "performed no more work, through the week, than their regular task," and they "were not able to provide themselves with good clothes; and many of them suffered greatly from the cold, in the course of winter."[9]

The Willson slaves were better situated than some described by Charles Ball: they had more options, and the evidence suggests that they usually made sensible choices. By calculating the income earned by individual slaves on this low-country plantation and using the sum as a measure of immediate and extended family group productivity, it becomes clear that the earnings of certain families were sufficient as to create economic and social distinctions in the slave quarters. Willson's Family Number 1 in March 1847 contained twenty-four members (figure 1).[10] At its head was eighty-seven-year-old Nancey. Her two daughters, Binah and Peggy, had provided her with fifteen grandchildren, the last being Peggy's son Isaac, born in 1841. Yanty, second son of Binah and her husband, Peter, appeared on the 1847 Willson list of slave accounts as having received $6.01 from the sale of 5.5 bushels of corn and 278 blades (fodder). Bess, his sister, earned $9.40 for seven bushels of corn, two and three-quarters bushels of peas, and 280 blades. Peggy's daughter, forty-one-year-old Edy, sold a bushel and three quarts of corn and 218 blades in October 1847, for which she received $2.95. Bess's sister, Caty, who worked as cook and whose husband lived on another plantation, managed with her three daughters, aged seventeen, ten, and eight years old, to earn $3.38 from sales of 1.5 bushels of corn and a 45-pound shoat. Earlier in the year Caty had sold Willson four hogs for which she received $15. Her eldest daughter, Mary, earned $2.76 for corn and blades. Through cash earned for hogs and small quantities of corn and blades, Caty's family, with herself no doubt frequently busy in the kitchen, was able to earn the not inconsiderable sum of $21.14. When this is added to the sums earned by the other members of her

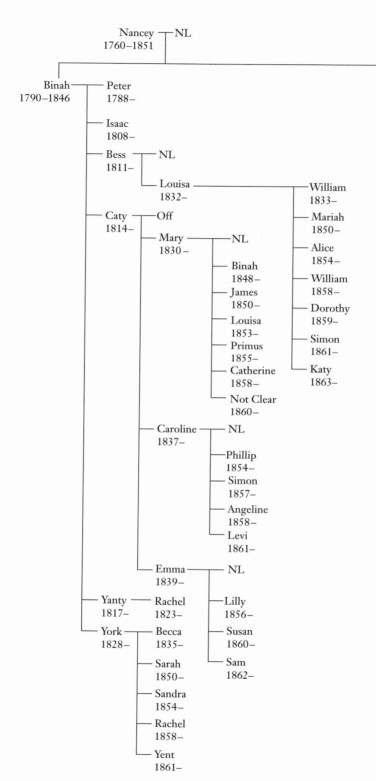

Fig. 1.   Willson Family Number 1

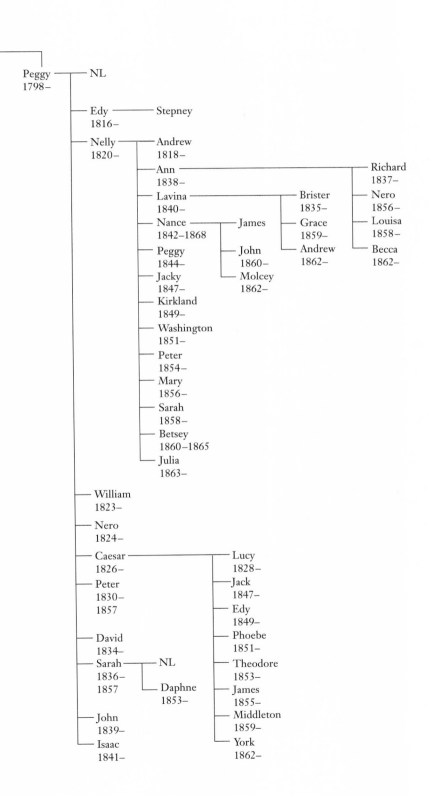

Peggy
1798–
— NL

— Edy ————— Stepney
1816–

— Nelly ——— Andrew
1820–   1818–
            — Ann ——————————————— Richard
            1838–   1837–
            — Lavina ——————— Brister — Nero
            1840–   1835–   1856–
            — Nance ——— James — Grace — Louisa
            1842–1868   1859–   1858–
            — Peggy   — John — Andrew — Becca
            1844–   1860–   1862–   1862–
            — Jacky   — Molcey
            1847–   1862–
            — Kirkland
            1849–
            — Washington
            1851–
            — Peter
            1854–
            — Mary
            1856–
            — Sarah
            1858–
            — Betsey
            1860–1865
            — Julia
            1863–

— William
1823–

— Nero
1824–

— Caesar ————————— Lucy
1826–   1828–
                  — Jack
                  1847–
— Peter   — Edy
1830–   1849–
1857   — Phoebe
                  1851–
— David   — Theodore
1834–   1853–
— Sarah ——— NL   — James
1836–   1855–
1857 — Daphne   — Middleton
      1853–   1859–
— John   — York
1839–   1862–
— Isaac
1841–

extended family, it gives some idea of the volume of goods and money a large, able-bodied, skilled, and industrious family, working together, could have accumulated for their own use.[11]

The Willson slaves are not listed as having produced any cotton of their own, a practice that might have been prohibited by Willson as it was by Edgefield County's James H. Hammond, among others. There is no record of Willson purchasing cotton from the slaves even though they would have been very familiar with its production and could conceivably have produced some in their gardens for sale or worked out for neighboring planters for which they would have been compensated.[12] Some of the slaves with whom Charles Ball lived and worked took advantage of the opportunity to increase their earnings by working off the plantation on a Sunday for wages. Many of the slaves on Ball's plantation, "perhaps forty in all, went out through the neighborhood, to work for other planters." One of the men, Ball wrote, "cleared to himself, included his Sunday work, two dollars a week, for several weeks; and his savings, on the entire crop of cotton, were thirty-one dollars." In addition, "one of the women cleared twenty-six dollars to herself, in the same way."[13] Therefore, the recorded earnings of the Willson family groups might reflect only a fraction of their actual earnings.

Willson encouraged slave family members to work together in a work and garden system. It is not clear whether Willson used coercion to ensure the compliance and good behavior of his work force, but it is clear that the Willson slaves took advantage of their opportunities to gain better control over their work and family life.

The work and garden system both encouraged and strengthened the development of a corporate family structure wherein senior family members could supervise the labor of junior family members. Accordingly, the thirty-six-year-old Bess, for example, could have expected her fifteen-year-old daughter Louisa and her brothers Isaac and Yanty to assist with the family responsibilities. If they did not, her younger siblings, Caty and York, could be of assistance whenever required. Of course, house servant and cook Caty could expect her siblings, as well as her two daughters, to help her with her own garden. Caty would have been in a position to return such favors with little "extras" from Willson's kitchen.

If the Peter credited with over $16 in earnings for hogs, beef, and corn was Bess's father and the nominal male head of the family, he probably exerted some control over the considerable amount of land used by his extended family. His seniority under such a family structure would have permitted him to call upon individual family members to assist the family group and to perform a variety of services in time of need. Division of family-produced goods and services would require a workable and equitable system of distribution. That Caty's daughter, seventeen-year-old Mary, produced crops independent of her mother suggests several interesting possibilities. The Willson slave families may have worked on a share system with each contributor taking an agreed portion of the final produce for his or her own use in return for labor. This may have been the case only for the younger slaves who had not yet reached prime hand status, whereupon they would become entitled to a piece of land for which they would enjoy sole responsibility. Those already "seated" on their own land may still have been entitled to some compensation for work performed for the extended rather than the immediate family unit. Family heads, such as Nancey, Bess, or Peter, would then have had the important responsibility of distributing to the right person whatever land came under their jurisdiction, in the right amount, and at the right time. In this way, certain plots of land would have remained within the same family under the control of the family head to be shared with new members once they came of age or handed down to successive generations. For example, if Binah, a senior member of the Willson slave quarters community, had been allowed a sizable piece of land during the second half of her life, what would have happened to it after she died in 1846? Would her husband, Peter, have continued working it along with his own, or would it have been given over to another member of the family or to another family? Might Willson have recovered the use of the land, or would it have been too late for a master to intrude, in a forceful and potentially disruptive way, upon a productive and settled community without risking the good order and morale of the plantation?

Caribbean planters sought to avoid this risk to the good order of the plantation and the slave quarters community. Bryan Edwards described a practice which he considered universal in Jamaica by 1793: "I do not believe that an instance can be produced of a master's interference with his Negroes in their [gardens]. . . . They are permitted also to dispose at their deaths of what little property they possess; and even to bequeath their grounds or gardens to such of their fellow-slaves as they think proper. These principles are so well established, that whenever it is found convenient for the owner to exchange the negro-grounds for other lands, the Negroes must be satisfied, in money or otherwise, before the exchange takes place." [14]

There is no evidence that South Carolina planters conducted their affairs in this way, but, as Sidney Mintz observes, the alternative would have been the equivalent of an "unworkable estate tax system of one hundred per cent death duties on the 'property' of deceased slaves." [15] That some of South Carolina's slaves escaped death duties on their property was revealed by Edward Brown and William Drayton of Beaufort before the SCC in 1874. Brown, a young man under slavery, had been left a mule by his grandfather and had "used the mule as his own property for two or three years before he left to join the Union Army." Drayton testified that his father had died and "left me the means with which I bought the Jenny mule" that constituted a large part of his claim. His father had left "the means and property he left for his children" with his oldest brother ("my uncle"). Drayton had purchased the mule on the advice of his uncle and had made payments in three installments. The first was $100 in gold and silver, then a second payment of $50 "all in silver," and a final payment of $100 in "state bank bills." [16]

The economic experience of Willson's "second" family suggests that the family head enjoyed some influence over members of her extended family group. Furthermore, these family members were particularly well-equipped to exploit the opportunities available to them. In October 1847, Nancey from Family Number 2 (figure 2), which numbered less than half the twenty-four of Family Number 1, produced and sold one bushel and four quarts of corn and a quantity of peas for total earnings of $4.73. In December, this mother of seven increased her earnings by $12.50 with the sale of more corn and a "steer." It is not clear who Nancey's husband was, whether he lived nearby, or if he was still alive. A full hand in 1844, Nancey could have called upon her brothers, Isaac (nicknamed Solomon), one of the plow hands, and Andrew, who was also a full hand in 1844, for assistance with her crops. Her nineteen-year-old daughter Lucy's contribution to the family enterprise would have been reduced because she had

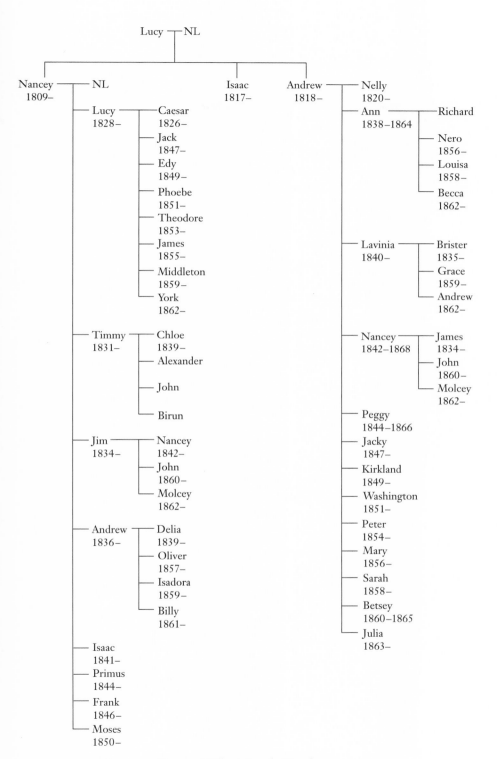

Fig. 2.   Willson Family Number 2

given birth to her first child in June 1847. What time and energy she had was probably given to working land belonging to herself and her husband, Caesar, who managed to earn for himself, his wife, and newborn baby over $5 for corn and fodder. Nancey's brother Isaac, thirty years of age and a plow hand who probably enjoyed more free time than most, produced over fifteen bushels of corn for which he received $11.43. Her younger brother, Andrew, aged twenty-nine, who may have married a woman off the plantation, produced and sold six bushels of corn and 444 blades, for which he earned $7.41 in October alone. Later that year, another three bushels and two quarts of corn and a "beef" brought him an additional $14.53. If Andrew's wife and children lived on a neighboring plantation, they surely stood to benefit from his industry, as did his family on the home place. Of course, although Nancey (and other family members) probably shared in her brothers' productivity, this is not to say that as nominal family head she was able to manage their work. The very productivity of several individual members in a large family may have worked to

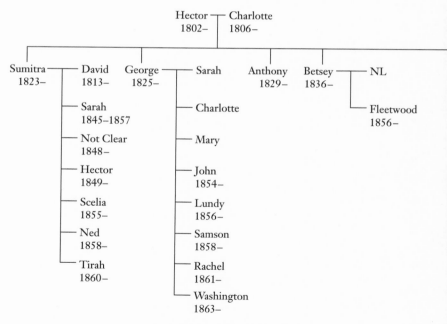

Fig. 3. Willson Family Number 3

reduce the authority of some family heads, effectively spreading it to include its most productive members such as Isaac and Andrew.

Some families on the Willson place did not produce and sell sufficient
goods to enjoy more than a basic standard of living. Members of Hector
and Charlotte's family, for example, do not appear with any frequency in
the Willson slave accounts (figure 3). It would have been necessary for this
family to have marshaled their meager resources if they were to ensure a
modicum of material comfort. Hector and Charlotte may have played an
active role in the economic affairs of their large but comparatively unproductive family. In October, their twenty-two-year-old son, George, sold a
160-pound hog for $6.40. Their eldest daughter and firstborn, Sumitra,
who had a two-year-old daughter, collected and sold a small quantity of
fodder for which she earned 50 cents. In December, Hector earned $1.85
for 247 blades. This low level of productivity from a group with nine immediate family members raises questions about its ability to provide extras.
The infrequent appearance of Family Number 3 in the account books is

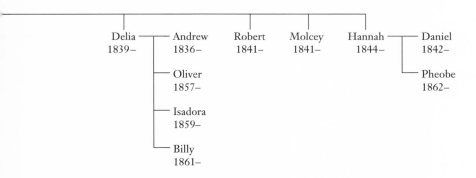

partly explained by its comparative youthfulness. Four of Hector and Charlotte's eight children were under ten years of age, and during the latter part of the 1840s Charlotte had three children and at least one grandchild under seven years of age; she and her eldest daughter, Sumitra, who gave birth twice between 1845 and 1848, may have given up much of their nonwork time to care for these infants. Families unable to take full advantage of the available opportunities were less able to provide for and protect themselves. These economically weak families would have found themselves wholly dependent on their owners and on the slave quarters community.

The experience of Hector and Charlotte's family shows that as important as a large family was to slaves, numerical advantage by itself did not necessarily indicate economic advantage. Gender and family structure and timing could significantly affect a family's economic and social well-being. A glance at Family Number 6 (figure 4), illuminates the linkage between these variables and economic productivity. The largest on the plantation with thirty-four members in 1847, this family was headed by Simon and Tirah, both born in the 1780s. They had produced nine children by 1829. Yet the family did not figure prominently in the Willson slave accounts, nor did it dominate any of the slave work groups. This failure is most directly linked to the presence of a sizable number of females of childbearing age in Simon and Tirah's family. Between the births of Phillis in 1803 and Susan in 1829, Tirah gave birth to five girls. By June 1848, all except nineteen-year-old Susan had given birth to at least one child. At the time when the accounts were being recorded, this family included fourteen children ten years old or younger and at least one adult in an advanced state of pregnancy. At this particular moment in time, burdened with a large number of very young children and its inability to produce extra income for itself, this family may have considered itself poor. Of course, the work and garden system encouraged the production of goods for immediate consumption and for sale only when a surplus existed.

Although Simon and Tirah's family's productivity might have been too low to provide surpluses for sale to Willson, we cannot be sure that the family did not produce sufficient provisions for its own consumption. Furthermore, like other families that produced their own crops, these slaves probably had some say as to which nonstaples they planted and adjusted their work routines accordingly and planted foodstuffs suitable for their immediate needs rather than for sale. Families with a large number of dependents would have considered it more appropriate to retain a greater proportion of their produce in reserve as insurance.[17] From time to time as their needs dictated, the family might choose to exchange some of these reserves for cash or other goods. Tirah and her three daughters, for example, received $2.62 for corn and blades in October, and Chloe sold corn and blades for $3.37. In December, Phillis brought in an additional $3.07 for corn and blades, and Benah sold a small amount of corn for $1.31. Although Tirah had few able-bodied helpers on whom to call, Phillis had three sons, aged twenty-two, twenty, and fourteen, as well as a seventeen-year-old daughter. Much of the goods that were produced by this family might not have materialized without the assistance of Phillis's adult male children. With time, however, as the children approached and reached adulthood, this family's fortune would improve, and, for a time at least, the family would produce at a high level. Until then, they were obliged to make do without many of the extras available to other families on the place.[18]

The records of Thomas Cassels Law of Darlington District provide an opportunity further to examine the relationship between family structure and economic achievement and to identify some of the advantages and disadvantages that could accrue to middle-country slaves who organized themselves into productive family units. Owning some eighty slaves at slavery's end, Law was one of the largest slaveholders in the middle country. Like many of his neighbors, he used a work and garden system that incorporated elements of both the gang and the task systems. Law was also typical in that he often divided his workers by both age and sex, as captured in an entry for January 12, 1841: "Fellows splitting rails, boys ploughing and women knocking cotton stalks."[19] The work and garden system under which the Law slaves labored enabled them to produce their own crops, which they exchanged with Law for cash or manufactured goods.

Cotton was the staple crop produced on the Law place, and it was from cotton that the Law slaves earned much of their extra income, unlike their fellows on the Willson plantation. In 1859, Law paid his slaves three cents per pound for seed cotton and two cents for "bad cotton," which was close to the 1859 Charleston market rate of about eleven cents for ginned cotton.[20] According to a list of slave accounts for this year, sixteen slaves, most of whom were family heads, produced and sold cotton to Law. Of the sixteen accounts, seven belonged to male slaves who sold their cotton for a total of $85.47; the nine female heads sold their cotton for $126.00. Additional sums of money were earned for various other work performed on or

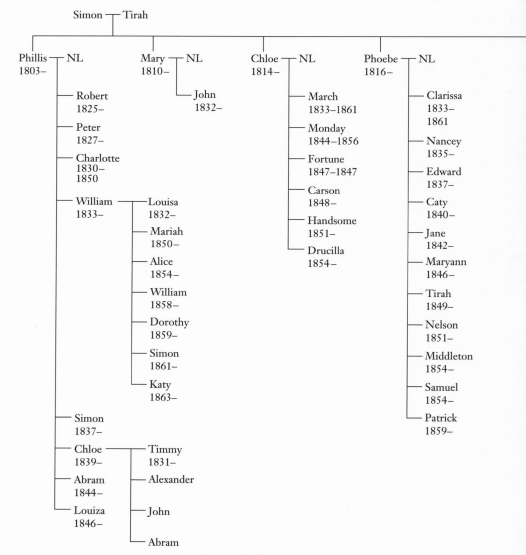

Fig. 4.   Willson Family Number 6

around the plantation. Henry, for example, earned $2 "by killing [a] dog (fox)" and for helping to build a house, Wesley earned 75 cents, and Sophy and Ann sold three and a quarter bushels of corn at $1.25 per bushel.[21]

Law's account book, detailing the family records of his slaves, reveals that Yenty, born in January 1764, and Bess, born on August 13, 1790, were

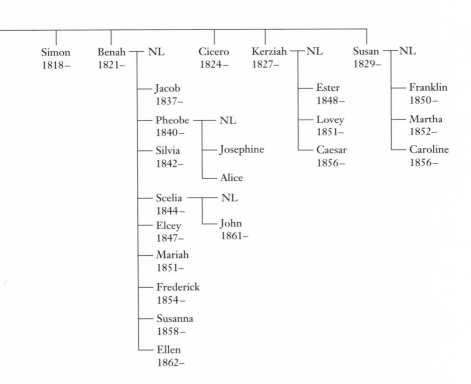

"married" sometime around 1810 (figure 5). By the time Yenty died, aged about seventy, he had fathered thirteen children, four of whom died before 1824. Bess's last child, Harriet, was born in 1834, the same year her father died. Her seventh child, Emily, and her family were sold in 1841, so from a total of thirteen births, Bess could boast a family of only eight children in 1859. These included five sons, Howard, Peter, Cyrus, Derry, and John, and three daughters, Dorcas, Hannah, and Harriet, all of whom were over twenty-five years of age. Dorcas had a daughter, Sarah, born in 1842, who by 1862 was married to a slave called Sidney. Sometime around 1846, Bess's second surviving daughter, Hannah, married Henry and had eight children before 1860, three of whom died in infancy. Her third son, Cyrus,

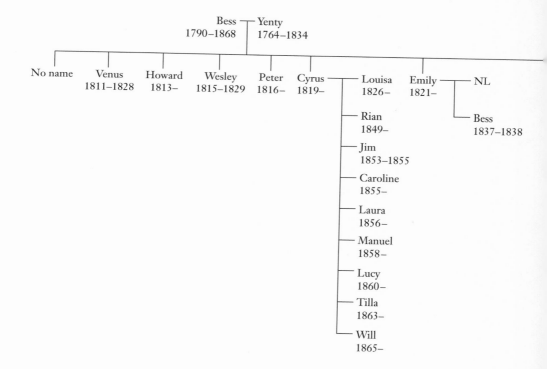

Fig. 5.   Law Family—Bess's Family

had married Louisa sometime around 1849, and their family had grown to six before 1860, the eldest surviving child being their ten-year-old daughter Rian. By 1859 Bess's other sons, Peter, aged forty-three, Derry, aged thirty, and John, aged twenty-eight, had either married women not living on the plantation or had remained single. Forty-six-year-old Howard, the firstborn son, held the position of plantation driver.[22]

As a unit with six mature males, six healthy females, and five children above five years of age, their family had considerable economic potential. With its senior male occupying the top position on the plantation, the family may have enjoyed additional benefits, and its economic strength and influence probably provided the political muscle that had placed and

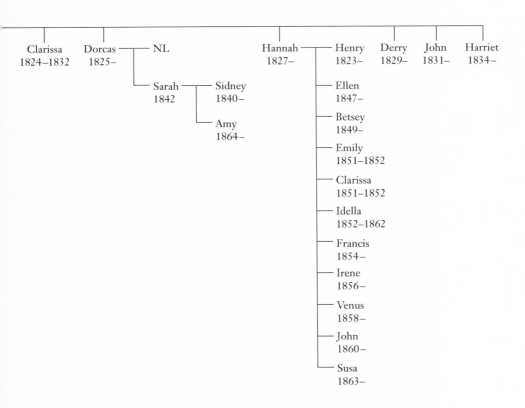

helped maintain Howard in the powerful but often precarious position of driver.[23] Under the work regimens that gave slaves opportunities to procure some of the benefits of their own industry and so improve the quality of their lives, Bess's family would have been better situated than most to have grabbed its share of anything that was offered, and even to have had some influence in determining the nature of those opportunities.

At the height of the 1859 cotton picking season Law ran a race conducted over four days, which he called "Race Week." During this week, the average cotton picked was 383 pounds. With the exception of Rose, who picked on only two days of the race, only one picker totaled less than 300 pounds for the period, while the top pickers all exceeded 500 pounds. Among the top ten pickers were five members of Bess's family, and her youngest son, John, picked 515 pounds, only 2 pounds less than the top picker. Even Henry and Hannah's twelve-year-old daughter, Ellen, who was probably not yet a half hand, added to the family's total with her 302 pounds. Using the slaves' performance during "Race Week" as a guide, it is clear that Bess's family constituted a considerable economic force in Law's plantation organization and in the private world of the quarters. In simple numerical terms, the family made up some 30 percent of Law's labor force and at least 50 percent of its best workers. Furthermore, its male head was also the plantation's headman. Consequently, Bess's family as a kin group was likely to have enjoyed a huge advantage over less well-situated families, not only in the number of males and able-bodied members but, perhaps more important, in the level of skill displayed in the often crucial task of picking cotton. Structural advantages, as we have seen, were not always successfully exploited, nor was the ability to pick cotton well always an indication of the ability, expertise, or desire to function as effectively in other areas. Charles Ball, for example, found that "at the hoe, the spade, the axe, and the sickle, or the flail, I was a match for the best hands on the plantation," but he soon discovered that when it came "to the picking of cotton, that I was not equal to a boy of twelve or fifteen years of age."[24] Ball, and no doubt many other slaves, would have been happier had he been more adept at picking cotton. Mastery of this highly prized and essential skill might very well have provided a solid base from which South Carolina slaves could build economic security while also strengthening their defense against sale. Few slave owners would sell one of their best workers without good reason, particularly if it risked creating disruption among a family of top-class workers.

Of the twenty-eight slaves listed as having accounts with Law in 1859, ten were from Bess's family, and they produced and sold a total of 3,278 pounds of seed cotton. Cyrus and Louisa, no doubt with some help from daughter Riah, produced and sold a total of 759 pounds. Henry and Hannah, with Ellen, aged twelve, and Betsy, aged ten, produced and sold 540 pounds. Dorcas and her teenage daughter, Sarah, produced and sold 334 pounds. Seventeen-year-old Sarah might already have begun to divide her time between her mother and her husband-to-be, Sidney. Peter, Derry, and John, not listed as married to women on the place, produced and sold 385, 366, and 320 pounds, respectively. Most revealing is Bess's personal achievement. At the age of sixty-nine, she produced and sold 574 pounds. With three sons without wives and families on the place and her twenty-five-year-old unmarried daughter, Harriet, still living with her, Bess could look to them for assistance, as well as to other members of her family, not in the least Howard, her driver son.

The volume of cotton she produced, over 60 percent more than that produced by three of her adult sons, also suggests that Bess might have had control of a larger portion of land than most of the other members of her family. If this were the case, it would support the notion that, irrespective of gender, family heads, particularly senior heads of families, had control over when (and which) members of their family received land, its size, and its location. Under such an arrangement, Bess could do as she wished with land originally controlled by herself and her deceased husband, Yenty, which passed to her upon her husband's death in 1834. It would not have been necessary for Bess to work the land herself because this could be done by other members of her family. And at a time Bess considered suitable, she would have parceled out pieces of the land to younger members of the family. This system would have operated as a kind of old age insurance policy for aged slaves while providing an economic reinforcement of the African practice of respect for elder members of the community.

Having been allotted land at an earlier time, Yenty and Bess would in all probability have received larger plots than, say, Sidney and Sarah could have expected. Sidney may have had to look to Bess, Sarah's grandmother, rather than Law, to obtain a suitable piece of land. If such a system operated on the Law place, or elsewhere, it would have given family heads a good deal of control over younger members. It would also have allowed the master to control, discipline, and punish younger slaves through their parents. A letter from Harriott Pinckney to her overseer captures the tricky relationship that sometimes existed between masters and slave family heads and the former's desire to hold parents responsible for their children's behavior. Writing from Charleston in 1855, Pinckney asked her overseer, William Winningham, to tell "Sambo that I received the Palmetto and will send him some coffee and sugar the next trip . . . tell him he don't deserve that I should send him the coffee and sugar because he brought up his son so badly."[25] Subtle, perhaps even humorous, the message nonetheless has clear implications. Although some masters would have frowned upon so much authority resting with senior slaves, discerning slave owners such as Sparkman and Pinckney might have endorsed this method of controlling and disciplining their slaves' large families through the family head.

How the members of Bess's family enjoyed the fruits of their labor reflected the structure and social organization of their family. Perhaps as payment for Harriet's part in the cultivation of her mother's cotton, and revealing her continued dependence, Bess spent $1.25 of the money she earned from the sale of her cotton on a "pair of shoes for Harriet." Hannah, with her considerable family of young children, at least five of whom were female, spent her income from 540 pounds of cotton on "12 yards of calico," probably for dresses; some "sugar"; and for her husband, perhaps, "2 shirt bosoms." Dorcas, whose main concern seems to have been herself (her husband lived on another plantation), and her daughter, Sarah, purchased "one hook," a bonnet for $2.50, and "half dozen iron spoons." Peter and John, with wives elsewhere or still unmarried, took most of their earnings in cash; Derry, also not listed as married and perhaps particularly concerned about his appearance, purchased a cloak for $1.75, two pairs of stockings, and two spools of thread. Sidney, who was probably already courting Sarah and hoping to join Bess's family, spent his earnings on a $4 coat, tobacco, two pounds of cheese, and a set of plates. The relative success of Bess's family seems to confirm the existence of a correlation between a slave's ability in one area of agricultural labor and a comparable ability in others. Furthermore, although the bulk of their earnings came from selling cotton, the Law slaves were not restricted to this single source of income. Old Sophy and her youngest daughter, Ann, twenty-one years old, produced and sold over three bushels of corn. And Charlotte used some of her "extra time" to earn 75 cents for one "days ditching."[26]

Bess's family's productivity placed them in a position to dominate the slaves' commercial activity on and around the Law plantation. Indeed, it was possible that had they so desired, they could have influenced the market on most goods by virtue of their numbers and their buying and selling power. With Howard as driver, they might even have had some influence over what came into the community's economy, legally or otherwise. Their ability to produce goods beyond their basic requirements meant that these slaves, in times of need, could look to family members for assistance. Whatever goods one family member did not have, another could supply. Charles Ball recalled an example of the exchange that probably often took place on South Carolina plantations. Following a comment on the slave allowance, Ball wrote that a peck of corn "is as much as a man can consume in a week, if he has other vegetables with it." This part of their diets these slaves were sometimes "obliged to provide for themselves." A fellow slave, Nero, had "corn in his patch, which was now hard enough to be fit for boiling," Ball wrote, and "my friend Lydia had beans in her garden." The age-old transaction was simple: "We exchanged corn for beans, and had a good supply of both."[27] This ability to satisfy their material needs allowed the slaves a level of autonomy that they would not otherwise have had. Furthermore, belonging to a large, economically productive family such as Bess's gave each member an increased ability to control some of the many variables that often brought unwanted fluctuations into the life of a slave.

As was true for the Willson plantation, families' work and economic experience differed greatly despite structural similarities. The next largest family on the Law plantation, unlike Bess's family, was not well equipped to take advantage of available opportunities. Born in September 1810, Old Sophy had seven children between 1828 and February 1841 (figure 6). By Christmas 1859, she had lost three of those children, and the worst blow must have been in 1849, when her firstborn son, seventeen-year-old

Colon, died. Her oldest surviving children in 1859 were Charlotte, aged thirty-one, and Serena, aged twenty-nine. Wesley, the only male, was twenty-five years old, and the youngest child, Ann, was almost twenty-one. The family had expanded through Charlotte, who had eight children before 1860, and Serena, who gave birth to five children. Like their mother, they too suffered: of Charlotte's eight children, three failed to survive their first year; Serena fared less badly, losing one child within the first year of birth. Ann, Old Sophy's youngest, lost her firstborn after a little

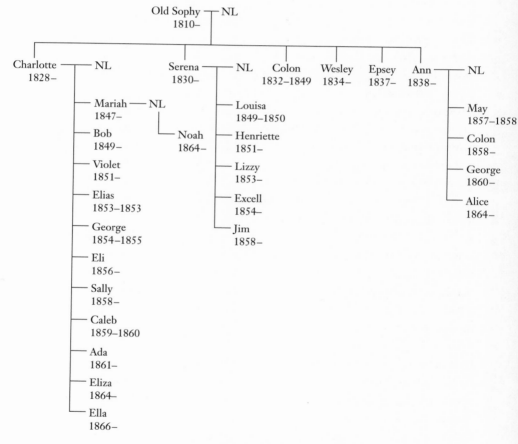

Fig. 6.   Law Family—Old Sophy's Family

over a year. Perhaps because Sophy and her young family were a gift Law received from Captain T. E. Hart, there is no information about her husband or exactly when she arrived on the Law place.

As the 1859 cotton picking season approached, members of Old Sophy's family were not well placed fully to exploit their opportunities. Sophy was forty-nine years old, Charlotte was pregnant with her eighth child, having given birth the previous spring, and Ann was pregnant with her third child. Although not pregnant, Serena had an infant not yet weaned. Furthermore, Serena had her last child at age twenty-eight (Charlotte had her last at age forty-six), perhaps indicating some illness or disability that both prevented her from having more children and hampered her ability to work for herself.[28] What is significant, however, is the different positions Bess's and Sophy's families found themselves in at this crucial stage in the agricultural season.

It is not surprising that only Sophy's name appears in "Race Week" and for a total just above the average of 384 pounds of cotton picked. On the lists of slave accounts the family fared a little better. Charlotte, although not credited at this time with any cotton sales, did purchase some $2 worth of guano (fertilizer), which indicates not only that she had some land under cultivation but also that she was willing (or was forced because of its poor quality) to take extra measures to make her land more productive. She purchased the fertilizer on credit and settled her debt in part with the seventy-five cents she earned from doing a day's work ditching. In this venture, assistance may have come from her children, Mariah, Bob, Violet, and Elias, aged twelve, ten, eight, and six years, respectively. Sophy's second daughter, Serena, with two daughters of her own aged eight and six years, had not yet credited her account. She had, nonetheless, purchased for her young family—two under the age of five—"a set of six bowls" and "two iron spoons." Wesley, the only adult male, also failed to appear on Law's list of creditors for cotton received. The money he earned had come from "building a [wooden?] horse for Cy," for which he was paid $1.50. This sum went toward paying for the $3 worth of tobacco he had purchased. Slave accounts often recorded purchases of twenty-five cents worth of tobacco so for Wesley to spend $3 probably means he was reselling the tobacco. Rather than laboring on his or the family's land,

Wesley may have exploited the slaves' internal economy to earn extra money.

Only Sophy, her daughter Ann, and her two young children were credited for cotton sold. For the 179 pounds of cotton and three and a quarter bushels of corn Sophy and Ann sold to Law, only three pounds of cheese had been purchased.[29] That Ann was working with her mother might suggest (as was the case with Bess and Harriet) that she was still at home despite having two children of her own. It also adds weight to the notion that land was not freely given out to anyone who might want it but that younger members of the family, like Ann, had to attain a certain age or status before they were considered ready to manage their own household, whereupon they would receive exclusive use of a garden. Being a young mother, Ann may have been deemed not yet ready to take up this responsibility. Questions such as the likelihood of her receiving suitable assistance with her land in case of need would have been high on the list of factors to be taken into account before such decisions were made. Until then, she was probably obliged to remain with her mother. Furthermore, that Sophy and her family were given to Law as a gift may have restricted the amount of land available to these late arrivals.

Although information about slave earnings is incomplete—we do not know the exact amount of cotton the slaves eventually sold or what other goods and services might have earned them additional income—certain criteria for economic success can be determined. Of course, family members had to be willing to work extra hard and to learn necessary skills, but there were other factors that were beyond their control. Economic advantages were more likely to accrue to a sizable family with able-bodied males and females who were not in the process of producing their own families. Unlike Bess, who was blessed with a large and talented family, including several sons, Sophy's family was less well blessed and, as a result, would have to struggle to put an economic "space" between itself and the master. The families that could not meet at least some of these criteria were likely to find themselves in strained circumstances. The unwillingness of certain family members to pull their weight may have been a major cause of family disruption, and weaker families may have found themselves being referred to as "poor" or "no count," while families such as Bess's would have been considered "well off," if not "rich," and the dominant political and cultural force in the slave quarter community.

Of course, Sophy's family may have received some compensation from their master for their disadvantages. Law may have supplemented the allowance of female slaves such as Charlotte and Serena, who, being pregnant and burdened with young children, were less able to perform their normal routines. So-called rewards for childbirth—an incentive bonus given to mothers whose children survived beyond the dangerous first twelve months—probably compensated slave mothers and their families for the loss of earnings while they were away from their work; it was a form of supplementary family income. Pregnant women usually did less work and received more attention and rations than nonpregnant women. Designed primarily to ensure the good health of mother and fetus alike, this improved treatment would also have acted as an incentive for over-worked slave women to have children.[30] I doubt, however, that women who labored under the work and garden system and who appreciated the economic difficulties the burden (however temporary) of a large family of young children could bring would have considered extra attention and rations a sufficient short-term incentive to have large numbers of children. Of course, once the earlier stages of family formation had passed and young children became productive, slave women could expect to benefit from a family that could meet the criteria for economic success.

Richland District's Keziah Goodwyn Hopkins Brevard left an intimate account of her dealings with her slaves. Her diary covering the period immediately before the outbreak of the Civil War provides a revealing glimpse into slave work and family life. Brevard had many problems disciplining some of her slaves, particularly the females. She "indulged" them, partly in an attempt to win them over and partly out of a genuine concern for them. As did many slave owners, Brevard allowed her slaves to work their gardens and encouraged them to develop stable families. Those of her slaves who worked hard earned considerable sums from the production and sale of crops and livestock and took steps toward making a life of their own. In October 1860, Brevard reluctantly allowed her two "house boys," Ned and Dick, to spend three days in the fields picking cotton. Although she was concerned for their welfare because, being house boys, they could not "stand the sun as the field hands do," the young men appreciated getting away from the house and their mistress and the opportunity to pick cotton with their fellow slaves. Furthermore, both had been growing their own crops, and the following month Ned was paid $12.50 for his crop of corn, which "netted him $8.50 all due for his crop [after] he paid me $3.50 for . . . flour."[31]

Several other slaves were paid for crops, and money was given to Abraham Rawlinson, the overseer, to pay the nonhouse slaves for their corn. A busy commercial exchange also existed between Brevard and several of her slaves, as indicated by the following entries in her diary: "Nelly let me have one dozen eggs. I paid her in tobacco, sent it by Dick one and a half plug, 15 cents, I give 15 cents for a dozen eggs." And "Harry paid me for flour he got and I paid him for the two baskets I got from him." Brevard fully appreciated the financial rewards and subsequent benefits that could fall to particular slave families. She found that certain families were too powerful for her to control and resented the complacent well-being of some of the slaves on the place. On January 23, 1861, she recorded a picture of Jim bringing a cart load of wood for his family. "Perhaps if he were free," she pondered, "he would have to buy this wood . . . maybe have a poor house and a dirty chimney." Instead, Jim had "a house . . . brick fire place with three rooms—one to sit in—two bedrooms." Brevard associated the most unruly slaves with the largest and most powerful families on the plantation. She struggled to feel any affection for these slaves and wrote that she "didn't wish them very bad luck." She only wished them to "feel like they are no better than other servants." But these slaves were formidable opposition for Brevard because they were "prop[p]ed up by a large family and presume on it by making others succumb to them." She only wished to have these slaves realize (somewhat ironically) that "power is not always to the strong." Brevard felt sure that if all the slaves were "freed in a day—these very families would enslave the small families."[32]

Among the troublesome large families singled out by Brevard was that of the "independent" Jim. His family and Old Dick's descendants, she wrote, "are enough to kill anyone who thinks to manage them." As for the importance of family stability and longevity, she wrote of Old Dick's and Old Jacob's descendants that they were "the next high in power & the ruling spirits" at the plantation. Despite the "bad" treatment by some of her more powerful and richer slaves, Brevard neither neglected them nor, as she put it, did she forget her "poor." An entry for early December 1860 reads: "Paid John for his corn and fodder. $4.20 payment in full. John has made so little I forgave him the debt he owed me, one glass 25 cents, one for cloth goods 20 cents . . . these are my poor," she reasoned, "why not give them some things." John was not the only "poor" slave on the Brevard place. Later that month she recorded the plight of Dick, to whom she had paid all the money due to him, $2 for 132 pounds of fodder. Apparently some hogs belonging to Henry Strikland, a neighbor, had eaten all Dick's corn. Brevard wrote, "Dick owed me $3.50 for a bag of flour [but] as the hogs destroyed his crop I forgave him the debt and paid him for his fodder $2." Frank, whose crops were also damaged, also had his debt with his mistress canceled.[33]

Brevard worked hard "to make her negroes happy," and she encouraged both slave enterprise and stable families.[34] Her "indulgences" testify to the precarious nature of the slaves' agricultural exploits and how quickly the economic base of the slaves and the resultant "space" between the slaves and their owners might disappear. Even for the "better off" slaves, one bad harvest could destroy their economic base and all the associated benefits. Like others involved in the somewhat risky business of agriculture, having invested their nonwork time and all their resources in the cultivation of their crops, the slaves remained at the mercy of the vagaries of weather and other unnatural as well as natural disasters. Without caring and understanding owners like Brevard, one bad harvest could throw most slaves back into a state of total dependence. Although it was at times such as these that slaveholders could exercise their paternalism to good advantage, and in so doing remind the slaves of their lack of "real" power, such crises would also have reminded individual slaves of the importance of large, well-organized, and productive family groups. As in many African societies, slaves who were outside of a family unit were more vulnerable than those secure within such groups.[35] Single slaves, therefore, would have tried to form productive family units. Indeed, for many slaves, this search for a stable family and the maintenance of its integrity constituted the most immediate and attainable steps in their search for freedom from the most debilitating aspects of their life under slavery, if not from slavery itself.

A high level of trust, loyalty, and mutual support within the slave quarter community was most clearly evidenced when the white world forcibly intruded and slaves were forced to muster their relatively meager political power to protect themselves. At such times, large, well-established families, although no guarantee of protection against the destructive forces of slavery, would have been better placed to protect their members. A case tried before the Spartanburg Magistrates and Freeholders Court reveals that while on patrol duty one night in January 1847, John Zimmerman came across some of "his property" in the possession of several slaves. Five large tablespoons and five teaspoons were found in the possession of Phillis, a slave belonging to A. W. Thompson. Also charged with eight other slaves was her husband, Jim, who belonged to M. Moore. Mooney, another member of the patrol group, testified to Phillis's claim that she had purchased the cutlery from a peddler "and that she could prove it." Mooney had also found a spoon in the possession of her mother, who claimed that her mistress had given it to her, but later Phillis claimed the spoon. Smith, the third member of the patrol, reported that he had heard Jim say he bought the spoons from a peddler some seven or eight years previous and that "his master gave him $5 and he had 50 cents and he gave $5.50 for the set." Liza, a slave, said she saw Jim bring the spoons to his wife's house three to four years earlier. The court was given sufficient cause to find the defendants not guilty.[36]

The evidence suggests that Zimmerman and his patrol had entered Phillis's house without just cause and certainly without authorization. When they found cutlery that may or may not have rightfully belonged there, the slave Phillis was asked to prove she had not stolen the spoons. Suspecting a theft, the patrol conducted a random search of all the slave houses and found other pieces of cutlery, Mooney finding one in Phillis's mother's house. The large number of defendants—nine, six of whom were women—suggests that cutlery was found in other slave houses. Had they originated from Phillis's house, brought there by her husband, Jim, it would indicate that a high level of sharing or exchange and a high level of interdependency operated in the quarters, confirming the generally supportive nature of the slave quarter world. If the spoons had originated from diverse sources, the widespread ownership of the cutlery would indicate that a large number of slaves had legal (or illegal) access to manufactured goods.

Particularly noteworthy is Phillis's mother's instinctive response to the patrolman's question, which was to protect her daughter. "Her mistress gave it to her," she volunteered. Several postures were being struck here. The patrol's authority was set up against that of the mistress—public law against private practice and white superiors against white subordinates. The claim of generosity on the part of one's master or mistress was a frequently used defense for slaves forced to prove ownership of property, and their claims could be checked easily. The patrol, however, in this case having violated custom and overstepped its duty by entering the plantation and searching the slave houses without the owner's permission, may not have wished to confront a master or mistress whose property had been so intruded upon.

In setting the mistress's authority against that of the patrol, the slaves were also calling on her for protection. It would have been very easy for the patrol to check Jim's claim that he had received $5 from his master; such a large sum would have been recorded in a journal or diary, and most slave masters would have appreciated knowing when, where, and on what their slaves were spending such large sums of money. Jim's claim, therefore, is likely to have been true.

That Jim spent his money on his wife reveals a high level of commitment between the two and is evidence that slave husbands kept their property at their wives' houses when they did not share the same master. Their joint ownership of property is further suggested by Phillis's willingness to inform the patrol that she "bought them from a peddler" and that "she could prove it," whereas the evidence indicates that Jim's money was used to purchase the goods. For Phillis, the source of her husband's money was not pertinent in this case, nor was it important who actually had paid the peddler. What was relevant was that the money had belonged to them, and the goods were purchased by them and for them: not acting as individuals, theirs was a joint existence; they were man and wife.[37]

Having outlined the economic and social benefits slaves could expect to receive from working together and organizing in productive family units, it is necessary now to take a closer look at the organization of work and slave life on a selection of farms and plantations and to examine how these processes affected the public and private lives of the slaves and their families. Work systems had a profound impact on slave family structure, affecting its economic well-being and public and private behavior, determining the contours of family life, and shaping each member's worldview. How the majority of slaves arranged their working life, then, is of crucial importance for any understanding of the development, function, and form of the black family under slavery.[38] In the public world of the master the slave's economic activity signified little more than a reduction of slaveholders' responsibility for the slaves' immediate welfare and a broadening (but increasingly subtle) panorama of control mechanisms. In the private world of the quarters, however, the slave family economy echoed far louder and had profound effects on the slaves, their families, and the structure of the community in which they lived. The ownership and working of land was the fulcrum in a world where, short of actual freedom, the family and family stability became the immediate and more tangible goal.

The harder the slaves worked for themselves, the better able they were to take advantage of the available economic opportunities; the more they could contribute to their material comforts, the more protection they could accumulate against physical punishment, the ever-present threat of sale, and the many other abuses that characterized life under slavery.

Evidence of slaves working hard, accumulating property, and moving toward stable family formation was not restricted to any particular part of the state, although low- and middle-country slaves may have enjoyed certain demographic and spatial advantages over their up-country counterparts.[39] Nonetheless, whenever opportunities presented themselves, most slaves quickly grabbed them. Low-country slaves in Beaufort District took firm hold on the life chances that came their way and even made some of their own. Sam Mitchell was born in 1850 on a Ladies Island plantation owned by John Chaplin. Sam's father doubled as a carpenter and plow hand. His mother worked as a hoe hand. Both parents worked under the task and garden system and had "'bout two task ob land to cultivate fer se'f." They could also raise a pig. Mitchell's father worked hard in the daytime to complete his task, then he was likely to take his boat and was "gone fishing." He would sell his catch. Chaplin also allowed him to "cut post and wood at night," which he sold.[40]

Another Beaufort slave, Sam Polite, born in 1844, was old enough to fend for himself before the end of slavery. His master, B. Fripp, practiced the task and garden system, allowing Sam and his family about "two or tree tas' ob land" around their cabin. When they "knock off work you kin wuk on your land." They were also permitted to "hab chicken, maybe hawg." The results of their efforts could be sold, the eggs and chickens to a "store," and master "will buy your hawg." Sam recalled that money earned might be spent on items such as "fish and w'atebber he want." As he explained, "We didn't get much fish in slabery 'cause we nebber hab boat." Even without a boat, Polite seems to have stretched the bounds of slavery and made his life bearable if not comfortable for himself and his family. His comment on his experience under slavery is particularly relevant to our discussion: "I t'ink," he reflected, "it been good t'ing. It larn nigger to wuk." Polite's words indicate a direct correlation between the slaves' willingness and ability to work hard in their own time and their general welfare under slavery. The ability to take those important steps toward making a life of one's own did not require that slaves possess any special skill or talent or that they work in the master's house; given the willingness to make the effort, quite ordinary slaves could succeed. Polite and his fellow slaves had to work hard if they aspired to do more than simply survive; if they hoped to make something of their lives, they had to work extra hard. While a slave, Polite had worked until dark even on Saturdays, "just lak any odder day." More often than not on those Saturdays and during those late nights, he was working for himself and his family. And as he told the WPA interviewer in 1937, "I still does work 'till dark on Saturday."[41]

Without the support and assistance of family members, few slaves would have found it easy to create a niche, a space for themselves under slavery because individual slaves could not always muster the energy and willpower to make the extra effort to provide a satisfactory economic and social foundation. Aunt Margaret Bryant, born about 1850 on Sandy Island, recalled her industrious mother, a seemingly tireless weaver. After receiving an order for three or four yards of cloth from a "po buckra," her mother had to weave day and night to make the cloth. The purchaser had no money and settled his debt with a "hog and such like as that to pay." Bryant's mother, like countless other slave parents, had to labor and make sacrifices to provide extras for her family. Henry Brown of Big Island was acutely aware of his responsibilities as a father. He recalled that "men didn't have time to frolic 'cause they had to fin' food for the fambly" because their master "never give 'nough to las' the whole week." Another low-country slave, Sabe Rutledge of Horry District, recalled a scene that reveals the tireless efforts of some slaves in their struggle to maintain even a minimum of living for their families. At night in their cabin, Rutledge's mother would be spinning, there would be "a great oak log, iron fire dog. [She] would have we chillin sit by the fire place. . . . We four chillin have to pick seed out of cotton. . . . Work till ten o'clock at night and rise early. . . . Pick out cotton seed be we job every night in winter time . . . 'cept Sunday." When they were old enough, their mother made "one card. One would spin and then Mudder go to knitting."[42] In such situations it would have been likely that the whole family, irrespective of age or gender, would contribute its share to the work, and, of course, here as in their gardens, the more hands the better.

In 1850, Michael Gramling of Orangeburg, owner of some thirty-eight slaves, was a successful middle-country planter. His records provide an opportunity to examine the working life of middle-country slaves.[43] Gramling used a highly sophisticated form of the work and garden system whereby the slaves not only worked under the task system but were assigned the same piece of ground for the season. No doubt Gramling wanted to instill in his slaves a sense of personal responsibility for, and attachment to, their place of work.[44] As was typical of the whole state, however, he also operated a fairly rigid system of labor that was gender-based and divided between able and less able workers. In "laying off" thirteen acres in his Barnville field, for example, he divided it up into cotton tasks at "three quarters of an acre large [with] Bob's half acre tasks next by the gate. Sophy back of the garden. Then follows Judy, Delia, Deborah of the women, the men behind to take slips to suit themselves."[45] Clearly, Bob was not in the same category as "the men" who were working to "suit themselves." He did not even have the same status as the women with whom he had to work, working only a half acre task to their three-quarter tasks.

Although involved mainly in the production of cotton and corn like most Orangeburg County slaves, the Gramling slaves also produced a little indigo, rice, watermelons, pumpkins, peas, potatoes, turnips, and wheat. Furthermore, in March 1846, Gramling began making "mudsills" for the local railroad. They were thirty-six feet long by seven inches wide and sixteen inches across the stump, and Gramling would be paid "at 2 cents the running foot." He delegated this work to two of his slaves,

Anthony and Tom. The former would be tasked "15 pieces a week," the latter only twelve pieces. "I make this difference," Gramling explained, "because Tom has never hewn before and Anthony has."[46]

The available evidence suggests that Gramling's work systems generally operated smoothly and fairly successfully for all concerned. An entry for May 4, 1848, reads: "Started to shaving down my cotton—Thursday afternoon and Friday forenoon, negroes ploughing their own corn." Another for Monday, April 19, 1852, read: "After dinner . . . negroes went to planting their own cotton just as regularly on as they do mine." This account conjures up images of an organic relationship between Gramling and his slaves and, perhaps, something about the latter's attitude to their labor which facilitated this smooth transfer from the master's to the family's field. Such a relationship would have required the acceptance of agreed roles and responsibilities by master and slaves, engendered by, and reflected in, the successful operation of the work and garden system.

One immediate benefit to the slaves for their cooperation was goods they produced and sold to Gramling. During the 1850–51 season, five out of approximately eighteen working hands produced and sold cotton to Gramling for a total of $36. Anthony's 302 pounds of seed cotton purchased by Gramling at three and a half cents a pound brought him a sum of $10.56, which was the largest amount sold. Ned, with the smallest amount, received $3.85 for 110 pounds. Three other men earned money from their cotton sales: Chance earned $6.75, Lewis $6.81, and Tom $8.05. Other goods sold that year included manure and fodder, sales of which placed a further five slaves (and the first female) on the Gramling account book and pushed the total recorded earnings up to $48.85.

The following season, a total of 3,482 pounds of seed cotton was produced by twelve slaves, two of whom were females (Delia and Judy) for an average of 290 pounds per slave. Among the best producers were Anthony, Adam, and Charles, whose total sales exceeded the average by 200, 195, and 150 pounds, respectively. At the other end of the scale were Joe, Judy, Ned, and Delia, all of whom failed by 130, 118, 104, and 54 pounds, respectively, to reach the average of 290 pounds. With 10 pounds of Tom's cotton carried over from the previous year, the ginned cotton weighed 1,169 pounds, which Gramling recorded as "all sold and negroes paid on the 13 January, 1852." Two years later, eighteen slaves, including four females, produced 4,494 pounds of seed cotton at an average of 250 pounds. Among the female slaves were two house servants, Milly and Delphy, whose combined total crop was only 131 pounds, and with a low of 37 pounds for Judy and 126 pounds for Bob, who in 1847 had been given half hand status, the average was drastically reduced even though six slaves had produced in excess of 300 pounds and two, Harry and Tom, produced 466 and 416 pounds, respectively. Some other notable achievements also occurred that year. Ned, who had produced 110 pounds in 1850, increased his crop to 172 pounds in 1851 and reached a high of 331 pounds in 1854. Hercules's wife, listed separately from her husband in 1854, was credited with 343 pounds, her husband with 217 pounds, which would have given them a total family income for their cotton of $25.20. In the 1856–57 season Hercules topped the table with cotton earnings of $20.56, Adam was close behind with $18.25, followed by Hercules's wife, Delphy, with $14.58 and Delia with a similar sum. The smallest sums were earned by Judy, $5.55, and Old Harry, $5.35. Even Charles, the plantation cook, was able to earn an extra $8.10 for his cotton. Production for 1858 remained about the same as in 1854, with fourteen slaves producing 3,482 pounds of seed cotton at an average of 284 pounds. That year Adam and Charles topped 400 pounds, and eight hands exceeded 270 pounds. Neither Judy nor Joe managed more than 14 pounds, and, along with Bob with 54 pounds, and Delphy, the house servant, they were the smallest producers of cotton.[47]

Those who extended themselves on the Gramling place, particularly in family groups, were always likely to earn substantial sums of money. One late entry in his journal shows that Gramling paid out over $200 to sixteen slaves for the year's cotton crop. Such a sum for the cotton the slaves produced and sold provides some indication of the amounts that might have been available to slaves of the middle country and the "wealth" that could have been accumulated by hardworking and enterprising slave families.

Although Gramling encouraged all his slaves to produce their own crops and purchased what they had for sale, it is clear that they did not all fare equally well. Nor did all the slaves produce only cotton. Other crops would have provided a more immediate supplement to their allowance and a subsequent boost to their standard of living. The yearly income from cotton was likely considered their cash crop, paying out only once a year.

If they grew corn, they could have produced a harvest several times each year. Gramling noted that he gave the slaves the afternoon of May 4, 1848, and a Friday morning "to plow their corn." Producers of smaller amounts of cotton probably concentrated their main efforts on corn or on some other edible or more easily marketable crop rather than on cotton. Slaves had to be fairly well supplied with the basic necessities before they could consider committing the bulk of their available resources—garden space and perhaps money for seeds—to cotton. Although cotton remained the main cash crop and could legally be sold only through the master, alternative outlets for other products were certainly available in the slaves' internal economy.[48]

The Gramling records make it clear that female slaves on the plantation generally produced less than the men did. The vulnerability of individual slaves outside of strong families is most noticeable when those individuals were single mothers with very young children. Any such women on the Gramling plantation would have found themselves in a less than comfortable situation.[49] The small number of slave women on the plantation— eight out of a working population of thirty—suggests that they were either married or related to male members of the Gramling slave community and probably worked their land as a family concern. The benefits of their labor would have been recorded under the name of the male (or female) family head. Deborah, for example, a hoe hand not credited with having produced any crops for sale, had given birth to a child on December 4, 1846, and to another on May 2, 1849. Sophy, equally unproductive in her garden, gave birth on January 6, 1847, and again a year later, and had a third child in May 1852. Both Deborah and Sophy, along with Judy and Delia, were hoe hands who were usually asked to work three-quarter tasks and were regularly listed as picking cotton. There is nothing, therefore, to suggest that any of these women had been chronically sick and exempt from work or that they had not been expected to produce crops for sale. Because tasks for hoes and pickers took longer than those for plows, the lack of female plow hands on the place was an immediate disadvantage for unattached female workers. And given women's additional responsibilities for domestic duties, most may have found comparatively less time to work in their gardens. Indeed, single women may have been expected to work and remain with their families until they married. Of course, married women with husbands living on nearby plantations could have looked to them for assistance. But when women do appear in the accounts with masters they generally registered a small crop and received a small payment in return. On this point Bob's situation may prove a useful test.

Gramling's work organization was highly segregated. The males were responsible for plowing and executed tasks such as felling trees, hewing wood, and making barrels, while the women's primary responsibility seems to have been restricted to the less arduous but more tedious jobs of hoeing, picking cotton, and "dipping" indigo. An entry for November 8, 1847, reads: "Started Tom, Hercules, Adam and Anthony . . . with half shovels to breaking ground. . . . Women clearing up before the plough." When, in April 1848, Joe was "sick with piles," Anthony rather than one of the women was taken away from the highly lucrative enterprise (for Gramling at least) of barrel making and put to Joe's plow. The group picking cotton on October 2, 1848, included Sophy, Deborah, Judy, and Bob—who worked only a half task compared with the women's three-quarter task. Also included were three children who on their first time in the cotton field only a year before had made Gramling very proud when the "three little ones picked together . . . forty pounds." That Bob was working in this company suggests that he was either old, disabled, or "sickly," the former being more likely because he was vaccinated against smallpox along with Tom, Rufus, and "the whole of my little negroes."[50] Given his presence in such company, we should expect Bob's production to be low. He produced and sold 154 pounds of cotton in 1854, and his next contribution of 54 pounds came two years later. Thus, as with Judy, his productivity was markedly below the average for all the slaves and more typical of those who were either not adult, not able-bodied, not fit, or not male. The correlation between the nature of the slave's work on the plantation and the amount of land he or she was deemed capable of tending and, by extension, the amount of crops particular slaves and slave families could produce, meant that women without close family attachments on or near the plantation would have been totally dependent on the master for the necessities of life, as would the old, the very young, the infirm, and the disabled. Given the seemingly smooth relationship that existed between Gramling and his slaves and the latter's relative well-being, the underrepresentation of women in the slave accounts should not suggest that the female slaves were in dire economic straits but simply reflects the extent and stability of slave family organization in the Gramling slave quarters.

Not all middle-country slaves were as well settled into their work routine as the Gramling slaves, and the life experience of slaves whose work experience differed markedly would been affected accordingly. Although one of the oldest and most populous slave states, South Carolina retained some characteristics of the frontier. James D. Trezevant arrived in Orangeburg District in September 1845 to begin clearing and preparing his land. Short of slaves, he frequently "borrowed" slaves from neighbors or hired in slaves. September and much of October were spent clearing land and building houses for the slaves. By March the following year he was still relying on foodstuffs from outside the plantation, purchasing "a years supply of meat . . . 60 sides of bacon and 10 fowls." After completing his first season's planting on Friday, April 25, Trezevant "gave the hands holiday until Monday."[51]

By 1849, Trezevant no longer had to purchase meat. January found him waiting for "a cold spell to kill hogs." He was unsure exactly how many he owned. The same year he listed twenty adult slaves who were assessed as fourteen working hands. Thus, like Gramling, Trezevant would be considered a medium-sized planter. A further and important addition to the plantation was the "50 head of sheep" bought in May 1849, which was almost twenty head above the average for the district. The presence of a large number of sheep, penned to separate them from other livestock, would have reduced the amount of land available for slave gardens.[52]

The work organization on the Trezevant place, in part because of the newness of the enterprise and the size of the work force, tended more toward the gang system than the task system, further reducing the opportunities for the slaves to demonstrate and benefit from their industriousness. In 1851, Trezevant worked his plantation with eleven full hands and one half hand. The rest of his work force consisted of Doll and Old Mary, both over fifty years old. Doll was useful as a nurse, but "Old Mary was useless." Old Simon, however, was earning his keep as a hog minder and "mule feeder." Feb, the cow boy, and a handful of young children completed his workers outside the house.[53]

Trezevant did operate a work and garden system that allowed his slaves occasional days or half days to work for themselves. On these occasions and during the late evenings the slaves were able to cultivate their provision grounds to produce for their own consumption and have a surplus to sell for cash. Trezevant's list of slave earnings is a clear indication that even where the gang system might have had ascendancy over the task system and the slaves' time was in great demand, they could still have the opportunity to plant for themselves.

Even in this small community, the Trezevant slaves displayed significant differences in earning potential. Old Simon, the hog minder, no doubt past his prime, sold five bushels and three pecks of corn and some fodder and earned $4.55. Feb, the cow boy, earned $7.50 for his corn and fodder. While all the male full hands did fairly well, each selling at least three bushels of corn and Joe doing exceptionally well with eight bushels, the female slaves, once again, appear to have fared less well. Only Mary and Hoby were listed as having sold corn or fodder, yet five of the eleven full hands on the place were females.

Most of the women of childbearing age were having children. Hoby gave birth to a boy named Simon and a girl named Dolly. Hannah, another full hand, aged about thirty-three, gave birth to a boy in 1847 who failed to survive a full year. In the summer of 1848, she gave birth to a girl called Eve, who outlived her brother by only a year. Another son, Adam, born in May 1851, survived his first two years and was joined by a brother named Prince in October 1853. Peggy had a son, William, in September 1850. These three full hands constituted over 25 percent of the plantation's senior workers and half of the senior female workers. Pregnancy and the rearing of young children must have substantially reduced the amount of time these women were able to spend looking after their plots of land. And, of course, absence from Trezevant's field because of pregnancy, childbirth, and postpartum responsibilities also meant absence from their own gardens. These factors help to explain the comparatively poor performance of the women in general and of childbearing slave women in particular. Women who had passed this period were much more likely to perform well in the production and sale of crops. For example, Mary Chapel, for whom there is no record of childbirth, had earnings of $5.47 for her corn and fodder, and Hoby, whose two pregnancies were separated by some six years, is the only other female full hand to appear on the list of slave accounts, though then only with the relatively small sum of $1.25 for corn and fodder.[54] The dependent position of some categories of slaves is here again emphasized. Without a husband or able-bodied relatives on or near the home place, women of childbearing age ran the risk of becoming dependent upon their master or on the slave quarter community, both unenviable positions.

There were additional reasons why women's earnings were lower than men's. Like Gramling, Trezevant distinguished between men's and women's work. His plow hands were men and his hoe hands women. An entry for March 17, 1852, reads: "All hands on the island today. The men cutting and the women burning bush." On April 28, he put "all hands . . . to planting rice." They finished at noon, and the "ploughs then went to the island and the hoe hands to chopping seeds of[f] the cotton." The plow hands enjoyed more time to themselves and would have been trusted to work larger pieces of land for their own use. Being male, the plow hands probably set the standard for all males, making it necessary only to be a male, and not even a plow hand, to have been allocated a larger plot, thus reinforcing a gender-based system that accorded women an inferior position in the public world.[55] Furthermore, because Trezevant had only recently purchased the plantation, a massive overhauling and extensive clearing of land for cash crops as well as for the provision of large gardens probably took primacy over other work. Those best able to do this work on their own time would probably also have received larger plots, an additional factor in favor of the men.

The Lancaster District plantation of William J. Connors was not untypical of the up-country. The Connors work force consisted of probably no more than fifteen or sixteen hands, the majority of whom were women. Perhaps because of this small work force and the small size of the plantation, Connors kept the division of labor to a minimum. Beyond their designation as "plows" and "hoe hands" and the occasional reference to women working with cloth, the Connors women could be found plowing, picking, and even digging "in the canal for the foundation of a dam," work described as "very tedious [as] there are so many roots." Perhaps less typical of the up-country as well as of the small planter was Connors's use of a work and garden system based on tasking. He also encouraged his slaves to work for themselves in their spare time. As elsewhere, the time these slaves had available for their own work depended to a large extent on their plantation occupation. Connors's plow hands, for example, enjoyed more free time than those hands whose main responsibility was with the hoe. On the morning of July 3, 1841, Jim and Elvira, two of Connors's plow hands, began their task, which they were "able to complete . . . by 12 noon, after which they worked for themselves." A later entry reveals that the "plows finished the 19 acre field by mid-afternoon, after which they worked for themselves."[56]

The hoe hands could anticipate much longer days in the fields even though the work might have been considerably lighter. An entry for July 27, 1841, reads: "The hoe hands drew up cotton in the thirty acre field, but about 11 o'clock, before they got through their task we were blest with a good heavy rain." A dry spell had delayed planting, and following the downpour, the hands were directed to the more immediate task of planting slips. Several days later Connors complained that the female hands hoeing slips had not completed their tasks but that they would have "had it not been for Emma that was somewhat behind." Emma had to return to the same task the following day, but her workmates had the day free because they had "finished their tasks and doubling tasks." Having struggled with her task for the second consecutive day, Emma was next recorded as "sick today."[57]

When Connors's female plow hand, Elvira, was not plowing she could be found doing what would have been considered women's work. Usually Elvira and Jim worked as a plow team, but Jim and Emperor were mending rails while the females, including Elvira, "layed by corn." On August 18, 1842, Elvira was teamed with Daphney, who "with three spinners commenced stripping fodder."[58] If fodder gathering, another particularly unpleasant job, was considered women's work, it might explain why women often appeared in masters' account books as having earned money only from the sale of fodder or blades. Connors's reference to women digging in the canal, usually considered men's work, was qualified by the information that the job was "very tedious." To Connors, this physically demanding task was appropriate for women.

Connors did not record exactly how his slaves spent their free time or whether they produced crops and sold their surplus. He does, however, provide several clues. On September 6, 1841, after stripping fodder in the old field, the "negroes stripped and brought up theirs and mine too." Both Connors and the slaves were growing corn; they both had crops from which the fodder could be stripped and used to feed the livestock. The entry suggests, therefore, that the Connors slaves had both gardens and livestock and so produced goods for their own consumption and probably also for sale. Indeed, Emperor is recorded as having "brought a hog of his from Johnson's," and later that month, Ben, who had been recovering for some time from "a very bad rising on his foot," collected some poles to make an outhouse for provisions. A few days later, when "the others were permitted to work out [for themselves], the fellows were employed putting up Ben's house." Perhaps it was a sizable provision house for a sizable amount of provisions. Furthermore, on several occasions two or three slaves were recorded as having worked off the plantation; on September 29, "Jim and Emperor assisted my neighbor Elisha Blackman about his mill dam." For this work these men might have received some financial reward.[59]

Despite the absence of any concrete evidence of the Connors slaves' extra work activities and any financial rewards they might have received, there is enough in his journal to show that the slaves were not forced to work from "sun to sun" for six or more days each week. On the contrary, they were given time from work that was spent working on their own crops, on neighboring plantations for pay, or tending their livestock. Furthermore, when one of their community was in need of assistance, as Ben had been in the construction of his provision house, they were willing and able to come to his aid.

The record of the slaves' efforts picking cotton over a two-day period and the brief but untidy accounts J. B. Witherspoon kept of his dealings with his slaves reveal another dimension of the up-country slaves' world of work. Some forty-seven slaves worked on this plantation. It is not certain that they all belonged to Witherspoon; some might have been brought in for cotton picking. On November 2 and 3, 1852, the Witherspoon slaves picked cotton in a manner their master "considered something extra good." As a result, he decided "to make a record of it for future references."[60]

Witherspoon was one planter who believed in the use of positive incentives to motivate slaves to perform at their best.[61] Rather than setting a task for picking cotton, some masters made the cotton harvest an occasion for merriment and gaiety, often bringing slaves from other plantations to help. Cotton pickings and cornhuskings were among the events best remembered by former slaves and were a focal point of the master's overall strategy to encourage his slaves to work and live in an orderly, peaceful, and contented manner. The festive atmosphere of the cotton pickings, created by both master and slaves and facilitated in part by the awarding of prizes to the best performers, might be considered one of the few mutually satisfying occasions on the plantation. This would have been one of the few work-related activities that allowed large numbers of slaves to come together for a social occasion.

During a particularly busy period in the cotton picking season, Witherspoon encouraged his slaves to pick as much cotton as they could by "running races in twos." The winners would receive prizes of "tobacco, flour, sugar and such like"—the very luxuries slaves were often deprived of, particularly if they were not able to earn extra income. The incentive of competition, the excitement of the occasion, or the allure of the prizes motivated the slaves to a high level of industry. The forty-seven slaves averaged 132 pounds picked on the first day and 159 pounds on the second. The top five pickers, two of whom were females, picked a total of over 480 pounds for the two days, and Peggy was the top picker with 530 pounds. Those at the other end of the list were probably the inexperienced, the young, the old, and the disabled. Three hands had totals for the two days of less than 100 pounds, Dilsey and Jacob picking the least with 92 and 76 pounds, respectively. Of the twenty-three pairings formed to take part in these cotton races, only one contained members of the opposite sex—that of Peggy and Anthony, who were the two top pickers.

These records indicate a significant correlation between a slave's success in one area and a generally high level of industry. It would seem that the slaves' ability to succeed at important tasks such as cotton picking might have had a distinct bearing on the style and quality of their life—their opportunity to control a large piece of land.[62] Accounts kept by Witherspoon for William and George, who picked over 800 pounds between them, support this contention. In 1852, George produced and sold fourteen bushels of corn at 75 cents per bushel, receiving at least $7.50 in cash and 1.5 gallons of molasses in part payment. William earned $5 for six bushels and three pecks of corn and was paid with twelve yards of cloth, 35 cents worth of sugar, and a dollar in cash.

The physical and technical abilities a slave was able to command were crucial. One who was unable to do the required tasks well and within an allotted time would have struggled to maintain any but the most basic standard of living. Those who were best able to master the labor requirements under slavery were most likely to improve their economic position and go some way toward making a life of their own. One up-country slave, Jessie Williams of Chester District, lamented the absence of this opportunity. He recalled how disappointed he was when, after having earned useful sums of money picking cotton, "they took me out de field in November to drive de mules to de hoss gin." Williams had lost the opportunity to earn a "shin plaster" every time he picked over one hundred pounds of cotton.[63]

In another part of the up-country slaves engaged in the same activities and with similar results. The sixteen cotton pickers on T. C. Means's Fairfield District plantation did not match Jessie Williams's efforts, much less those of the star pickers among the Witherspoon slaves. On the best three days of a five-day cotton picking week that commenced October 3, 1858, most of the Means slaves failed to total 300 pounds. Again it is significant, however, that the slaves with the best performances in the cotton field were also those who shone elsewhere. The best pickers on the Means place included Charles, Jim, Bacchus, Bill, Nancey, and Abe, all of whom picked above the three-days average of 300 pounds; Adam and Daniel topped the list with 400 and 380 pounds, respectively. With the exception of Robert, who was not listed as having been involved in the picking, and Nancey, who was not mentioned again, these slaves dominated Means's slave accounts. In 1858, nine slaves produced and sold some 34 bushels of corn; with the exception of Joe, all had been among the top cotton pickers, and both he and Patsy, the only female in the nine, had sold the smallest amount of corn—1.5 bushels. Jim, who picked over 330 pounds of cotton, was credited with 7 bushels of corn, the largest amount. Robert, who was probably the headman, was not credited with either a quantity of cotton picked or corn sold, but he did receive $25 for services rendered, which he collected by way of a part payment of a pair of shoes, $1.50, and "to cash lent you, $15." Robert clearly had not been given something for nothing. His account for 1860 credited him with a regular income from sales of chickens and eggs to Means and debited him for purchases of sugar, wheat, and "2 hats." Bill, who was one of Means's best pickers, outdid Robert in the dairy market. In addition to sales to Means of rice and groundnuts, he outsold Robert by seven chickens at 20 cents each and 3.5 dozen eggs at 12.5 cents per dozen. Jim's account with Means included, as well as rice, groundnuts, eggs, and chickens, two mats and six partridges, payment for which was collected in flour and sugar. Only one female slave was listed as having an account of her own. One of the better cotton pickers, Patsy was able to extend her income through the sale of eggs to her master and in payment received eight yards of homespun.[64] Six of the top male pickers earned money for hay and fodder gathered and sold to Means.

Male physical domination does not completely explain the discrepancy in slaves' earning potential, nor do the slave accounts indicate that males dominated the slave quarters' economic activities. But females, particularly those pregnant or with infants, who were not members of productive families, might have found themselves hard-pressed to provide needed extras. The above evidence highlights the importance slaves placed on their own work time and how profoundly the results of their efforts could affect the most intimate areas of their lives. Clearly, the slaves' work and garden activities introduced visible economic and social divisions into the quarters and provided a major stimulus for the organization and maintenance of stable, productive, and cooperative family units. Furthermore, the economic productivity of the large family units working sizable pieces of land increased heads of families' authority over younger members.

Those who belonged to large, able-bodied, and healthy families were better placed to improve the material conditions of their lives and maintain the integrity of the family by providing its members with a modicum of protection against family disruptions, especially those caused by illness and untimely death.[65]

3

In Sickness and in Health:
Disease, Death, and Family Disruption

Throughout South Carolina, slaves worked hard to take advantage of the opportunities available to them. Their extra work activities and their efforts in forming and maintaining stable families gathered pace as the antebellum period wore on. The very factors that contributed to the slaves' productivity, strengthened families, and generally improved their life chances also helped to mitigate the power of an outside force that could not be ensured against, foreseen, or prevented but which often had dire consequences for the slave family—the frequency of untimely death. A strong, well-organized family could provide its members some protection against illness, disease, and death.

By far the greatest single threat to the stability and material interests of the slave family was early or untimely death.[1] In her study of the low-country Ball family slaves, Cheryll Ann Cody estimated that of unions begun when both partners were between the ages of twenty and twenty-four little more than 80 percent could expect their union to last five years, some 60 percent could expect ten years without the death of a partner, and less than half could expect unions to survive fifteen years, at which point the proportion would rapidly decline. Thus, she calculates, only about 15 percent of slave couples could expect their union to survive until both partners had reached fifty years of age. Cody's list of the main determinants of adult slave mortality includes old age, respiratory diseases, nervous system diseases, dropsy, typhoid fever, childbirth, and tuberculosis.[2] If these figures for the 620 Ball slaves studied were applicable to the state as a whole, single-parent families and orphans would have been a common feature of slave life, and South Carolina slave families would have struggled to maintain their productive and emotional unity. Yet the regional variations discussed above also affected the health of slaves.

The American Slave narratives for South Carolina provide only occasional references to death and family breakup, but death was no stranger to the slave quarters; its arrival was always traumatic, reverberating on the immediate family and often on the wider black community. The personal effect of the untimely loss of a loved one to individual slave families is not altogether clear. If only in economic terms, however, a family's ability to provide for itself could have been seriously impaired by the loss of a significant member. Furthermore, there existed something of a regional variation in the frequency and structural impact of untimely death on the slave family. Where a slave lived was a crucial factor in determining his or her life chances.

In the low country, Amos Gadsden of Charleston, born in 1849, had a grandmother who "lived over 100 years" and had worked as "nurse to the children." Dadsden lost his mother, Ellen, during "the first part of the war," when Amos was about twelve years old. Ellen had worked as a laundress, and following her death, Amos grew up "with the white children in the family" and "sometime I slept at the foot of my mistress bed." His father had "'tended the yard and was coachman." As well as receiving training to work in the house when he was older, Amos was also trained "for a yard boy." Because his parents were part of the white household within which he had been trained to fit, the loss of his mother perhaps had a less disturbing effect on young Amos than might have otherwise been the case. Maria Jenkins's mother, Ellen, died the "first year of the war." Her family had lived on Hugh Wilson's Wadalaw Island plantation. Soon after Ellen's death (and perhaps as a direct result), her father, Aaron, "put heself free off to New Orleans," never to be heard from again. Maria was about fourteen years old.[3]

Celia Woodberry of Marion District in the middle country drowned sometime before the end of the Civil War. She had received word that her mother had been struck down with the fever "en was bad off." Needing to cross the river to Sand Hills when it was "a might high," Celia was advised by Pa Cudjoe that crossing would be dangerous but that he was willing to risk it to take her and her young daughter Louisa across. While they were crossing, the boat overturned, Celia was drowned, and Louisa was "raised up a motherless child" by Pa Cudjoe.[4] In 1846, Dolly Haynes was born on Charlie Baumer's Euta plantation. When her mother died, leaving four children, her mistress was "mighty good to us . . . call us her children." Her father, who was probably an underdriver, "rung de bell on de plantation fer ter wake de slaves up fer to go to de fiel," would have been some help, but he might have sought out another eligible female and so begin again the process of family formation.[5] The premature death of slave parents was not restricted to any one part of the state, but it may have been more frequent in the low country, where the malarial conditions generally placed the slaves' health at greater risk. Slave women were particularly at risk living in a part of the state where childbirth and normal and otherwise manageable illnesses could become complicated by the fevers prevalent in the area.[6]

The difference was most marked between the low and the up-country, yet in the mountainous regions of Cherokee District untimely death was not uncommon. Elias Dawkins, born in 1853, lost his mother when just "a wee baby." An only child, Elias was left with his mother's mistress, Kissy Sims, who, along with Stake Simms, her master, "helped my granny to raise me." Another likely result of untimely death is evidenced in the following account. Soon after Leah lost her husband, Will, she and her child, Bill, were given away by her owner as a gift to his married daughter. Will had belonged to the Rainey family of York and had to get a pass to come visit his wife and child, who lived near Chester Courthouse.[7] After her husband's death, they were moved from York to Fairfield. Whether this gift would have been made while Will was still alive is open to conjecture, but it is likely that Leah, with just the one child, was considered young enough to start over again and so made an ideal gift. Because many of the former slaves interviewed in the 1930s had been either children or young adults while slaves, it is to be expected that the few references to untimely death refer to loss of a parent.[8] Several plantation journals shed some light on slave health, the cycle of life and death, and the frequency and likely impact of untimely death on the structure of the African American family under slavery.

81

Established late in the antebellum period, Exeter plantation in the low country in St. John's Parish had some features more often associated with frontier plantations. J. R. Motte acquired Exeter in 1845 and staffed it with two slave families and some single domestics. Between 1848 and 1857 he purchased or received as gifts thirteen families of plantation slaves, two families of house servants, and some single slaves. Although the early history of many of the Motte slaves is not available, the health records for some of the family units provide useful insights into slave health and family structure and the impact of one on the other.[9]

Recorded first in a list of slaves purchased in 1848 were Manny, Flora, his wife, and James, their son (figure 7). Born around 1803, Manny died in July 1865, and Flora, born around 1808, survived slavery and lived until 1876. By any standard, these two slaves lived long lives. Their son, James, however, did not fare as well. Born sometime in 1828, James died in July

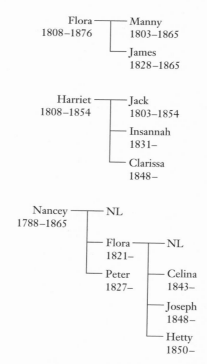

Fig. 7.   Motte Plantation Slaves Purchased in 1848

1865 and left a wife, Clarissa, and a son, Nat, who was born in February of the year his father died.

Also purchased in 1848 were Jack, born in 1803, his wife, Harriet, born in 1808, and their child, Insannah (figure 7). Both parents died in 1854, Jack of consumption and Harriet of "appoplexy." In August 1848, soon after arriving at Exeter, Harriet gave birth to a daughter named Clarissa. Thus when Jack and Harriet died in 1854, Insannah, aged twenty-three, and Clarissa, aged six, were left alone. The following year, Insannah was sold for $650 and seven-year-old Clarissa was taken into the house to live with a family of house servants. Death broke up this family of slaves. That Insannah was sold after her parents' death attests, once again, to the special vulnerability of slaves without a family. The presence of parents who were senior members of the slave community could be enough to influence masters whenever they had to wrestle with the difficult question of which slaves to sell. That Insannah was twenty-four years old and without children would have been an additional consideration.

Nancey, born about 1788, was purchased in 1848 along with her children, Flora and Peter, and granddaughter Celina. Nancey died in 1865. Flora had been born in 1821 and was the mother of five-year-old Celina. She was pregnant on her arrival at Exeter, and her son Joseph would be the plantation's firstborn. Joseph died at the age of nine in 1857 from "congestion of the lungs." A third child, born to Flora in August 1850, survived slavery, as did Flora herself. Celina, aged eight in 1851, was not so fortunate; she died of "gastro." Two of Flora's three children, then, did not survive into adulthood but suffered from respiratory problems and died. Her brother, Peter, was sold in 1850 for $600. Thus, through death and sales, less than three years after having been purchased and moved to a new home, Nancey's family was severely disrupted.

A list of slaves purchased in 1852 included a family of plantation slaves: Paul, born about 1817, his wife, Chambers, born about 1821, and their children, Cuffee, aged fourteen, Hannah, aged ten, and Abram, aged five (figure 8). Also in this unit purchased for $2,190 was Sue, a nurse, aged about fifty-five, who might have been the children's grandparent. Five years later, Sue died from pneumonia. Paul and Chambers both survived slavery, Paul dying "suddenly" in 1872 and Chambers in 1876. Their children formed families of their own under slavery, Cuffee marrying Jessy,

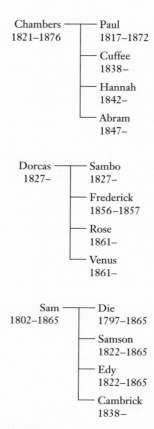

Fig. 8.   Motte Plantation Slaves Purchased in 1852

who was purchased in 1857. Her sister-in-law, Hannah, whose husband lived off the place, had her first child when she was about twenty-one years old. The child survived for only four weeks, and a second child, Betsey, was born in February 1856. In 1865 Hannah, twenty-three years old, was still living in her parents' house.

Sambo and Dorcas were purchased in 1852, both aged about twenty-five, the parents of a young infant (figure 8). Soon after their purchase, the child died of "dropsy," and it would be another four years before Dorcas had a second child. She gave birth to twins, Rose and Venus, and in February 1865 to another girl. The twins and their father survived well into freedom, but the mother and youngest child both died soon after the child's birth.

A large group of slaves purchased in 1852 for $4,960 might have been an extended family. At its head (if measured only by age) was Sam, the gardener, aged about fifty-five. His wife's name was Die. They were followed by Samson, the engineer, aged about thirty, Edy, about the same age, and Flanders, aged about thirty-five, and his wife, Alice, aged about thirty. Next on the list were fourteen-year-old Cambrick and sixty-year-old Bella, who cooked for the slaves (figure 8). Bella died in March 1861 of "paralysis." Sam, Die, Samson, and Edy all died within months of one another in 1865, Edy of "congestion of the lungs." Cambrick was left with her parents and her young daughter Celia. Flanders and Alice remained together and childless. Whether a family unit or not, this group of slaves had more than their share of untimely deaths. Indeed, this seems to have been the normal experience for Motte slaves.

Not all of the Motte slaves, however, had so much experience with death. For example, Isaac and Charlotte's family was purchased in 1857. Born around 1807 and 1817, respectively, they had two children, Boston, aged seven, and Bob, aged four. All four survived slavery. Therefore, apart from the experience of separation from their wider kin which preceded their arrival at the Motte place, this family remained intact.

Living and working in the house might have ensured slaves a longer and more healthy life. Motte purchased a group of "House Negroes" as a unit in 1846 for $1,050. Nanny, aged about sixty, was a seamstress; Willoughby, aged about twenty-six, was a washerwoman. Her children included Edward, aged about eight, Susan aged two, and Patsy, born about four months before the sale. A fourth child, Moses, was born in 1848 (figure 9). Nanny died after being struck by paralysis in September 1857. Willoughby and her children would all live on well into the 1880s and

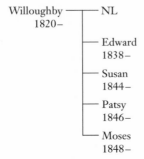

Fig. 9.   Motte House Slaves Purchased in 1846

beyond. Her two daughters remained in the house, Susan becoming a nurse and Patsy, like her mother, a washerwoman. Here again, families of house slaves (like Amos, the yard boy) lost one or both of their parents but remained within the domestic structure of the big house. Both sons were also still with the family in 1865.

Ambrose and Jenny, also house servants, were purchased in 1856. Two years later, at the age of fifty-two, Jenny succumbed to "paralysis" and died, leaving Ambrose a widower (figure 10). Purchased the very next year was Moll, aged about twenty-seven, a seamstress, and her two children, Henry and Sarah. By 1859, Ambrose and Moll were married. Their first child was born in March 1858 and named Jenny after her grandmother. Moll had arrived on the plantation as a single woman with two infants so for the sake of herself and her children, it was in her best interests to find a husband. The vulnerability of single women is attested to by Elizabeth Botume, who recalled meeting a slave woman, Jane, who found herself in

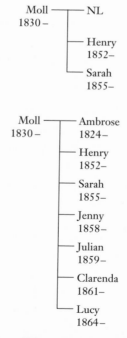

Fig. 10. Motte House Slaves Purchased in 1856

86

similar circumstances, having lost her husband through sale. With her mother's blessings, and for very practical reasons, Jane had quickly remarried: "You see, ma'am," Jane explained, "when I come here I had no one to help me."[10] Like the pragmatic Jane, the smaller families in the Motte slave quarters had to replace significant family members in order to maintain the family's standard of living and its ability to protect itself. As Jane's mother said in defense of her daughter's hasty remarriage, "I tell you . . . it been a hard fight for we."[11] Inability to respond quickly to the changes brought about by the loss of family members through untimely death increased the family's dependency upon the master and better-off members of the slave quarters.

The Motte slave community's growth from fifty-one to fifty-seven between 1859 and 1865 is remarkably low, even allowing for the slaves sold away. The main reasons were that Motte purchased families that often included aged members and that the infant mortality rate was high. Twelve of the twenty-one children born on Exeter did not survive beyond infancy. The most common causes of death for those who survived beyond the first few months were "overlaying" and "congestion of the lungs." A total of fifteen adult slaves (nine females) died before the end of slavery, and seven were sold away. It would seem, then, that if one were an adult rather than a child, male rather than female, a house rather than field slave, and lived on a settled rather than a new plantation, one would have had a much better chance of living to an old age.[12]

The records of J. O. Willson, a low-country planter with a much more settled slave quarters, provide a closer look at the slave family's response to the loss of members through death and suggest that better situated slaves were less likely to experience the shock of untimely death and, when such events occurred, they were far better equipped to ride out the psychological and economic storm.

The history of the Willson slaves extends back into the 1760s, when Nancey, the progenitor of Family Number 1, was born. At her death in 1851 of "paralysis and old age," Nancey was nearly ninety-one years old (figure 1). Her daughters, Benah and Peggy, both born sometime in the 1790s, produced a large third generation. Benah and her husband, Peter, had five children before she succumbed to "dropsy of the chest" and died in May 1846. Peggy had ten children before disappearing from the records sometime after 1844. Two of her children, Peter, born in 1830, and Sarah, born in 1836, died during a typhoid epidemic in 1857. Deaths among the children constituting the fourth generation of this family were few. Peggy's daughter Nelly lost three of her children, two of whom died after slavery and after they had reached their majority. The third, Betsey, born in May 1860, lived for only five years. Peggy's first daughter, Edy, married Stepney, who was listed as "diseased," which might explain why Edy was the only daughter who failed to reproduce. When Sarah died of typhoid fever in 1857, her four-year-old daughter went to live with her grand-mother, Peggy.

The men who married into Family Number 1 also survived slavery. Of the sixty-four direct members of this family and those who married into it, only three suffered what might be considered untimely deaths before the end of slavery. By any standard this is an extremely low mortality rate. The economic well-being and the "political" muscle of this family would have had a significant impact on its health and general well-being. Their poten-tial for self-help and mutual assistance would have positioned this family well to take care of its own.

Willson Family Number 2 also seems to have experienced death infre-quently (figure 2). Lucy, the head of the family, had her first child, Nancey, in 1809. Nancey's first daughter was born in 1828 and was named Lucy af-ter her grandmother. Although this family had little experience with un-timely deaths, it does seem to have had several disabled members. Among Nancey's family, Jim, the eldest son, was "deformed"; Primus, born in 1844, had a "withered arm"; and his younger brother Frank suffered from a "swelled knee." These factors were likely both a cause and a result of their relative economic powerlessness and consequent inability to provide those much needed extras when they were most required: when children were very young and when members of the family were sick or injured and so in need of special care and attention.[13]

Willson Family Number 3, headed by Hector and Charlotte, contained eight children, including twins Robert and Molcey, born in 1841. The first daughter, Sumitra, lost a baby during the early months of 1848, and her fifth child, Ned, died before the end of slavery. Sumitra's husband, David, was deaf. Her brother George died of bronchitis (figure 3). In 1863, Char-lotte was listed as "very old," her husband, Hector, as "diseased," and their second daughter, Betsey, as "paralysed." Delia, the next daughter, married Andrew from Family Number 1. Of the third generation, Sumitra's daughter Sarah, born in 1845, died in 1857 of whooping cough. Although not a frequent occurrence, death was not unknown to Family Number 3, but the disabilities that had afflicted Family Number 2 were largely absent. Such disabilities would have affected the economic viability of the family unit, requiring them to draw excessively upon already limited resources. The marriage of Delia to Andrew from Family Number 1 probably added to the economic stability of this family.

A glance at Family Number 6, similar in size to Family Number 1, allows a more direct comparison between these two potentially powerful families living on the same plantation (figure 4). Simon and Tirah, who headed this family, had their first child in 1803 and their last in 1829, with seven in between. Both Simon and Tirah survived slavery. Their son Cicero, born in 1824, was sold away at the age of thirty. Kerziah, their second to last daughter, died in 1856, when she was about thirty years old. The youngest daughter, Susan, died in 1856 of typhoid fever at the age of twenty-seven. The youngest of Susan's children were taken in by their grandmother. Kerziah's eldest daughter, Ester, born in 1848, died five years later of "burns," leaving behind her siblings Lovey and Caesar, who were brought up by their grandmother. Among the second generation, Simon and Tirah's daughter Phillis lost her first daughter, Charlotte, in 1850, when she was twenty years old; she died of "phrinetis [a] very violent case." Her second girl, Chloe, born in 1814, had six children between July 1833 and December 1854; the first three failed to survive slavery, and her firstborn, March, died in 1861, aged twenty-eight, from an "affection of bowels." March's brother, Monday, died in 1856, "disease unknown." The third child, Fortune, born in 1847, lived only three weeks before he died "by suffocation overlaid by his mother." Pheobe, Simon and Tirah's fourth daughter, had eleven children between November 1833 and May 1859, including twins Middleton and Samuel in 1854. All but the first child, Clarissa, who died of hepatitis at age seventeen, survived into freedom. For this family, in marked contrast to Family Number 1, death was a frequent visitor, if not through diseases then through accidents such as that which struck young Ester, who died of burns. Of the sixty-four direct members of Family Number 6 (including those marrying in), five adults and three children died between 1803 and 1865, a mortality rate much higher than that of Family Number 1 but proportionately much lower than that of the smaller (thirty-four members) and less economically productive Family Number 3.

Another sizable family of Willson slaves serves to highlight the advantages Nancey's family (Family Number 1) may have enjoyed over the other slave families. Born in 1790, Mary, the progenitor of Family Number 7, had her first child in 1809 and her seventh and last in 1831 (figure 11). She died in 1858. Aphe, her firstborn, died in 1843 of "serophila" at age thirty-four, leaving behind four children aged between two and thirteen. Sometime before 1853, Sarah, her daughter, married and had Washington, her first child. She would have been about twenty-two years old. She had five children before the end of slavery. Diana, who was a surviving twin, the other having been "smothered before being named," had her first child at the early age of fourteen, and her second was born some four years later. Mary's second daughter, Elcey, born in 1811, had her first child in August 1829 and her tenth and last in 1857, when she was forty-six. Her first daughter, Molcy, born in December 1832, had her first child when she was nineteen. Molcy's second and third children, Priscilla and Dorcia, died. In 1859, during the birth of another child, Molcy died, leaving behind Margarette, her firstborn. In 1863 Margarette was with her uncles Tom and Jerry. Elcey's seventh child, Betsey, born in 1843, died three years later of a "fever neglected in commencement by being in Charleston." Her ninth child, Josephine, died of "infantile incompetent fever" in 1852, aged four years and three days. She had died in convulsions. Of thirty-six family members, three adults and five children died between 1809 and 1865. Although Mary's family lost fewer adults through untimely deaths than Family Number 6, this family would have been at a particular economic disadvantage with two of its males of prime age being rated as "unsound," and their infirmities probably rendered this sizable family unable to provide adequately for all its members, thus increasing its susceptibility to disease and untimely death.

Analysis of a selection of Willson slave families suggests that the death rate on the Willson place was markedly low; it was proportionately much lower than the eight deaths experienced by the slave families over twenty years on the Motte place. Nevertheless, the longer-established and much larger Willson slave quarters was very familiar with death. An "Alphabetical List of Negroes," including slaves born as early as the 1760s, provides some general information about the Willson slaves. The last reference to a death was in 1862, and over the whole period, some forty-six deaths occurred, variously attributed to "old age," "accidentally killed by a gun going off in hand," "appoplexy," "epilepsy," and "smothering by mother."

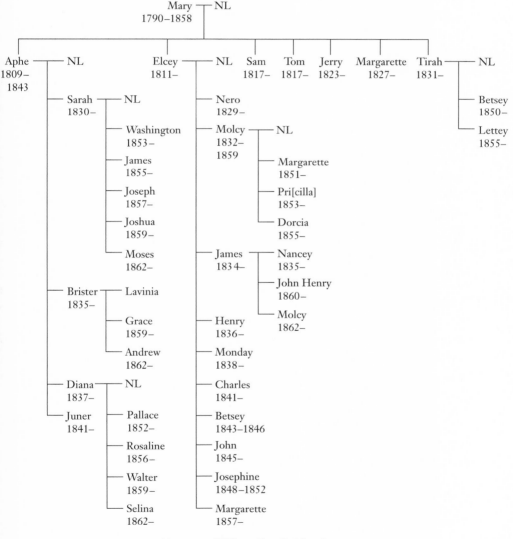

Fig. 11.   Willson Family Number 7

For most of the Willson slaves, then, death was a constant reality. If not touching the intimate lives of the whole community, it deeply touched the slave quarters. Given the large number of members in Willson Families Numbers 1 and 3 and the number of recorded deaths on the Willson place, that these two families experienced a comparatively low mortality rate suggests that those families best able to protect themselves materially were less likely to suffer untimely deaths.[14]

It cannot be said that diseases such as hepatitis, "phrinetis," or "unknown" would have been avoided or rendered more curable had the victims been better protected through superior food and living conditions and other material comforts provided by themselves, for we cannot be sure that they were not all well nourished and satisfactorily cared for. But where slaves were likely to have had a high level of control over their diet and access to extra food and medicine and were able substantially to increase their income, there does seem to have existed a correspondingly low level of death and illness caused or exacerbated by nutritional deficiencies.

Investigation of another low-country plantation provides an opportunity to look more closely at slave families' experiences with disease and death and their impact on slave family structure. The Fripp plantation slave community was perhaps typical of the low country. Containing some seventy-three slaves in 1857, this slave quarter enjoyed a relatively even gender balance of some twenty-two male hands and nineteen female working hands. During the period of the journal, from March 1857 to November 1858, four births occurred on the place. On May 16, 1857, Pat had a baby boy and was attended by Milley, the midwife. Four days earlier she had been in the fields planting peas. Pat and baby remained in the Negro house (hospital or sick house) for a month, as was customary on the Fripp place. On Monday, June 15, the day before she was due to leave hospital, Pat's baby girl was reported to be "very ill," and the next day she died. Some four weeks later, Pat was again in the hospital complaining of "pains about her body."[15] On May 23, 1858, Pat gave birth to another child, and exactly four weeks later she was back in the fields "chopping." On October 16, 1858, Molly, mother of three, had a baby boy. Sadly, the child lived for only six days. When Jane had her baby in May 1858, Milley was again in attendance. Some four weeks later, the young mother was out doing some light work "chopping grass" in front of the hospital. Not fully recovered or simply not having spent her full term "laying up," Jane did not return to her regular work until exactly one month after she had given birth. Even then, she did not join a team of full hands, as she was listed working with Sibby and Pat, who had both given birth the previous month, "chopping yesterday and today." This close adherence to the rule that mothers convalesce in the sick house for a calendar month must be balanced with Fripp's marked tardiness in removing pregnant women from the field. Fripp appears to have been one of those slave owners who were more concerned with their slaves who were alive than with those yet to be born. His care in keeping his slave mothers away from the fields and their babies in the hospital until they were both strong was consistent and in line with nineteenth-century southern medical practice.[16]

Fripp was strict about the care of his young mothers and their babies, and mothers were held primarily responsible for the care of their infants. When one of Molly's three children took sick in April 1857, it was she rather than a nurse, midwife, or doctor who was called in to do the "minding." Early the next year, when Silvey's baby was badly burned, the mother was taken from her work and sent into the Negro house to care for her baby. When Dennis became "extremely ill," he was attended by Will and Ruth, who were probably his parents. They were with him when he died at twelve o'clock that night.[17] Nonetheless, Fripp's tardiness in hospitalizing the mothers-to-be may have been partly responsible for the early deaths of both Pat's and Molly's children.[18] Indeed, overwork may have been the cause of Elsey's miscarriage in April 1857 and another the following January, when she became so sick that Old Nelly, the plantation nurse, had to remain with her for two weeks. Belle also suffered a miscarriage in April 1857. The experience of Lavina supports the contention that overwork was a decisive factor in the high rate of infant mortality and miscarriages on the Fripp place despite his policy of allowing a month of postnatal convalescence. On April 22, 1857, Lavina was working with Milley, the nurse/midwife, which may suggest that Lavina was not altogether well, and as was customary, Milley, with her experience and knowledge, would have worked with the women who were recovering from illness or those who were about to give birth. Thus, rather than having members of the latter group inoperative in the hospital, they would be in the fields doing some light work under Milley's watchful and expert eye. An entry for February

1858, for example, reads, "three sickly women working in the cowpen." In April, instead of resting in the Negro house or working a short day, Lavina and Milley "planted until 3 o'clock"—a full day for many low-country slaves. Later that day, Lavina miscarried, and Milley was attending to her.[19] Fripp's policy of paying little attention to women in the later stages of the pregnancy proved counterproductive because slaves spent more time in the hospital than would otherwise have been the case, and some may well have lost their lives.[20]

Although the number of deaths on the plantation for this eighteen month period was low—only one recorded death that was not an infant—the Fripp slave quarters was far from healthy. Apart from the pregnant women and mothers of newborn babies, who were likely to spend more time in the hospital than other slaves, there were slaves who suffered complaints that would have made their lives miserable and rendered them regular visitors to the plantation hospital, affecting their productivity both for their master and their families. Among these was Nelly, described as being "in delicate health," yet, despite her "complaining," she was expected to do some gentle hoeing. Among the males, Plato was perhaps the best example, being sick "off and on all the time." He complained of an earache; Fripp made more references to Plato's poor health than he did to Nelly's. Two long-term sufferers were Clarissa and Margarette, who were sick with the "pox." Also afflicted were Hector and Dennis, presumably their "husbands," because the disease was confined to the four of them. Although Dennis seems to have recovered quickly, the other three were not sufficiently cured to leave the sick house for any length of time and so were unable to execute their regular tasks on the place, but they did show signs of improvement. An entry to the effect that the two women had been "poxed months ago" suggests that the outbreak of the disease originated with them, which raises questions of fidelity among the Fripp female slave population. Frustrated at her continuing condition, which was not responding to any treatment, Clarissa complained that the physician, Dr. Ellis, "does her no good." Some eight months later, still suffering from the disease, Clarissa was visited by a Dr. Morral, who had her taken to the town of Grahamville "to be cured of the pox."[21]

Although most masters advocated what they considered to be kind treatment of their slave women and their newborn babies and followed a practice similar to that on the Fripp plantation, there were exceptions.[22] Susan

Hamlin of Charleston recalled that pregnant women on her master's plantation "were jus' given time 'nough to deliver dere babies." Hamlin, who was born in 1833, reported that if a woman delivered her baby about "eight in de mornin'" by "twelve [she] had to be back to work."[23] No similar examples were found in the plantation journals consulted, but if the woman felt physically capable and so desired, she may have found it natural to return immediately to working in her own fields or at other matters she deemed important. Slaves who had responsibilities over and above those to their masters probably had a good deal of say about the timing of their return to the fields because too much effort working on one's own land could not be continued for long without a similar effort being expended in the master's fields. Nursing mothers on the Fripp plantation may have been keen to return to regular (but light) duty long before their month's convalescence was completed so they could also be free to tend to their own affairs.

Middle-country resident Joseph Howell worked his slaves harder than most masters in the state. He seems to have been somewhat inconsiderate of his pregnant slave women. "Seven days in de week . . . made us all work," Henry Jenkins reported. Even "women in de perils of child birth, dropped cotton seed and corn kernels." He explained that their doctor, Dr. Turnipseed, "low dat light labor lak dat good for dem." Although some labor might have done little or no harm, the line beyond which the mother and child became exposed to severe risk must have been very narrow, and hard labor in the fields would increase the hazards of childbirth. Movements necessary for picking and hoeing, for example, became more difficult as women became swollen by pregnancy.[24] Andrew Flinn of Abbeville advised his overseer to treat pregnant women and "sucklers" with "great tenderness." They were to be "worked near home and lightly." Pregnant women were not to plow or lift but "kept at moderate work until the last hour if possible."[25] Given the general acceptance of the practice of requiring slave women to work well into their third trimester, slave owners and their overseers might have struggled to distinguish between "working" and "working lightly." Even well-intentioned masters may have inadvertently ill-treated their pregnant slave women. These masters would then go to great lengths to ensure that mothers and newborn babies were nursed with care.[26]

Slave families living with Ryer Emmanuel on a Claussens plantation in

Marion District had a better chance of reducing the health risks to mothers and their newborn. She recalled that her master, Anthony Ross, always allowed his slave women to "stop off work en stay dere to de house [hospital] a month till she git mended in de body way." After this time, at the start of each working day, the mother would take the child to the "big house and leave it in charge of an old woman . . . and then get back to work in de fields." The children would remain there until their parents came to collect them after having completed their work for the day. Gracie Gibson, born in Richland District, had been owned by Captain John Kinsler, a man with strong feelings and respect for the slave family. Although he "wouldn't sell his niggers and part de members of de family," Kinsler was another slaveholder who believed in keeping his pregnant women busy. Those "bearing children, not yet born, did cordin' wid hand cords." [27]

The small farms and plantations with only a few slaves prevalent in the up-country may have had increased pressures for slave masters to minimize the amount of time their slave women spent in the sick house before and after giving birth. Adeline Jackson was born in 1849 on John Mobley's plantation in Fairfield, where the slaves were sometimes attended by Dr. Henry Gibson. Here and elsewhere in the state, pregnant women "worked up to near de time." Just before their time, "they was took out and put in de cardin' and spinnin' rooms." The work required before a woman could move to the relatively sedate occupations of carding and spinning would have been more physically demanding, putting both mother and child at some risk. When William J. Connors of Lancaster District had pregnant women on his place he had them do light work. An entry for August 30, 1841, reads: "Molly in consequence of her pregnant situation spins." [28]

Clearly, slave women presented slave owners with sometimes problematic decisions, particularly when they were pregnant. The dependency of masters both on the labor and the reproductive powers of the slave woman sometimes caught them on the horns of a dilemma, the resolution of which was not always in their hands because it was not always clear which course of action was in the master's best interest.

The health problems Fripp and other slaveholders had to address were not all gender specific. Most of the slaves on the Fripp place who were listed as having some complaint other than childbirth suffered from viral infections. Sabine, for example, had occasional dysentery and fever, as did

Seth. In June 1857, Kate was hospitalized for at least five days with an earache. In April that year Molly was out for three days with "colds and fever," and Edmon suffered a bout of colic in December. Toward the end of September 1858, Miley, Bram, and Plato were sick for two days with "colds and fever from cole." Although the ailments affecting over half the women were not stated and were possibly menstrual or related problems, many of the men seem to have suffered from boils or "risings," which seldom prevented them from working for any period of time, although it sometimes determined which jobs they could or could not do. Seth, for example, "has boils on his arms cannot gin so assorting [*sic*] with others . . . 7100 pounds assorted." And Ben had a dreadful-looking ulcer on his foot "which kept him inoperative for two weeks."[29] The division of labor on the Fripp place suggests that he placed far more importance on his male hands than on the females. Therefore, the health records for his hands, measured by the probable number of working days lost, would have been incomplete. Perhaps because the place was so unhealthy, at least three different doctors visited at one time or another, and the slaves were well attended. Prompt and regular attendance by doctors, however, could present its own problems given the state of southern medical practice and the profession's perceptions of the physical differences between white and black patients and how the latter should be treated.[30] Even allowing for the presence of a "hospital" on the plantation and the regular visits of doctors, the Fripp slaves were expected to be responsible for some of their own health care, a sizable proportion of which may not have reached the master's attention. Furthermore, because Fripp was away for most of the "sickly season"—the months of June, July, and August—the full amount of sickness and the nature of treatment (by slave or white doctors) was not recorded. Therefore, sickness on the Fripp place, as on most low-country plantations, was probably greatly underreported.

Middle-country slaveholders were much more likely than their low-country counterparts to remain on the home place for the full year. Thus their records provide a fuller picture of disease and death in the slave quarters, and the farther the slaves were from the malarial coastal areas the lower should have been the incidence of their suffering from the maladies prevalent in the low country. If the latter was indeed the case, the disease-producing environment in which low-country slaves were obliged to work would have rendered them overall less advantaged materially than their

middle and up-country counterparts, whose exposure to the less sophisticated variations of the work and garden system decreased their potential
for property accumulation but who lived and performed their labors in a
far more healthy climate that would have placed fewer demands on their
material resources.

Following her husband's death in 1843, Mary H. Brockington took over
the administration of their middle-country Darlington District plantation.
A record of births and deaths from December 1843 to April 1851 provides
an opportunity to assess the health of the Brockington slave quarters over
a period of several years and to discern the health problems and crises with
which slave families had to cope. The picture of slave health that is revealed is one of steady improvement—measured by a decrease in mortality
rates—with each passing year. A significant reason for the overall improvement of these slaves was their increasing ability to provide important
services for themselves.

December 1843 was a cruel month for the Brockington slaves. Two
births occurred during this period. The first, Hannah, daughter of Kittey,
was born on the first of the month and was so unwell that her survival
through to the end of the month surprised Brockington. Another child
born around this time was Silvey's daughter, Ruth. In between these happy
occasions there were eight infant deaths, among them Lizer's first child,
who survived only one week. Brockington believed "it would be the only
one she ever had," but it seems Lizer did have another child in 1845.[31]

The new year began more propitiously for the Brockington slaves with
six births taking place before the first infant death was recorded in July
1844. The quarters had also lost Ellick, a slave born in February 1826, who
passed away on the morning of May 17, 1844, "after alonge sickness and
the Doctors attention." In July a daughter was born to Dianer, and on the
last day of the month, Annemarie gave birth to a son named Baldwin, who
would live for only five days. August closed with the death of Peter, whose
sisters and son George were at his bedside when the end came. October
brought an additional blow for this family when George suddenly died. He
"had for a year or better suffered from an acute headache" but had recovered about three weeks previous and had gone back to the plantation "a
grate deal better at his work." Ironically, his last trip to the Negro house
had been to visit someone there, but he had "staid longer than the negroes

that he went to seay [see]." While visiting in the hospital George suffered a stroke or cerebral hemorrhage, as he "dide in one or two breaths." Rose, a child of Lurindar, born the previous March, died in December. The birth of Murtilla's child, Peter, may have added some joy to the Christmas festivities, coming as it did on the twenty-sixth, particularly because Murtilla had lost all her other children. In April, Lizer, whose infant child had been born in December and died within the month, had her "secant child," but it also died. Two months later, Lizer herself died, "in the morninge— sometime after the dawn." In between these sad events, Judy, aged thirty-five, gave birth to twins, Cloey and Daffy, in May 1845. On June 1, Anney suffered a miscarriage, and before the close of the year, another two births and one infant death took place on the plantation.

May 1846 saw the birth of a girl, Frances, Anney's seventh child. The next day, however, Frances was "taken with spasiams and dide in a short time." Elizabeth's daughter Jacqulin died in August after an illness. Murtilla's son Peter died in September "after alonge sickness and the Doctor and myself could not save him," recorded Brockington. She also recorded at the close of her journal for 1846, "eight negroes dide this yeare. Six . . . little negroes and one grown negro." Three children were born. Because over the previous two years the slave quarters had experienced eight and four deaths, and eight and seven births, respectively, the Brockington slave population was clearly struggling to increase itself at anything like a natural rate.

The following year, 1847, brought seven births and five deaths to the quarters. Two adults died. Early in December, Brockington recorded that Rian, one of her wagonners, had been "sick all the time" since June 3 "with consumption . . . a coffee and shillin constant hellfire." I "believe he can't stand it longe," she wrote. During this time Rian had his wife to "nurse him for three munce and now," and she remained by his bedside until his death.

Another major disruption for black and white alike came about 5 A.M. on the morning of September 29, 1847, when Nancey, the Brockington nurse, died after "five days seviar sickness." This was particularly sad for her family because her death followed that of her firstborn son, who had lived for only a few weeks. In 1847 the Brockington slave community enjoyed seven additions and suffered the deaths of three infants and two adults. It seems that whoever looked after the Brockington slaves—the doctors who were frequently called upon, Brockington herself, the almost constant bedside visitors, relatives in attendance, or the slave nurses—the patient had, at best, only a small chance of recovering.

The record for 1848 reveals a balance of five births and five deaths. The latter included Eliza's child, who died of measles; Lurindar's child, who died of "worms"; Hennder's child Jenny, who died of a bowel complaint, and Jane's third son. The following year, 1849, was somewhat more auspicious, producing twelve births and only five deaths, one of whom was Milly, who died after "two years sick and considerable epidemience of Doctor bill at dif[ferent] times." From 1850 through to April 1851, eight births occurred, two infants died, and two adults died, including Dinah, who "died suddenly" in April 1850. For the total period from December 1843 to April 1851, the Brockington slave community welcomed the births of some fifty-two infants and suffered the deaths of thirty-three infants and thirteen adults, for a net increase of only six slaves.

A list of births and deaths on the Brockington place from January 1853 to July 1858 reveals a marked improvement in the condition of life for the slaves. Of the twenty-three entries, fourteen recorded births and nine recorded the deaths of slaves. Two of the deaths were adults, including "Old Betty," who died in May 1858. A subsequent list, covering the period from July 1858 to December 1864, recorded continued improvement in the health of the Brockington slaves. During this period there were twenty-two births and eleven deaths, three of which were adults, including Old Daphne. One of the eight children who died was Larinda's Charles, who passed away in September 1862, having suffered from "brain fever and worms." Overall, these figures reveal a continued improvement in health of the Brockington slaves over the three periods from a ratio of twenty-six births to twenty-three deaths from 1843 to 1851, to fourteen to nine from 1853 to 1858, to a healthier eleven to five from 1858 to 1864. Clearly, a child born on the Brockington place after the 1840s would have had a better chance of surviving past infancy, and the rate of adult deaths also declined from an average of nearly two per year before 1850 to less than 0.5 per year. This improvement can be attributed to a number of factors, not least of which was the slave family's increasing ability to influence its own health and general welfare, that is, to protect itself.

The Brockington slaves were ready and able to do what they could for their relatives at times of sickness; it was not unusual for family members to nurse their relatives and to be at their bedside when the end finally came. No doubt slave families could supply more than emotional and moral support during moments of crisis. But what could they do to reduce the frequency of those crises and improve their ability to cope with them when they did occur?

The records of another Darlington District plantation provide the opportunity to examine the effect of family stability on sickness and death in the slave quarters and to highlight the correlation between a family's economic well-being and an increased ability to protect its members as measured by a low mortality rate. On T. C. Law's plantation the slave community was organized around five main family groups, the largest of which with twenty-seven direct family members (excluding family marrying in) was the family headed by Bess. Yenty died in 1834. His wife, Bess, survived slavery and lived until 1868 (see figure 5). Of her children and grandchildren whose births spanned the period from June 1811, when her first child, Venus, was born, until the end of slavery, the only adult death was that of Venus. What is perhaps startling, considering that this was the same period when the Brockington slaves were experiencing such high levels of sickness and mortality is that only four infants died during the entire period. If nothing else, this family, highly productive economically and the best situated family in the slave community, was able to look after itself.

Not all the families in the Law slave quarters were able to provide a similar level of protection for their members. Old Sophy's family, from December 1828 when she had Charlotte, her first child, until the end of slavery, embraced some twenty-eight members (see figure 6). This family suffered nine infant deaths and that of Old Sophy's seventeen-year-old son, Colon, in December 1849. Old Sophy's eldest daughter, Charlotte, suffered more acutely than her sisters Serena and Ann. Ann's first child, born when she was eighteen years old, survived only into its second year. Ann lost another child in February 1862, her fourth, which died only a few days after its birth. Serena also lost her firstborn, conceived when she was seventeen years old. This infant, although surviving the first critical months, died before reaching a year. Charlotte had experienced problems with her firstborn, conceived when she was about seventeen years old, but the child, Mariah, survived and had her own child in 1864. In 1853 Charlotte had her fourth child, Elias, who lived for only three months. Eleven months later her fifth child, George, was born. This pregnancy may have followed too soon after the last and probably affected the health of both mother and child because, having survived his first year, George died four months later, in September 1855. Before George's birth Charlotte's children had been separated by about twenty-two months. In 1859, only eighteen months after the birth of her seventh child, Caleb was born, only to die eight months later. In the last full year of slavery, Charlotte's tenth child, Eliza, was born, but the child did not did survive past infancy. In 1874, Charlotte, at forty-six years of age, had her fourteenth child. This family's experience, even without that of Charlotte, compares unfavorably with that of Bess's family. It is perhaps not surprising that Old Sophy's family did not fare too well economically and was thus less able to provide the little extras that for so many slaves made the essential difference between good health and sickness, even between good health and untimely death.

Ellec and Sophy's family was much smaller and younger and started from a stronger and healthier foundation than Old Sophy's family. Ellec and Sophy were about twenty-two and seventeen years old, respectively, when their first child was born in September 1842; their last was born in November 1862 (see figure 12). During this time, the family group reached thirteen, and only one death occurred before the end of slavery, that of Ellec and Sophy's second daughter, Caty, who had been born in 1848. In December 1863, fifteen-year-old Caty gave birth to a son, Zack; less than three weeks later the young mother was dead. The girl's youthfulness may have contributed to her inability to survive her first birth because the relatively good health of this family correlated with their economic well-being. Not only were there a good proportion of young, healthy males to work their gardens (four aged from ten to twenty in 1863), but their father, Ellec, was the "Head home man," an office that no doubt had advantages such as Ellec not having to "pick as long or as often" as the other slaves, thus freeing him to concentrate his efforts on other matters. Furthermore, the skills and talents that would have helped to qualify him for the position of headman would certainly have been put to good use in the family interests.[32]

An example of a middle-country plantation smaller than those of Brockington or Law was that owned by Michael Gramling of Orangeburg District. With the exception of Joe, who had piles in 1848, and Tom's occasional problems with fits, which Gramling, with the help of white doctors, endeavored to arrest, the Gramling slave community seems to have been a most healthy one. Unlike most slaveholders, Gramling displayed a marked willingness to use preventive medicine to ensure the health of his slaves. For example, in the spring of 1851, following a report of "eight or ten cases [of smallpox] in the neighborhood," Gramling immediately had the young and the very old—the most susceptible groups—vaccinated. His journal, running from March 1846 to August 1852, reveals a certain intimacy between Gramling and his slaves, which involved more than Gramling's ability to list his slaves' hat sizes by comparing their head sizes with his own—"Joe's is a little larger than my head, Toms Chance Rufus & Lewis is the size of my head[,] Hercules, Anthony & Ned a fraction

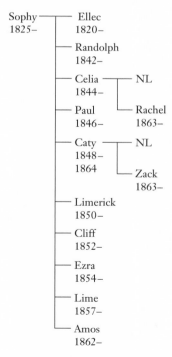

Fig. 12.   Law Family—Ellec and Sophy's Family

smaller & Adam & Charles is a little smaller still." An air of mutual respect and interdependency appears to have prevailed on the plantation.[33] When Gramling embarked on a barrel-making venture, for example, his slaves were soon fully committed to the new project, and Gramling's pride in their ability to learn quickly and to produce barrels with conveyor-belt efficiency was probably only an indication of the level of pride that slaves such as Anthony and Tom displayed in their work and accomplishments on the Gramling place. No deaths were recorded during the six-year period, and three women, Deborah, Sophy, and Delphy, produced six children among them. Tasked and allowed to tend their gardens, these slaves produced and sold their surplus to Gramling.[34] As well as having enjoyed a fair amount of autonomy, they also enjoyed extremely good health.

The healthier climate of the middle country is not sufficient alone to explain the different experience of middle-country slaves on both large and small plantations. Of course, the concern Gramling showed for his slaves would also have affected their general welfare. The role slaves played in this important area of their lives cannot be ignored. Slaves working in the middle country's healthier climate, under masters like Gramling, living on smaller plantations and working under work and garden systems, had significant advantages over their low-country counterparts—not least of which was superior health. It remains to be seen if the benefits of the more salubrious conditions of the up-country were sufficient to offset the reduced economic opportunities of up-country slaves, enabling them to enjoy an overall standard of living comparable to that of their materially better off low- and middle-country counterparts.

The up-country Lancaster District plantation of W. J. Connors was fairly free from sickness. Except for Ben, who had a badly infected or damaged foot that required an operation, sickness was almost entirely restricted to Connors's female slaves. From July to September 1841, the warmest and probably the busiest part of the year, only one person on the plantation succumbed to the intense summer heat. On July 14, Connors recorded that it was the "warmest we have had this year and that Maria was so overcome by the heat that she had to leave the field." Five days later Maria was still "indisposed with her old complaint" and was confined to her sickbed even though the weather was not "So expiringly warm as it was." Maria's complaint was probably menstrual and aggravated by the heat, but, because Connors referred to it as her "old complaint," it may have been a more serious ailment. Late in August, problem-free for nearly three weeks, "Maria was taken again with a flooding." "Her old complaint" was menstrual and seemingly of serious proportions. On August 12, having failed to complete her task two days previous, Emma reported sick, which probably explained why only she of all the women she had been working with had failed to complete her "task and doubling task." The same month Hannah and Satira were both reported as being sick. A day later Satira had recovered and was back in the fields. Hannah's condition, however, had worsened. "Her disease," Connors recorded, "appears very stubborn," and the next day she was "very sick." It was probably Hannah's condition that had finally persuaded Connors to have a doctor visit his Negro house. Ten days after the visit, both Hannah and Maria were "well but too weak to do anything." Evidently, these plantation doctors could sometimes provide effective cures for serious illness. Only two days after Hannah had appeared to be on the mend, however, she again reported sick. And another woman who suffered badly from the heat, Daphney, "came sick out of the field about noon" on September 13. It would be over a week before she went back into the fields to pick her task of cotton.[35]

Few masters allowed their slave women a month to recover from childbirth. Some denied their slaves sufficient time to rest and recover from illness and childbirth and thus helped maintain a never-ending cycle of ill health.[36] A small planter, Connors did not hesitate to give his slaves, particularly the women, the care and rest they needed when sick. If nothing else was done to help the patients in the Negro house, rest was surely welcomed, and, more than the medical treatment they received, it probably helped to speed their recovery.[37] Connors, however (different from Fripp), tended to rush them back to work before they were fully fit, and the entry recording Hannah's partial relapse might have been a reminder to Connors himself for future reference. A note in August about Molly, who "in consequence of her pregnant condition . . . spins," supports the notion that Connors was concerned about the health of his slaves, even if he did not always know whether his slave women were deceiving him. This was probably characteristic of the up-country and wherever else plantations were smaller. Living and working closely with their slaves, masters were likely to be more reluctant to take risks with a valuable "species of property."[38]

An economically well-organized and cooperative family unit was in a good position to affect the life chances of its members. This was a crucial function of the family. The family, economically sound or not, however, might have constituted the determining factor between whether a slave became seriously ill or recovered or died. Slaves from all types of families could play a part in maintaining the stability of their families by helping to prevent illness and by nursing and caring for those who did become ill, thereby increasing the chances of recovery. And when death did come, family members did what they could to provide solace and comfort to those left behind. The realities of slavery, however, placed constant obstacles in the path of people who wished for little more than to maintain the integrity of their families.

An incident recorded by low-country Colleton District planter David Gavin highlights the difficulty some families had in responding to the simple needs of their members, their genuine desire to make themselves available for one another, and the dire straits in which slaves who either lacked a family, or were kept apart by their owners might have found themselves in at times of crisis. At the beginning of February 1856, Gavin purchased at a sheriff's sale Mary, a slave woman, and her six-year-old and youngest daughter, Tenah. Gavin allowed Mary and her daughter to remain with their former owner, James Grimes, "to assist his wife." Mary remained at the Grimes's until mid-August, when Gavin brought her to his plantation "to nurse her father," an act Gavin had been moved to do "in kindness to the old negro who I thought would soon die." About a month later, on September 13, Mary's father, Friday, aged about seventy-seven years, died of "dropsy in the chest." As well as receiving the care and attention of his daughter, Mary, he was also nursed "night and day" by Mike and Big Jim, Mary's husband. At a time of serious illness, this family, aided by their master, was able to come together and give much needed assistance and support. Grimes, a not too distant neighbor, had probably owned Friday's wife as well as Mary and her child. Finding himself in financial difficulties, Grimes was forced to sell Mary and her child. Because Gavin owned both her father and her husband, Big Jim, he took the opportunity to purchase Mary and to bring husband and wife and father and daughter together on the same plantation. Interestingly, when Gavin allowed Mary to return to Grimes after her father's death, she was no longer welcomed. As Gavin explained, Grimes had become "vexed because I took her to nurse her father." Had Grimes remained Mary's owner, she would have been deprived of the opportunity of being at her father's bedside with the rest of her close family to comfort him before he died. This incident emphasizes the difficulties slave families were likely to encounter when family members were spread over two or more plantations and the important role slave masters continued to play. Indeed, with different masters, one half of the family could have had an experience of slavery totally different from the other.[39]

Clearly, masters' intervention in the lives of their slaves continued to have a profound effect on the slaves' life chances. Some slaves, however, were sufficiently well organized to provide effectively for themselves and their families. The important role the family played in times of sickness and death cannot be overstressed because it was at times of greatest difficulty that the family—the larger and stronger the better—truly came into its own.

Antebellum masters made their most successful interventions in the private world of the slaves in the area of health care. By and large quite rational beings, most slave masters knew they "must guard their slaves' health as among the most vital of their interests; for while crops were merely income, slaves were capital."[40] Yet even when slave masters endeavored to provide adequate health care for their bondsmen, most slaves (with good reasons) looked to other slaves for their medical needs.[41] Slave families who had full access to the skills and services of community health care providers would have been better placed to take care of their own in times of medical crisis.

For a variety of reasons, slaves were discouraged from relying too heavily on masters and mistresses whose proficiency in medicine left much to be desired. They tended, therefore, toward medical self-sufficiency and, unlike the antebellum southern medical profession, used medical techniques that were more African American than European American, more medieval than modern, and more gentle than "heroic." The method of health care the slaves practiced often revealed an attitude to medicine and a worldview significantly different from those of their masters.

Accounts from former slaves who had lived in the three regions of the state reveal a variety of experiences with slave and white medicine. Joe

Rutherford, born on Morris Island, Charleston District, in 1845, recalled that along with the medicine his owner, Dr. Thomas Rutherford, gave his sick slaves, "some of the folks [the slaves] would make hot teas from root herbs." When the slaves were sick on Sam Polite's plantation in Beaufort District, the doctor was sent for. "If you berry sick, doctor gib you calumus (calomel) or castor oil." Sometimes "dead shot" was given for worms. For a bad stomachache, Polite's mother gave him "Juse-e-moke," which was something she "git outen de wood."[42] Many low-country slaves were exposed to the combination of white and slave medical practices that was common on South Carolina's plantations. In her work on "granny mid-wives" Vennie Deas-Moore found that these "black ladies . . . effectively combined their bitter herb and root teas with the medicine left by the physician or dispensed by the mistress."[43] Some overlapping would have taken place in the dispensing of slave and white medicine, particularly, but not exclusively, in the private world of the slaves.

If slaves' use of plants for medicinal purposes is evidence of African retentions, it would probably have been more prevalent in the low country, where there was a high ratio of Africans to Europeans among the region's colonial population.[44] The early Africans brought their "highly esteemed pharmacopeia with them . . . as part of their oral traditions," and in the semitropical low-country environment they found enough similarities with Africa "that such knowledge was easily adapted to somewhat new flora and fauna."[45] Slave medicine retained a strong flavor of Africa, and so too did other medical practices echo the African village. Sam Polite, for example, recalled the involvement of the slave quarters in the birth and care of slave children. "W'en 'ooman hab baby," he reported, "he [she] hab mid-wife for nine days and sometime don't haffa work for month w'en baby born."[46] It was common for slave parents to arm their children with a "little teeny bag of asafetida on a string around they necks to keep off diseases,"[47] a practice that originated in Africa. The use of such herbs and charms reflected both a general lack of confidence in the master's medicine and medical practices and respect for preventive rather than curative medicine.

Not all masters failed to take advantage of preventive medicines. The slaves, however, seem to have been far more concerned with safeguarding themselves against sickness and disease than were their masters, who seemed more concerned with curing the sick.[48] Margaret Hughes, a slave born near Columbia in the middle country, captured the duality of life in a slave society and the existence of two distinct forms of preventive medicine—one "scientific," white, and public, the other more traditional, black, and private. Hughes recalled that the slaves "used to wear garlic and asafetida 'round our neck to keep off diseases." These slaves were also "vaccinated to keep from ketching smallpox." No doubt the combination proved successful, which was all that anyone, master or slave, desired. The slave would not resist being vaccinated, and few masters would have prevented the slaves from wearing their small bags of asafetida around their necks. Henry Ryan of Edgefield, born in 1841 on Judge Pickens Butler's plantation, described his master as "good" and "de best folks in de country." When slaves got sick, doctors were called in to administer to them. The Butler slaves also used herbs, field grass roots, and herb roots, which were boiled and drunk for fevers. Also, garlic would be hung around the necks of small boys and girls "to keep away sickness."[49]

If the middle country was healthier than the low country, the climate and conditions of the piedmont and mountain country were even more conducive to good health. Victoria Adams grew up on Samuel Black's Fairfield District plantation along with some forty other slaves. Born in 1847, Victoria recalled that her mistress, Martha Black, looked after the slaves when they were sick. Medicines were made from herbs, leaves, and roots—catnip, garlic, tansy, and roots of burdock. The last was soaked in whisky and was considered "mighty good medicine." The practice of dipping asafetida in turpentine and hanging it around children's necks to ward off disease was also common in the up-country. It is noteworthy that Adams, like many of her fellows in this region, did not mention doctors visiting the plantation.[50] The scarcity of doctors in the up-country would have placed increased pressure on masters and slaves to take care of most if not all of their medical needs.[51] Millie Barber, another Fairfield slave, was born in 1855. She could not "member us ever had a doctor on de place; just a granny was enough at childbirths." Here, a slave woman would have her baby "one day, up and gwine 'round de next day singin' at her work lak nothing unusual had happened." Without a doctor, these slaves, belonging to Eliza Weir, probably took a good deal of the responsibility for their own care. If these slave women (along with those described by Susan Hamlin) were able to decide when to return to the fields after having given birth, those who were up to it returned immediately to "work," particularly if "work" meant working for themselves. Once the woman had declared herself well enough to labor for herself, she could not then argue that she could not handle the master's work. Under such circumstances, slave women may well have returned to their work "singing . . . lak nothing unusual happened."[52] In a few instances, little out of the ordinary would have happened. Indeed, some women were unaware that they were pregnant until they gave birth.[53]

High up in the piedmont near the foothills, Laurens District slaves found the climate conducive to good health, particularly those on Sam Fleming's plantation. In his lengthy account of life under slavery, George Fleming failed to mention doctors coming regularly to the plantation to examine and treat the slaves. Only when slaves were "bad sick" were doctors sent for. Otherwise, the administration of preventive medicine and care of routine and less serious illnesses were the responsibility of "some of the women" who knew how "to bile herbs and roots and make tea for colds and fevers." Pregnant women were taken care of by an "old granny woman," who remained with them "'til dey got up and well."[54] In the absence of regular visits from a white doctor, up-country slaves may have relied heavily on their own resources, particularly for childbirth and preventive medicine. Indeed, throughout the state—even where doctors were frequent visitors to the plantations—whenever slaves were sick and in need of care, it was primarily slaves rather than masters, mistresses, or doctors who treated them.

Such arrangements, informal or otherwise, necessitated the presence of several "old grannies" on any sizable plantation to provide the attention some slave women seem to have enjoyed before, during, and particularly after their pregnancies. On the Fripp plantation in the low country, for example, among the seventy-three slaves in March 1857, there were three such "black ladies" entrusted with the day-to-day health care of the slaves. When Elsey miscarried in April 1857, it was Milley, the nurse and midwife, who attended to her. In January 1858, when she again miscarried, she was looked after by Old Nelly "for two weeks." Salina, who was "quite ill" in November 1857, was attended by Olive. These women must have accumulated a great deal of experience in caring for the sick and pregnant slave women that could be passed on to other slaves. Their level of skill was probably very high as, over a long period of apprenticeship, "young grannies were trained by old grannies," and old, tried, and tested methods were combined with white medical practices to provide an increasingly sophisticated collection of home remedies.[55]

But who exactly trained slave midwives, doctors, and nurses? Former slave Gus Feaster sheds some light on this important band of slave professionals. The old women, Feaster explained, "too old to do any work . . . would take and study what to do for the ailments of grown folks and lil' chilluns." These women would make pine resin pills from "de pine resin what dropped from de pine trees, and give de pills to de folks for de backache." They also "gashed de sweet gum" to get gum to chew. This sweet gum was, apparently, very good for indigestion and for "de tooties" (teeth; it may have been the forerunner to chewing gum). Feaster considered resin pills the best thing he knew to "start your water off when it done stopped on ye."[56]

One should not get the impression that an impersonal band of professional "old folks," "black ladies," or "grannies" administered to the medical welfare of the slave quarters throughout the state. These women and men were members of slave families. Their secret (and not so secret) remedies seem to have been used statewide, with only slight variations, and effectively drew most members of the wider slave community into a common practice of preventive medicine. Slave nurses and doctors, as well as slave parents, administered to their families' needs. Solomon recalled that his mother, Suella Caldwell, "would take fever grass and boil it to tea and have us drink it to keep the fever away." She also used branch elder twigs and dogwood berries for chills. A variation on the bag around the neck, or perhaps the adult version, and a method to prevent chills that easily progressed to pneumonia was to "dip a string in turpentine, keep it tied around de waist and tie a knot in it every time you had a chill." The reputation of Nat Alexander of Spartanburg for meanness and cruelty must have stemmed partly from the fact that he "would not get a doctor to a sick slave until he dropped in the field."[57] No doubt, before a slave reached this desperate condition, experienced helpers in the quarters would have been doing their best to aid the sufferer. Shrewd or perhaps unprincipled masters like Nat Alexander might have simply allowed the slave medicine time to effect a cure and call in a white doctor only when it failed. The risks to the individual slave and to health of the slave quarters are clear, and all too often they led to life-threatening epidemics. Only foolish masters would allow matters to go this far because neither they nor their families were immune to the diseases that so frequently brought havoc to South Carolina's plantations.

As widespread as was the use of slave doctors and nurses, few former slaves reported unqualified satisfaction with slave medicine. Granny Cain, born in 1847, lived on Squire Kenner's up-country plantation in Maybinton, Newberry District. She "waited on" her mistress, Miss Lucey, who was "just like a mother to me" (Cain was not without her own mother). Living in the same house with the Kenners, Cain would have been familiar with the doctor coming to treat sick members of the family and may have put greater "store" in white doctors. She recalled that "we never put much store in herb root tea and such like."[58] Perhaps slaves who were closest to the white public world, having less faith in the ways of the slaves, would have been disinclined to indulge in the more traditional practices of the slave quarters.[59] Both parents of Lila Rutherford, who was born in 1851 on Ivey Suber's Dutch Fork plantation in Newberry District, lived on the Suber place. Lila was "hired by Marse Suber as a nurse in the big house," and she also "waited on my mistress when she was sick." Suber was described as having been "good to his slaves," giving them "plenty to eat, good place to sleep and plenty of clothes." If ill house slaves were treated by a white doctor, they probably acquired a jaundiced view of the slave quarters' folk medicine, similar to that of white doctors in particular and the white world in general. Rutherford, it seems, was very close to the Subers. Although she had married at the age of fifteen and her mother moved away after freedom, she had remained with the Subers. Granny Cain and her family had also remained with their master's family after freedom, working for wages and then hiring "out to other people for wages" after Suber died.[60]

Generally, slaves who spent most of their lives in the slave quarters or in intimate contact with it had fewer experiences with white doctors and recalled a more positive relationship with slave doctors and nurses. Ellen Swindler, born late in slavery on Tom Price's Enoree River plantation, recalled that the slaves "didn't have doctors much, but de ole folks had cures for sickness." Mary Veals had been owned by Judge J. B. O'Neall and grew up near Newberry. She heard her parents talk about slavery times and learned of "rabbit tobacco," which was a cure for colds. Small boys would chew and smoke this, as did some of the old folks. Mary Johnson recalled that the older slaves on John Johnson's Newberry plantation, where she grew up in the slave quarters, had used "life everlasting," now called "rabbit tobacco," to cure bad colds and pneumonia. She explained that it could also be boiled and a plaster made that would be placed on the patient's chest. Emoline Wilson, born in 1847, Dutch Fork resident, considered her master Lemuel Lane to have been "mean to most of us, but good to me." Lane may have ignored his slaves' more immediate medical needs, thus strengthening their belief in their own medicine. Wilson reported that "peach tree leaves boiled and drunk for fever, and wild cherry bark" were good for anything "if taken at night." The best cure, however, was turpentine and a little oil mixed: "swallow it and it will fix you up."[61]

Throughout the state, masters and slaves often worked in conjunction to ensure the health of the slave quarters and of the plantation as a whole. Milton Marshall, born near Goshen Hill, was owned by Burton Maybin along with some eighty-eight other slaves. Marshall described his former master as "all right." On this plantation, care for slave health was shared between the "big house" and the quarters. "Old folks," recalled Marshall, "made medicines from root, herbs and tree barks." It was also common practice for the master to call "his big chaps up to de house in de mornings and made dem drink chinaberry tea to keep worms from getting in dem"—adding weight to the argument that adult slaves received more and better care than did the young. Wallace Davis, formerly a slave on Bill Davis's plantation, provided another example of the two worlds combining on health care practices. He recalled that when "our slaves got sick we sent for de doctor [but] some of de old folks in the neighborhood believed in giving root or herb tea or tea made from chinaberry barks or peach leaves." John Davenport, born in 1848, was a slave on Pierce Lake's plantation in Newberry District. Davenport recalled a weed named "bonesalt" that grew wild in the woods. "It was good for chills and fever," but it was "awful bitter." He also recalled the "little bags of asefetida" that were hung around the necks of young children "to ward off fever and diphtheria."[62]

The two worlds of masters and slaves were linked in the sphere of medicine because the white world was occasionally obliged to turn to the black world for medical assistance. In Union District, George Briggs, Jessie Briggs's slave, displayed a special gift that might have brought great comfort to slave quarters far and near. George would be "carried . . . a hundred miles to cure a sick woman." He would simply put his "hand on any 'flux' man or woman and remove de pain, if dey have faith in my hand." This form of curative medicine was more usually associated with slave "conjurers," and George's patients (both black and white) needed a strong faith.[63]

Given the poor state of nineteenth-century medical practices, the slaves' faith in slave doctors and nurses was probably higher than their faith in the white doctors and masters and mistresses who were often called in only when the patient was at death's door. Their heroic remedies were more threatening to the patients than the herbs and spirit healing more frequently used by slave doctors and nurses. As suggested above, the white world might have come in contact only with the slave world's medical failures.[64]

Not surprisingly, slave nurses and doctors were sometimes better received and more trusted than white doctors, who, because they often arrived on the plantation when the patient had reached a critical stage, may have come to be associated in the minds of slaves and owners alike with failure and incompetence.[65] An example of slave owners who thought nursing, tender loving care, and prayer could cure their sick is provided by David G. Harris, a planter from Spartanburg. When it appeared that the above prescription would not be sufficient to cure the patient, the doctor was brought in, and, as was so often the case, he was "just too late." On October 20, 1860, Harris wrote in his journal, "I thought our little negro was nearly well. But she is reported to be in a dangerous situation this morning. Emily is nursing her with much care. I hope it will survive." Loving care, hope, and prayers were seldom enough to pull patients through serious illness. Later that evening, Harris added, "The child continues so bad, we sent for Dr. . . . But soon after he arrived she died."[66]

Despite a genuine desire and concern for their slaves' health, the majority of slaveholders probably took few steps to use preventive medicines and instead relied on a doctor to come and cure slaves once they had become seriously ill.[67] This neglect would have created and further encouraged the development of slave medicinal preventives and cures. The existence of an effective and accessible slave medical practice would have made it attractive, both economically and morally, for slave masters to have their slaves develop and operate the first line of defense against illness and disease. This, in turn, would have allowed for the creation of a sophisticated system of training people to enter the profession, bringing with it economic and social rewards based on service to the communities of both worlds.

However well trained these health care providers were, the most sophisticated nineteenth-century doctor—black or white—would have been hard-pressed to produce satisfactory cures for the numerous diseases suffered by South Carolina slaves living on farms and plantations in unhealthy conditions, few of whom were provided with a balanced diet to help protect against the ever-present danger of disease that could so easily culminate in untimely death. A slave family's ability to provide foods and other extras that constituted or contributed to a nutritious and well-balanced diet and to the general good health of family members would have been a major factor in determining the slaves' chances of staving off diseases, remaining healthy and productive, and thus able to provide some protection for themselves against the harsh conditions under which they were obliged to live and work. A strong, well-organized family could do much to protect its members and assist them in maintaining good health, but the conditions on many antebellum plantations were such that the most salubrious setting could all too easily become one full of disease and death.

The poor state of medical knowledge in the antebellum South, with its dubious natural and manufactured remedies, rendered even the best situated slaves acutely vulnerable when sick. The low level of personal hygiene and deplorable sanitary practices on farms and plantations almost guaranteed that the majority of slaves would experience at least one bout of sickness. Contaminated water, for example, made the simple act of satisfying one's thirst a highly dangerous activity. The primitive state of toilet facilities and the archaic notions on the use of human waste products as a useful source of fertilizer only added to the health risks faced by the slaves living on farms and plantations where it was common practice to use human "night soil." This fertilizer would be scooped up once a year and hauled off to enrich the soil. In the meantime, it presented a constant threat to one and all. During heavy rains, it was washed into springs and streams from which the slaves got their drinking water, and young slave children were exposed to parasitic soil. Adults too would have been at risk, particularly those who made frequent contact with the earth in areas where "promiscuous defecation occurred constantly."[68]

Eating dirt often brought hookworms into the body. Chronic sickness, Todd Savitt writes, was the lot of those infected, accompanied by an enormous appetite, retarded mental, physical, and sexual growth among children, extreme lethargy, generalized edema (swelling), and chronic leg ulcers. These afflictions were particularly worrisome for slaves whose working life was strictly regimented and whose access to food was often tightly restricted. The close proximity of buildings on most plantations ensured that infection was seldom restricted to certain slaves or to the slave quarters. The whole plantation community was constantly at risk, and members frequently succumbed to epidemics. Farm animals that devoured decomposed scraps would often develop parasitic diseases, especially tapeworm and trichinosis, which were then consumed by people in poorly cooked meat.[69] In addition to the proximity of slave houses and gardens to exposed human waste and the dangers already mentioned was the attraction piles of human waste would have had for rats and vermin such as bedbugs and body lice. These parasites were directly responsible for typhus—body lice transmitting the infection and fleas carrying the body lice from the rats. Of course, these infections did not necessarily cause serious illness or even death, although both were likely, and epidemics could occur because of the primitive conditions and ideas on hygiene and sanitation, the close proximity of slave houses in the quarters, overcrowding, and the quality of the culinary arts.

One crucial variable, of course, was the individual's physical ability to ward off disease and so prevent illness or to overcome sickness once infected. This ability was closely linked to the quality of the nutritional store held in the individual's body. This, in turn, was dependent on two crucial factors—diet and work. The slaves' world of work has already been discussed, and consideration has been given to some of the physical demands placed on slaves in the different regions of the state. What slaves ate and the amount of work they had to do had an important bearing on the state of their health and on the quality of life to which they could aspire. The better organized the slaves were in stable, interdependent, cooperative family units, the better were their chances of providing the goods required to help maintain an adequate nutritional store.

Savitt, Richard Steckel, and others have shown how poorly southern slaves were treated in the important area of nutrition and health. Were South Carolina's slaves any better or worse treated, were they better able to fend for themselves, or did they, as did their fellow slaves throughout the South, find their diets inadequate, ill-conceived, and generally dull? [70] *The American Slave* narratives provide a sample of the conditions of the state's slaves in the three sections and give us some idea of the basic food allowance the average slave could have expected to receive and if and how this allowance might have been supplemented. Of crucial importance were the opportunities the slaves had to supplement their basic allowance, the quality of this supplement, and its regularity. It would be of little long-term value, for example, if the slaves were well blessed with food in October and November after the harvest but short of the basics come the "sickly season" of the summer months, the very time they would have needed all the nutritional protection they could muster. There is nothing to suggest that even the most well-situated slaves would not have suffered from poor sanitation, substandard housing, poorly prepared and inadequate food, and incompetent medical care. But where slaves had opportunities to improve their standard of living by improving their provision of food, clothing, and shelter, they were able to reduce their chances of succumbing to diseases, increase their chances of recovery when sick, and so lower the risk of serious illness and untimely death.

The long-term health and well-being of the slave community was seriously threatened by a poor or inadequate diet. As Kenneth and Virginia Kiple have shown, strengthening the mother and increasing her nutritional store would improve her chances of producing healthier babies more likely to survive past infancy and grow up into strong and healthy adults. [71] The reality for most slaves, however, was that their regular diet of corn meal and pork could not have provided enough essential nutrients to sustain a moderately active twenty-two-year-old male or female, much less a hardworking laborer or a pregnant or lactating woman. [72] To increase their chances of remaining healthy and surviving slavery and going some way toward making a life of their own, South Carolina slaves had to work hard to supplement a diet that in most instances was insufficient for their nutritional requirements and also must have been agonizingly dull.

Sam Mitchell and his fellow slaves on John Chaplin's low-country Ladies Island plantation received a peck of corn every Tuesday, and whenever potatoes were dug, "we git potato." The slaves were also allowed to "raise one pig," and they could augment their allowance from the produce of their "two task ob land to cultivate for se'f." Mitchell's father owned a boat and went fishing at night; any surplus fish would be sold. Additional income was assured from his work at night cutting posts and wood, which he also sold. The Mitchells, then, thanks in part to a busy and innovative father, were in a good position to supplement their basic allowance with their own crops, fresh fish, and whatever other food might have been purchased with the cash earned from extra work activities.[73]

Sam Polite of St. Helens Island and the other slaves on his plantation received their allowance on Saturday afternoon. Every slave "dat wuks gets peck ob corn and pea, and sometime meat and clabber." In addition, the slaves could keep chickens and "maybe hawg." They could "sell aig (eggs) and chicken to store and Massa will buy your hawg." Polite did not "git much fish . . . 'cause we nebber hab boat." Sometimes, however, "you kin t'row out net en ketch shrimp." Failing that, the money earned from selling livestock could be used to "buy t'ing lak fish en w'atteber he want." In Polite's part of the low country hunting dogs were common and one's diet and earning power could have been further expanded by hunting "possum and raccoon wid your dawg." Polite and his fellows "nebber see any sugar or coffee," but the two or three "tas' ob land 'round your cabin" would have provided a source of fresh vegetables that could be used or sold for more immediate necessities as well as luxuries such as sugar and coffee. Necessities, of course, would have frequently extended beyond food requirements. Polite's master gave his slaves four to five yards of cloth every Christmas, out of which they had to make their own clothes to last them through the year. They were given shoes, but they "didn't git no coat." As a result, these slaves at some point may have had to choose between extra food to feed the body or a heavy coat to keep it warm during the cold winter months. Polite may have been particularly disadvantaged because Mitchell recalled a twice yearly issue of some six yards of cloth, "calico in spring and homespun in de winter." Either way, these slaves and those elsewhere in the state had additional demands on their "nonwork" time which they were obliged to concede if they were to maintain what they soon came to consider a basic standard of living. Mitchell recalled, for example, that some fifteen slaves lived on the "street" on the Woodlawn plantation. Each cabin had two rooms. John Chaplin, however, "don't gib nothing for yo' house—you hab to git dat de best you can." Having fourteen children, Mitchell's father was kept very busy for it was he who had to find material and additional time to make the "bed, table and bench to sit on," which made up the bulk of the family's furniture.[74]

Situated "by the river," Daphney Wright and her fellow slaves had certain advantages living on Robert Cally's plantation. Unlike Mitchell and Polite, the Cally slaves did not need a boat to enjoy the riches of the river. Wright's father would go out at night and catch fish using a seine (fishing net). Usually he caught "nice big mullets," which he would divide " 'round amongst de colored folks an he'd take some up to de white folks for dere breakfast." Wright recalled that the Cally slaves and other "people on de water don't eat much meat." No doubt this was reflected in their weekly allowance. But for twenty-five cents enough bacon could be had to last them all week and would be added to their basic diet as a variation on fish stews. They would cut the meat into little pieces, "fry them into cracklings den put dat into de fish stew." They were allowed to keep pigs, and whenever one was killed, rather than curing the pork and storing it, "dey take it to town an' sell den use de money for whatever dey want." Although not part of their regular allowance, these slaves' basic diet came to include large amounts of fresh fish: "oysters, crabs, clams" were accessible to the poorest, weakest, and least able-bodied on the plantation, for when the tide went out "you kin walk along an' jes pick up crab."[75]

Henry Brown of Charleston had no complaint about the allowance received from his master, A. G. Rose. Every Monday each slave was issued three pounds of bacon, a peck of corn, a quart of salt, molasses, and "sometimes meat and peas." A "pack of tobacco was given to the men. The wife got the same thing but chillin' according to age." "They had all the vegetables they wanted; they grew them in the gardens," which Brown and his fellows, at least those who decided against going to frolics and generally misusing their free time, would have worked in on the weekends.[76]

Life was probably less comfortable on Lias Winning's Cooper River plantation. Thomas Goodwater recalled that he and his fellow slaves "use to go an' catch possums an' rabbits so as to hab meat." They must not have gotten much of this wild game because Winning's driver showed little respect for his master's property. Sometimes he would shoot a cow during the night and "issue him 'round to all the slaves, 'special when cows come from annoder plantation." It is not clear whether the driver stole these cows because the slave rations contained insufficient meat or if such "theft," occurring on a regular basis, robbed Winning of the meat earmarked for his slaves. Either way, slaves took matters into their own hands and supplemented an inadequate diet, albeit through illegal means. A more generally accepted means of improving the diet was tending the vegetable gardens that made available "things for the year 'round so we could hab soup." Nonetheless, if the driver had been responding to the abject condition of the slaves, his actions, enjoying their support, would serve as a useful indication of their desperation and the measures some slaves were willing to take in an attempt to improve their welfare, in this instance, supplementing their diets. Such measures were particularly dangerous for these slaves because "nuttin' make Winning so mad as when one would steal. . . . Anyone he catch stealin' was sure to get a good whippin'."[77]

Joe Rutherford's master, Thomas Rutherford, gave his slaves a "good house or hut to live in." They "could hunt and fish, and got lots of game around . . . we had dogs but our master didn't like hounds." The Rutherford slaves were in a good position to supplement their allowances with fresh meat, and they probably also enjoyed the use of a garden, as was the practice in the region. Prince Smith had been a slave on Wadalaw Island. His master, Osland Bailey, allowed his slaves to "plant as much land as we would for our own use." In addition to the allowance that was given out "at de end of de week" of a peck of corn, "which you had to grin' on Saturday ebenin' when his work was done," the slaves could raise fowls and hogs. Smith also remembered his master as a "gentleman" who treated "de slaves good." An element of this good treatment was Bailey's willingness, whenever he went to town, to allow "any o' his slaves [to] ax him to buy t'ings fir dem in Charleston." He would also give the little children money to purchase goods from the "Jews en peddlars" who came on the place with "clothes an' ginger to sell." In contrast to the experience of the Winning slaves, "de people on his [Bailey's] plantation didn't hab any need to steal frum him fur he didn't 'low us to want fur anything." Despite this "good" treatment, and the fact that Bailey was a "gentleman," Prince Smith recalled some of the barbaric methods used to punish slaves on the Bailey place. Perhaps, as Smith said, the sweat boxes, stocks, and scaffolds were "for those who disobeyed" and may have functioned more successfully as a deterrent from, rather than as a punishment for, crime.[78] Their presence and occasional use would have constituted a constant reminder to the slaves of their relative powerlessness and the potential power of their master. That they were not frequently used may have reflected the increasing constraints upon slave masters that made it unnecessary for them to use brute force to discipline their slaves.[79]

Low-country slaves, producing rice and Sea Island cotton under the task and garden system and enjoying access to the sea or to rivers, as well as to large towns or cities, would have been in an excellent position to supplement their diets as well as their incomes. Here, some slaves would have been hired out to work on the river and to perform highly skilled tasks in towns and cities such as Beaufort, Georgetown, and Charleston.[80] As William Oliver, formerly a slave in Georgetown, recalled, some slaves would "hire dey self out as stevedore—and pay Massa so much for the time." It was only the "smart slave do that," Oliver added, clearly counting his father among this group. George Hollon of Georgetown caught and sold fish and came to own three "row boats and one flat boat." Fellow Georgetown resident F. Alonzo Jackson paid his master $140 every year "for my time and supported my family from my own earnings working for whom I chose." His wife earned money as a pastry cook and laundress. Jackson also had two horses at a stable for which he received extra money whenever they were used. One witness to his claim before the Southern Claims Commission was Job Mayrck, who had been a butcher by trade and had managed to earn money and purchase his freedom "about 16 years before the war."[81]

Although the economic benefits of life in the low country may have been offset by the relatively unhealthy conditions of the region, a solid, well-balanced, and varied diet would have increased low-country slaves' resistance to disease and improved their recuperative powers and thus reduced their chances of succumbing to untimely death.

Slaves farther inland ought to have been at less risk of contracting the respiratory diseases that were more prevalent in the low country. They were likely, however, to have fared less well at supplementing and introducing variety to their regular food allowance. Peggy Grigsby, born in 1831, lived on her master Alec Grigsby's place somewhere near the Edgefield and Saluda District line. Peggy described her master as "fair," but "his wife was awful mean to us." The Grigsby slaves were fortunate to have lived in the midst of natural abundance, and they did not suffer for want of food. Peggy recalled the "quiltings" they had on Saturday nights "with eats and frolics." Some of these "eats" would have been provided by the "men folks," who regularly hunted "doves, partridges, wild turkeys, deer, squirrels and rabbits." Older than the average respondent, Grigsby was able to remember times when there had been few if any restrictions on land boundaries or on hunting and when everyone might have taken advantage of the land's natural richness. During the later period, fencing and restrictions on hunting were introduced.[82] A similar account was given by Henry Ryan, who had been a slave of Judge Pickens Butler from near Edgefield Courthouse. Ryan and his fellows "had extra patches of ground to work for ourselves." They also had a big plantation garden "dat the overseers planted for all de place to eat out of." The Butler slaves also hunted opossums, rabbits, squirrels, wild turkey, and doves and set traps for partridges. These slaves "always had plenty to eat," and Ryan considered his master and mistress to have been "good, de best folks in de country." Not surprisingly, as well as feeding his slaves well, Butler "used to give us a little money too . . . for our work." With this "little money," the slaves were able to purchase "clothes and things we had to have." With food in abundance, some of these slaves were able to equip themselves with suitable clothing and cooking utensils and so improve their chances of remaining healthy and disease free.[83]

Natural abundance, however, was no guarantee of unlimited amounts of food and the absence of hunger. The slaves were forever being called upon to work hard, improvise, do whatever it took to maintain a standard of living a little above the basic. Mom Sarah Brown, formerly a slave in Florence District, recalled that food was plentiful. "Coarse de peoples had plenty sometin' to eat," she said, "like meat en turkey and chicken. . . . En milk en butter . . . dey didn't never be widout plenty of dat." But she was quick to point out that slavery was no easy time—"peoples sho had to scratch bout en make what dey had in slavery time." For coffee, for example, sometimes these slaves would use their garden patches to plant okra "en parch dat [the seeds] en make what coffee dey have." Sugar and salt "never run free wid de peoples den neither . . . salt was so scarce dat dey had to go to de seashore and get what salt dey had"—another blessing enjoyed by low-country slaves who lived along the coastline.[84]

Sylvia Cannon, formerly a slave on Bill Gregg's plantation in the middle country, painted a picture similar to Henry Ryan's. She recalled having had "plenty peas en rice en hog meat en rabbit en fish." The Gregg slaves, she explained, "had dey extra crop what dey had time off to work every Saturday. White folks tell dem what dey made dey could have." During the war these slaves made a great deal of money from their extra crop. If the slaves had not been freed, Cannon was sure that "peoples would have found we colored people rich." Hard work and a willingness to "scratch bout" would have provided not only ample food for personal consumption but enough of a surplus to earn money to provide those much needed extras that had to be purchased.[85]

Not all slaves, even those who were willing to work hard and "scratch about," were able to supplement their diets by purchasing luxury items. Wiles Gregg allowed his slaves to "hab a garden uv we own." Washington Dozier recalled that the Gregg slaves hunted opossums and fished. They may have been close neighbors to Cannon with similar experiences, but Dozier, an adult at slavery's end, did not recall ever being paid for his work, only that "dey gi'e us plenty sumptin' to eat."[86]

An absence of cash payment from masters does not automatically indicate either poverty on the part of the slave or meanness and cruelty on the part of the master. Charlie Grant lived on a plantation of "about 1000 acres" in Mars Bluff. He had "plenty to eat en plenty clothes to wear." His master, Dr. William Johnson, gave the slaves their allowances on Saturday and gave them "more any time they needed it." They received "meat en bread en molasses to eat mostly, but didn't have no wheat flour den." The Johnson slaves "had dey own gardens dat dey work at night en especially moon light nights cause dey had to work all day in de fields till sun down." Grant recalled that his mother had a "big garden" where she planted "collards en everything like dat you want to eat." These goods, assuming the

Grants produced surpluses, could have been exchanged for other goods or for money.[87]

The accumulation of extra income for food and the like was only one aspect of the slaves' struggle to maintain healthy and strong bodies. Another important consideration was the maintenance of personal hygiene. Peter Clifton was born a slave in 1848 on the Bigger Mobley plantation "tween Kershaw and Camden." Clifton recalled that food was not a problem: "Us was fed up to de neck all de time." His experience of slavery, however, was that "us never had a change of clothes" and therefore "us smell pretty rancid maybe, in de winter time." This low level of personal hygiene, brought about by the infrequent changing of clothes, could have contributed to any sickness and disease present in the Mobley quarters.[88]

A constant problem, and one found particularly in a society where the knowledge of personal and food hygiene and the storage of food was basic if not primitive, was the quality of food preparation on the plantation in general and in the quarters in particular.[89] Walter Long, born near Chapin in Lexington District, recalled that the food "was good and a lot of it." Long emphasized that the food was "cooked good and prepared for us by servants dat didn't do nothin' else but tend to de food dat de rest of de slaves had to eat." Care and preparation of food would have been crucial in a society where pork made up such a large proportion of the staple diet and wild game and domestic animals constituted a large part of the slaves' regular fare.[90] Sam Rawls had lived on John Hillier's place near Columbia. Slaves there hunted a great deal, rabbits, squirrels, foxes, and opossums making up the bulk of the game. They also fished. The Hilliers had brick ovens that were away from the main house where cooking was done on Saturdays. This food, prepared in large quantities, had to "last several days." Fresh vegetables—potatoes, turnips, collards, and peas—were grown in a big garden "dat furnished all de slaves."[91]

Louisa Collier of Marion District received her allowance on Saturday, and it had to last until the next Saturday. Her master, Colonel Durant, permitted his slaves to have their own gardens, and they also "raised us own chickens en aw dat." Durant was typical of the state's planters, most of whom would have preferred to distribute food to their slaves on Monday or Tuesday rather than on weekends and to establish a communal kitchen rather than allot portions of uncooked food to slave families. Yet the general practice seems to have been a weekend distribution, which may have been a result of pressure from an increasingly autonomous slave quarters made up of well-organized and self-disciplined slave families who used their weekends as special time for families and for religious activities. As former slave Hester Hunter from Marion County recalled, "de people sho cook dinner for Sunday on Saturday." The chance was always present, however, that some slave women, returning exhausted from the fields or preoccupied with family or religious matters, would carelessly prepare and serve food, putting their families' health at risk. But it was a poor wife who did not put herself out for her family on weekends.[92]

During the week, the plantation managers had more control over the slaves' eating arrangements on middle-country plantations. Hester Hunter described how the plantation hands working in the fields would come to the main house in the middle of the day to get their "dinner." Her aunt cooked the food in the main house kitchen for the workers. Interestingly, whether to safeguard their health, to ensure that older slaves had ample food, or simply to maintain a social distance between the generations, the little children were not allowed to "eat outer dat pot wid de field hands." Genia Woodberry had belonged to Jim Stevenson, who lived near Bretton Neck. Stevenson gave his slaves "mos' eve'ting dey hab en den he 'low every family to hab uh acre in land uv dey own to plant." Their allowance was given out every Friday. The Stevenson slaves would eat their breakfast "fore dey leabs dey quarter." If and when they had to remain in the fields all day, for their lunch they would carry "dey basket uv victual en pot 'long wid em and cook right dere in de field. Jest put dey peas en bacon in de pot en build up big fire 'bout it close whey dey wuz workin'." Food preparation under these conditions was most likely to lead to unhygienic and risky practices because the regular consumption of poorly prepared and reheated food could cause serious illness.[93]

Some slaveholders refused to allow any but qualified slaves to do the cooking. G. D. Harmon, for example, argued that in nine cases out of ten, they cooked with bad water, in dirty pots, and without salt.[94] On this matter, as on so many others, planters did not publicly agree. One South Carolina planter thought differently. "Many planters," he wrote, "argue that the negroes would enjoy better health to have their food cooked for them. Our experience is to the reverse—the field hands are always healthier than the house servants, or those who eat at this cook's table. The simplicity of the negro's diet, his victuals has much to do with his admirable digestion and good health."[95] The collected evidence clearly indicates that most masters, often against their better judgment, allowed their slaves to prepare their own food and intruded on this aspect of the slaves' world only when cooking and eating time was likely to interfere with the slaves' working time. Where the slaves had a good deal of control over their work time and functioned in well-organized families, they probably would have also controlled the important area of food and cooking. There is nothing to suggest that masters and slaves may not have worked out (perhaps passively on the part of many masters) a satisfactory arrangement on this aspect of slave life, as they did on so many others.

Other middle-country slaves received a regular food allowance as well as having a small garden to tend. Most could have expected their masters to furnish other important necessities, but this was not always the case, and slave families sometimes had to pool their meager resources if they were to enjoy any of life's basic comforts. For example, Hector Smith had lived on the Wahee Neck, where the slaves' allowance included a "peck of corn, quart of syrup—and meat," and the slaves were allowed to have a garden of "dey own." For further supplements, they hunted opossums and rabbits with their dogs. Smith's father, however, had died just before he was born, and perhaps this helps to explain why the family endured hard times, living in "log house in what never had but just one room," the furniture "was worser den de house," and beds were made "wid four stumps for de corners dat had boards lay across em to put de mattress on." His near neighbors, better situated slaves, had a different experience from Smith's. As he explained, "Some of the colored peoples had bag mattresses stuff wid hay en de others had homespun mattresses what was stuff wid dis here gray moss you see in de woods."[96] As well as the amount of free time slaves could acquire for themselves, the presence of crucial family members—in this case the father—would have made a great difference in the quality of life slaves experienced and could have determined the condition in which they came out of slavery or even if they survived the institution.

The involvement or noninvolvement of the master in the world of the slaves had a strong impact on slave families. The Smith family, lacking a male head, could have benefited from additional help from their master,

whereas slaves in the middle country (and elsewhere) felt their master's intrusion in different ways. Margaret Hughes lived on a plantation at Nipper
Hill, near Columbia, where her master and mistress, Mr. and Mrs. Daniel
Finley, were "so good to us . . . de slaves on the other plantations was jealous, they called us free niggers befo' we was freed." Besides enjoying having a shoemaker "what do nothing else much' cept make shoes," the Finley
slaves had plenty to eat. Hughes, born in 1855, was "too young to work" in
the fields so her "missis mostly keep me in de house to nurse de chillin."
Margaret's father "made chairs for de slaves" for which he would have
earned extra income. The Finleys were among the small number of slaveholders who took the sensible precaution of inoculating their slaves
against smallpox.[97]

Had Dave White grown up on a plantation adjacent to the Finley place
he may well have been one of those slaves who were jealous of his black
neighbors and considered them "free." Born in 1842, White had been a
slave on Bill Cooper's Richland District plantation. Both his parents had
belonged to the Coopers, and the whole family had a tough time under
slavery. White recalled that when his mother cooked a pot of peas "weevils
was always on de top." Their house had no furniture, and his mother, Jane,
would have to "turn mush an' clean a place on de floor." She would "make
a paddle an' we eat off de floor." The Cooper slaves "didn't know 'bout no
garden" of their own, nor could they get any news from outside. They
were expected to work on Sundays "if de week bin bad." And they were
sometimes brutally treated: White's father, Nat, had told him that Cooper
"use[d] to take de fork an' punch holes in dere bodies when he got mad."[98]

Tom Robertson was perhaps typical of many antebellum medium to
large slaveholders. Jane Johnson, born a slave in 1847, recalled that
Robertson kept his distance from the slaves. He came to the plantation
every day but "never talked to us slaves much just talked to de overseer
'bout us all." The black overseer, who Johnson thought "de meanest man
white or black" she ever saw, worked them "hard from sunrise to sunset."
The food, however, was good and might have helped compensate for
the overseer's meanness. There was "plenty of rations . . . no fancy vittles,
just plain cornbread, meat and vegetables. No flour bread or any kind of
sweet stuff for de slaves to eat." The overseer had been told that "sweet
things 'fected de stomach and teeth in a bad way." This policy may have

prevented these slaves from having problems with toothaches and related illnesses. In this case, it is clear that harsh treatment was not necessarily synonymous with slaves being underfed. When food and work were satisfactory and the sick and the poor were adequately provided for, the former slaves were quick to praise their masters as at least having been "fair" if not "kind" or "good."[99]

Henry Jenkins was born just below Columbia on Joseph Howell's plantation. His experience fell somewhere between the extremes reported by Johnson and White, as did many other accounts. Jenkins's recollections, however, lean more toward the harshness of slavery. On the Howell place, "everybody work, sun to sun, seven days in de week . . . made us all work, women in de perils of childbirth, drapped cotton seeds and corn kernels." Yet the slaves' food allowance seems to have been a little above the average, with farm hands getting the familiar "peck of meal, 3 pounds of bacon, plus a quart of molasses, a cup of salt, two cups of middlin flour (there was no white flour)." The Howell slaves were also given "good warm clothes in winter" and a "one piece cotton suit in summer." Their shoes for the winter "was made on de place, out of leather from our own tan-yard . . . from our own cow hides." Here, one of the two crucial areas of life under slavery affecting the general quality of slave life seems to have been way below the norm, the other just above. This evidence suggests that most masters accepted the basic equation that if they were going to work their slaves hard, they were also going to have to provide them with at least a basic diet. The Howell slaves had an additional and no less important problem to deal with: the water on "de place was no 'count." Safe drinking water had to be hauled on a sled with a mule. The proximity of the "no 'count" water may have been an indication of the general unhealthy condition of the area and would have presented a constant danger to younger slaves or those who did not have the time, energy, or wherewithal to haul good, clean water.[100]

The American Slave narratives and other sources suggest that the experience of Jake McLeod and the other slaves on Frank McLeod's Lynchburg plantation may have been more typical for the middle country and so present a more accurate picture of slavery. Jake described his master and mistress as "good people" who believed in "plenty work," but when a task was given, it had to be done or "dey put de little thing to you." The plantation had some twenty-five slaves living in "four slave house that was three or four hundred yards" from the master's house. McLeod did not give his slaves money, but they had "plenty to eat every day." He also allowed them to have a garden and extra patches that they worked in their spare time. These slaves were able to supplement their income and diet by hunting rabbits and fishing, which they could do as often as they wished. The McLeod slaves received at least two sets of clothes because they had to have a different set to wear to church on Sundays. Their shoes were made by a shoemaker who came onto the plantation to make "all the colored people shoes." It is not clear whether McLeod took the precaution of vaccinating his slaves, which would have indicated a sensible and genuine interest in their health, but he did take some steps to prevent the disease from spreading once it did break out. Jake recalled that the smallpox victims would be carried into the swamps, where a house was built for them to stay until they recovered (or died).[101]

As shown above, slaves in the low and middle country were likely to have had the conditions of slavery ameliorated by the work and garden system, by access to some external market (if only by way of the master), as well as by involvement in an active internal market within the larger slave community. These slaves might even have benefited from a generally more liberal attitude on the part of their owners, born of their longer experience with slavery, who had come to appreciate the importance of flexibility in their dealings with their "black family" compared with some of the less experienced and newer slaveholders and planters. The larger numbers of slaves on plantations in these areas may also have been a benefit for the slaves. In *Roll, Jordan, Roll*, Eugene Genovese points out some of the benefits that might have accrued to slaves who had regular access to large numbers of fellow slaves.[102] Liabilities may have been the climate and the problems of limited resources, which would have affected the quality of their lives. The upper part of the state may have had only the promise of a healthier climate in its favor, and the smaller than average land and slave holdings actually might have denied up-country slaves numerous "blessings" enjoyed by the state's other slaves.

A close look at the accounts from up-country former slaves will help us better understand the conditions of life in the slave communities in that region. Benjamin Russell, born in 1849, lived on a plantation near Chester. As a young man, Russell sometimes received small sums of money from "white folks and visitors," which he used to "buy extra clothing for Sunday and fire crackers and candy at Christmas." Russell and his fellows on Rebecca Nance's plantation did not want for food. "We had good food," he recalled, and explained that "in the busy seasons on the farm the mistress saw to it that the slaves were properly fed, the food cooked right and served from the big kitchen." The Russell slaves were also permitted to have "a fowl house for chickens"; they enjoyed "warm clothes and stout brogan shoes in winter" even though they "went barefooted from April until November" and "wore cotton clothes in summer."[103]

Had food been in short supply, these former up-country slaves might have reported spending their money on food rather than on manufactured luxury goods. The slaves living on Jim Aiken's Winnsboro plantation had an allowance that included "three pounds of meat, a quart of molasses, grits and other things." These items were received every "Monday night." William Ballard, born in 1849, and his parents, John and Sallie, thought Aiken had been good to his slaves. He "gave us plenty to eat and good quarters to live in." Aiken had a "very big garden with plenty of vegetables." He raised more wheat than corn and not much cotton so that life on the Aiken plantation may have acquired a more gentle routine than it did where large amounts of rice or cotton were produced. Sugarcane was also grown, from which molasses was made on the place. Aiken's son was a physician, which probably explains the existence of both a "sick house" and a "drug store" on the plantation. Aiken "didn't use old time cures much, like herbs and barks, except sassafras root tea for the blood." All in all, the Aiken slaves were in an enviable situation: a healthy environment, a gentle work routine, and the presence of a physician who may have had considerable interest in the long-term health of his patients.[104]

In contrast, Millie Barber and her fellow slaves on Eliza Weir's plantation seldom saw a doctor, but that lack does not seem to have damaged the healthy and robust condition of the Weir slaves. Barber complained that they "never git butter or sweet milk or coffee," but they seem to have had plenty of the basics. She recalled that as a young child she was fed "peas, hogmeat, corn bread, 'lasses, and buttermilk on Sunday." They also indulged in "greens, turnips, 'taters, shallots, collards, and beans through the week." With these "rations," the young slaves on the Weir place were "kept fat" and perhaps even healthy. As another former slave, D. Cunningham, suggested, "Marse like to see his slaves fat and shiny." [105]

Caleb Craig grew up on Ed Mobley's Blackstock plantation, home to some three hundred slaves. Mobley had a reputation for working his slaves on Sunday. Perhaps because of the large number of people on the plantation, the slaves may not have enjoyed the exclusive use of gardens, nor did Craig recall having earned any money. Their food allowance, however, had included "corn-meal, bacon, 'lasses, bread, milk, collards, turnips, 'taters, peanuts and punkins," which must have provided as wide a choice as most could have expected. The variety of basic foods available to up-country slaves seems to have been much wider than in the state's other two regions, which may have simply reflected a greater emphasis on subsistence farming common to the region. A young child under slavery, Phillip Evans grew up in Winnsboro. He, too, recalled having had a wide variety of foods on the home place. As well as "peas, beans, okra, Irish 'tators, mush, shorts, bread, and milk," the slaves fished in the Melton Branch with hooks and caught "rock rollers, perch and catfish." Because their master, General Bratton, was a "great sheep raiser," no doubt that meat was a regular part of the slaves' diet. William Brice's slaves were "quickly 'tended to by de doctor" when they became ill, and Andy Marion, born in 1844, recalled "gallopin' for old Dr. Douglas many a time." Working as a carriage driver, Marion had no time for fishing or hunting, but perhaps the other slaves were kept less busy and had more control over their time and pace of work. Brice encouraged his married slaves "to have their own gardens." On Mondays he gave the slaves their rations of "meat, hominy and cornmeal," and on Saturdays they were given "wheat bread, lard and 'lasses." [106]

Poorer and less well-situated slaves could also be found in the up-country. According to a former slave, Sena Moore, Jim Gladney was "not a big buckra, he just had a handful of slaves." Their quarters were not the healthiest: "Us had to fight chinches, fleas, and shuters (mosquitoes)." They had no money but "plenty to eat" and made their own clothes from cloth "dat us spin of de cotton dat us picked out of de field." The Gladney slaves "raised their own chickens," which would have supplemented their weekly allowance to some extent.[107] The condition of the quarters and the prevalence of mosquitoes and other bugs suggest that the Gladney slaves would have been particularly susceptible to disease and infection. Given the absence of a well-balanced and ample diet and the slaves' inability to add substantially to it, they probably were frequent visitors to the sick house and generally unable to function at their best.

Gordon Bluford, born in 1845 in Laurens District, recalled having had "a pretty good house to live in slavery time." Although her master, Dr. Felix Calmes, used a lot of his "corn and apples, and peaches [to] make whisky, brandy and wine," the slaves "had plenty to eat." The men on the plantation "hunted some squirrels, rabbits, possum and birds." Fellow Laurens slave George Fleming also had positive recollections of food on the plantation of his master, Sam Fleming. Along with "collards, turnips, and other vegetables wid cornbread," the slaves enjoyed "chinets of meat . . . and lots of butter milk." Most of the field hands would have had their food cooked for them in the fields, although these slaves had "lil gardens of deir own." They were also provided with at least two sets of clothes and "better clothes for Sunday," and Fleming would "give 'em a li'l change sometimes" with which they were able to purchase small luxuries. George recalled that all the household items in their cabin were homemade, "but we sho had good beds . . . shelves and hooks to put our clothes on . . . benches and tables wid smooth boards." For domestic cooking "kitchen (hooks) was on de side of de fire place whar big iron pots hung to bile and cook. We had pans and leads (lids) and things to bake on, too." These slaves apparently enjoyed a wide variety of foods that were probably well prepared, helping to reduce the likelihood of spreading disease.[108]

If slaves in the up-country engaged less fully in the task and garden system and were provided with smaller gardens, if any at all, they would have been more dependent on their masters than their fellows in the low and middle country. Although masters throughout the state continued to enter powerfully into the life of the slave, accounts from the up-country suggest that the quality of life experienced by the slaves was unpredictable and not uniform.

Milton Marshall grew up on Burton Maybin's Goshen Hill plantation of some eighty-eight slaves. Marshall and his fellow slaves "got food and clothes for our work," which usually means they were denied the opportunity to earn cash money. These clothes were made at home, "spun and wove by de women . . . and made by them." Their shoes were made by a local shoemaker and were brogans made with wooden soles that were so hard that sometimes they "had to be soaked in warm water and grease wid tallow or meat skin so de slaves could slip [them] on de feet." According to Marshall, his master and mistress were "all right"; on Sunday they would give each slave a "quart of flour extra for breakfast," a special bonus because Marshall thought some masters in the neighborhood "didn't feed de slaves much."[109]

Victoria Perry and her mother had an extremely hard time under slavery in Newberry District. They were owned by Bert Mabin. Victoria recalled being woken at night by her mother, Rosanna, "crying and praying, her back . . . sore from the beating her master had given her that day." Victoria had always been "scared of her master as she was of a mad dog." Whenever Mabin "got mad at any of the niggers on the place, he would whip them all . . . he was a mean master," Victoria reported. Perhaps not surprising, then, Victoria and other slaves "went hungry many days." Sometimes she "would have to pick up discarded corn on de cob, wipe the dirt off and eat it." The problem was not simply a scarcity of food to eat. As Perry explained, "Sometimes during slavery . . . we had plenty to eat but my master would give us just anything to eat. He didn't care what we got to eat." Such behavior seems abnormal now and was probably out of the ordinary even then. There are numerous examples of masters who behaved as cruelly as Mabin (indeed, some more so) who were indicted and punished for not feeding their slaves or for ill-treating them in other ways. There is no evidence to support any argument that whole neighborhoods or communities actively condoned the ill treatment of slaves by their masters and much evidence to the contrary. Clearly, most masters would have realized that it was counterproductive to underfeed their slaves.[110]

Madison Griffin grew up on Billy Scott's Spartanburg plantation with some forty-eight slaves. Scott was described as "a fair man, not so good not so mean." He gave the slaves "poor quarters to live in" and sometimes "plenty to eat," but sometimes "we went hungry." Scott kept a big garden and cows, hogs, and sheep. The slaves' rations consisted primarily of "corn, collards, peas, turnip-greens and homemade molasses." On

Sundays the Scott slaves had wheat bread "made from flour grind at our mill." They also made their own clothes out of cotton and wool and made "our own shoes out of leather tanned at home." These slaves, as was to be expected in this part of the state, lived on farms and plantations that were self-sufficient. For special treats at cornshuckings they could expect "pumkin custard to eat and liquor" to drink.[111]

Nat Alexander was another master who failed to endear himself to his slaves. Unlike his brother Bob, who owned a nearby plantation, Nat was "mean and cruel." He made his slaves work at night and on Sundays. At the end of the day's work he would come "to their one room log house and lock them up until morning." The well was also locked "so they could have no drinking water." Denied a garden of their own, they had to use the "white folk's garden." The four or five slave families who lived on the Alexander place, nonetheless, "had plenty to eat." Flour was given out once each week, "also a little meat some molasses and corn meal." They never had any sugar and "only got coffee when Lucinda's father would bring it to her mother" from Bob Alexander's plantation, where he lived. Overworking his slaves and liberally using the whip, Nat Alexander was considered a cruel master, but he did feed his slaves, probably as well as he could, as the overwhelming majority of masters seem to have done.[112]

Milk, which often played an important role in the diet of young slaves, was not always available in the slave quarters.[113] Bouregard Corry, a slave in Gaffney, Union District, recalled that the slaves on the plantation of his master, Mike Montgomery, had "plenty of bread and milk." They also raised hogs and "killed all kinds of wild things like turkeys, ducks and birds, and caught fish." He also remembered the men having guns which "dey used every day." Gus Feaster recalled the slave children eating "mush and milk" for breakfast. For lunch, they had "plenty cow peas, meat, bread and water," and at night, "us drink milk and et bread, black bread made from de shorts." On Friday the slaves received their weekly allowance of four pounds of bacon, a peck of meal, a quart of flour, and a quart of molasses. On Saturday "came de shoulder of meat for Sunday morning breakfast, and de flour also." His master, Berry Richards, gave them "hominy for Sunday mornin' breakfast." The Richards slaves were also in the habit of setting mud baskets to catch catfish, sometimes catching up to "75 or 80 fish" at one time, which would likely have been distributed around the quarters and elsewhere. Of course, this was not a reliable food source because the catch was not always good, and they would "sometimes have none." When they did have a good catch, however, they could expect to enjoy the "cat fish stew and cooked ash cake bread" that was made "fer us to eat." The Richards slaves took their "rations to de fields every morning," where the women would "slack work round eleven by de sun fer to build de fire and cook dinner.[114] Food cooked in the field may have increased the number of dietary and hygiene problems faced by slaves.

"Duty, humanity and self-interest," writes James O. Breeden, "demanded that masters fed their slaves well," and, as shown above, most tended to do so.[115] Not all plantation journals offer explicit details of the size or nature of the food allowances given to South Carolina's slaves. There is no record of the allowance given to slaves on John Edwin Fripp's low-country Beaufort District plantation, where they worked the task and garden system. The slaves, however, were allowed time, above and beyond that earned from tasking, to plant corn and other crops. Although their proximity to swamps increased their chances of succumbing to sickness and disease, access to a river provided them with the opportunity to fish and thereby supplement their food allowances. On November 9, 1857, for example, a slave, Abel, "caught several fine whiting." Later the same month, when "two cows had their legs broken by the others in the pen," Fripp "made Abel kill them for the Negroes." On Friday, April 16, 1858, Abel "caught one of the largest Drums [Fripp] ever saw . . . weighing 80 pounds." The following Saturday, Will and Dick, two slaves on the Fripp place, "caught 7 drums."[116] Fripp had to have been informed of these catches or he would not have recorded them; the size and number of fish caught, therefore, were probably exceptional. No doubt numerous other slaves caught fish for their own use. As for the routine (some planters thought it monotonous) of keeping a record of the most regular plantation business such as the issuing of daily, twice weekly, or weekly food allowances, many planters seem to have left this to others or not to have bothered at all.[117] That mistresses, overseers, or drivers often had responsibility for this chore perhaps reflects the routine nature of the Monday, Friday, Saturday, or Sunday issue of slave rations.

William E. Sparkman may have found the process tedious, but he endeavored to record each distribution. His plantation book for the Springwood plantation for 1844 to 1847 provides details of the allowances given to his slaves. In 1844, Sparkman had ninety-eight slaves on his 138 acres of rice land. Each Sunday he entered the items given out to the slaves, most frequently corn and peas, corn and rice, sometimes corn and potatoes, other times corn and meat—meat was not a regular part of the allowance. Between March 31 and December 22, 1844, there were only three references to bacon or meat among the weekly entries for cereals or vegetables distributed. For the Christmas period, however, Sparkman "gave the people" a half bushel of rice, ten pounds of beef, a pint of molasses, and some tobacco. Interestingly, an entry for January 12, 1845, notes that the "fellows received meat, and the women molasses," a combination repeated the following Sunday. On February 16, the slaves received the "whole allowance" of corn, bacon, and rice; the following week the "whole allowance" consisted of "corn and molasses." In March 1845, Sparkman had to purchase 513 bushels of corn at fifty cents per bushel and bacon to supplement his food store. With "30 weeks to 26 October" he calculated he now had "888 bushels [of] provisions and about 10 bushels of peas." It was at such times that planters would have sensibly given themselves a reminder for the future as to the exact amount of provisions required and what had to be purchased to feed their slaves. Such preparation would have facilitated planning and helped keep costs down. Either because he was short of bacon or simply for a change, for three weeks in January Sparkman's hands enjoyed fish as part of their diet (the previous year's supply of meat had probably run out and the current "killings" had yet to take place). Later that year, Sparkman wrote in his journal that he allowed his hands "molasses and water as average during the whole harvest." He even gave them whiskey twice but then decided that in future "no whiskey," only tobacco to those "who chew and smoke and extra rations of rice to those who prefer it to tobacco."[118] If the Sparkman slaves had not been able to supplement their diets and had to subsist only on what they received from their master, they might have considered themselves unfortunate.

When John Berkeley Grimball had cause to be concerned about the state of his provisions, he made detailed calculations. On March 7, 1832, for example, he visited one of his plantations "and measured the corn—10

bushels in corn house, consumption on the plantation including everything but poultry—amounts to 11 [illegible] bushels—There are therefore about 10 weeks allowance." In March 1834, after receiving news from
his overseer that the corn had been "used up," Grimball calculated back-
ward. On February 26 he "gave to women who have young children and
sick people 1 bushel 2 pecks and 3 quarts." On March 3 and 9 the same
quantities were given out. On March 16 he noted, "to the hands 12 bushels
and 3 pecks . . . the children get 2 pecks per day." With allowance for
Grimball's horse and two pecks per week for the poultry, the total weekly
corn requirement was 18.5 bushels. The next month Grimball had to bor-
row half a bushel of salt "for the use of the Negroes."[119] Except for these
occasional references to the availability of adequate provisions for the
slaves and the farm animals, Grimball recorded no other details.

Another low-country planter, David Gavin of Colleton District, kept a
plantation journal from 1853 to 1873. On November 9, 1855, he recorded
his trip to court, where "several persons were indicted for trading with negroes" and a Mrs. Wilson was indicted "for not feeding and clothing her
negroes." In April 1858, he recorded that one McGuire "was indicted for
trading with a slave and selling liquor to a slave." His reaction to other
owners not feeding their slaves might suggest that Gavin's slaves were am-
ply fed, yet there are no references to the nature, quantity, or frequency of
the food rations he gave them. We do know, however, that several of
Gavin's slaves earned extra money that could have been used to supplement their food allowances had it been necessary so to do. For example, on
December 1, 1860, Big Jim was paid a dollar for three horse collars. In
May the following year, Mike earned thirty-five cents in cash and sixty
cents worth of syrup for "ditching." The young boy Tom earned five cents
in May for catching a rabbit and twenty-five cents in November for a basket he had made. These were the sums former slaves often recalled as "a
few coppers," but considering that for twenty-five cents a week's supply of
meat could be bought from a store, they were not trifling; rather, they
could have determined the quality and quantity of food at one's disposal.
Furthermore, the opportunity for slaves, even young children like Tom, to
have some control over this important area of their lives, to provide extras
through their own efforts, must have had a positive effect on their self-
respect and self-esteem. In addition, the Gavin slaves were allowed to

plant their own crop, and Mike, Little Jim, Big Jim, Abb, Jane, Henry, and Moses all earned money from selling their corn and fodder to Gavin for which they were paid in goods and cash.[120]

Michael Gramling, a middle-country Orangeburg District planter, kept a plantation journal from March 1846 to May 1849, which was quite detailed and full of information on the organization of a small to medium-sized plantation but contained only one direct reference to the slaves' food allowance. An entry for November 5, 1847, reads: "14 bushels given to the negroes, half allowance till 15 November. The other half corn and just about 15 or 20 bushels in the potato house for the children." It would seem, then, that planters tended not to make weekly records of these transactions except when they feared that provisions were running low and had to be replenished. The slaves, who worked the task and garden system, were able to earn fairly large sums of money for the crops they sold to Gramling. The variety of the crops they produced for their own use may have ranged as widely as those they produced for Gramling, which included watermelons, peas, potatoes, indigo, cotton, corn, rice, turnips, and wheat. If the slaves were not allowed to plant some of these crops, they would still have had access to them, if not by purchasing them with the money they earned on their own crops then by extralegal means.[121] The absence of detailed accounts of rations issued to slaves does not indicate the absence of such practices on South Carolina's farms and plantations.

The slaves on Harriott Pinckney's Charleston District plantation received their allowance of food plus extras such as molasses. The hands would "usually have a quart given out to each at Christmas," and the rest would have been "kept for sickness" and to give to the "old people a little when they ask." In May 1855, her new overseer, William Winningham, asked what to do with three barrels of molasses and three boxes of soap Pinckney had sent to the island. The overseer wondered whether she wished him to "sell [them] to the negroes or give out as you did not say anything to me about it." Winningham knew only that William, the slave driver, had told him that Pinckney had said that she "was going to send up some molasses to sell to the people." Having only recently taken over as overseer, Winningham needed to know at "what price I must sell" the molasses. The Pinckney slaves clearly had the means and time to earn extra money, as was common in the low country. Pinckney's willingness to give to those slaves less able to fend for themselves was offset by making those who could pay for these extras supplement the less well off.[122]

Another such slaveholder, and another female, was Keziah Goodwyn Hopkins Brevard of Richland District. Brevard had experienced great difficulty managing some of her slaves. A Christian woman, she wrote that she wished "to be kind to my Negroes." Her slaves were allowed to work their gardens, and she would purchase their produce. Although most of her slaves mentioned in her journal had done very well for themselves, there were some whose efforts had been less rewarding. A Brevard slave by the name of John would have fallen into this category. In the middle of December 1860, Brevard paid John $4.20 for his corn and fodder. "John," she wrote, "made so little I forgive him the debt he owed me." Slaves, like farmers the world over, were always at the mercy of unforeseen occurrences. Early in the new year, Brevard forgave Frank his debts, refusing to accept his offer of payment for some flour because "the cows (not my cows) destroyed his crops." Under Brevard's guardianship, her slaves were able to manage their losses, without having to suffer dire consequences, and supplemented their diets. Her kindness was not restricted to those slaves in her immediate environment. In December 1860, she "gave lard to Old Sary, Young Jenny, Old Fanny, Dolly, Lucy B., Hagar, Jim's daughter Dinah" [but] "sold to Israel lard" for fifty cents and "to Nell, Parker, Lard—50 cents." Brevard did attempt to look after her poor and her sick; her problem was with her more wealthy and powerful slaves and their families.[123] Even James Henry Hammond of Edgefield displayed no qualms in helping those less able to help themselves: "Some negroes," he wrote, "have unnatural appetites and do not keep in health without more allowance than others. Whenever such is ascertained to be the case and is not a symptom of sickness," he instructed that "a larger allowance must be made." [124]

J. D. Ashmore, a much smaller planter than Hammond, had operated plantations in Sumter and in up-country Anderson District. Ashmore did not keep details of the allowances given to his slaves. He did, however, keep a record of the meat killed and prepared on the plantation but said nothing about how the meat was divided and issued.[125] Once planters had issued basic instructions to plantation mistresses, overseers, and drivers as to how much, when, and how food allowances were to be made up and distributed, and as long as ample provisions remained in store, few would have occupied themselves with what was a routine, if not tedious, operation. Of course, if masters, particularly those on larger plantations, were ignorant of the allowances their slaves were actually receiving, there was the possibility of abuse on the part of unscrupulous overseers and drivers. One imagines, however, that slaves would have found some way of bringing the matter to their master's attention. That there are so few detailed references to slaves being issued weekly rations does not suggest that they were deprived but rather probably reflects plantation hierarchy, as well as planters' priorities when keeping their journals.[126]

The ability of slaves to expand and improve their diets, thereby helping to safeguard their health, depended to a large extent on the very qualities and abilities needed to increase their economic independence. The slaves who were able to work under some type of task and garden system and who were encouraged to sell their surpluses and cash crops and those who lived and worked within a family structure that could offer support and assistance whenever it was needed were much more likely to have a more comfortable lifestyle. Slaveholders may have tried to give most to the able-bodied and least to the sick, the young, and the old, thus encouraging the survival of the fittest. Slave families in turn may have followed similar practices with the largest and strongest families becoming the most powerful and eventually distancing themselves from the weaker families. Stronger families, under the guidance of their senior members, would have operated a strict policy of selecting suitable marriage partners for family members. Disabled, sickly, or otherwise underproductive members of the slave community—those completely reliant on the master and thus most vulnerable to sickness and sale—may have become the slave quarters' charity cases and dependent on the stronger and more powerful families. Young men wishing to marry a young woman from the richer and more powerful families would have experienced considerable pressure to display their ability to provide for themselves before they could anticipate any success in winning their heart's desire.

4

To Love and to Cherish: The Slave Family

The family was the primary institution in the slave quarters, and the efforts slaves made to establish and maintain the integrity of the family provides the broadest expression of their worldview.[1] Although supportive family units helped to protect slaves from the harshest aspects of a cruel, arbitrary, and frequently inhumane system, slaves knew that the formation and maintenance of a family, much less a productive unit, was not an easy and painless process. On the contrary, the vast majority of the slaves had to overcome a multitude of obstacles in the path of forming a stable family. In 1820, the state of South Carolina was home to some 260,000 slaves; in 1850, there were approximately 385,000 slaves and 25,600 slave owners. Even if he was lucky enough to live on one of the hundred or so South Carolina plantations that had 200 or more slaves in 1850, there was no guarantee that a single male would find an eligible female on the home plantation.[2]

Most eligible males seeking to marry and begin a family had to look for someone off the plantation.[3] The numerous problems many would have encountered were expressed succinctly by Andy Marion, a Fairfield District slave. Born in 1844, Marion lived on an up-country plantation containing some seventy-two slaves under the supervision of Will Brice, a master described as "cruel" and who was in the habit of selling "off slaves" when they "git too many." Marion explained that slaves "had a hell of a time gittin' a wife." If an "eligible" female was not to be found on the home place "to suit you and the chances was you didn't suit them, why, what could you do?" Marion continued: "You couldn't spring up and grab a mule and ride to de next plantation without a written pass." These slaves had their work cut out for them. "S'pose you gits your master's consent to go? De gal's master got to consent, de gal got to consent, de gal's daddy got to consent, de gal's mammy got to consent."[4] Andy Marion's statement suggests that, had there been a suitable partner available on the home place he would have had no qualms about marrying someone there, that is, if he could get the consent of all concerned—the girl, her master, and her parents.

Confirmation of the role of the master in this important area of slave life was provided by Beaufort District resident and former slave Sam Mitchell. His master, John Chaplin, had to be informed as soon as slaves "begin to cote." And if Chaplin refused to give his blessing, "den dat settle it you can't marry." Chaplin, typical of many masters, preferred his slaves not to "marry slave on nodder person plantation." Writing in 1833, one planter summed up what was probably the view of most masters: "In allowing the men to marry out of the plantation, you give them an uncontrollable right to be frequently absent." For, "Wherever their wives live, there they consider their home; consequently they are indifferent to the interest of the plantation to which they actually belong." Perhaps of greatest concern to this planter was that an "abroad" marriage "creates [in slaves] a feeling of independence from being, of right, out of the control of their master for a time." However much masters desired their male slaves to marry on the home place, they were not always able to prevent them from doing otherwise. Living in a community with some twenty or thirty others, eligible men and women among the Chaplin slaves would have been hard-pressed to find suitable partners on the home place. Their only alternative would have been to look "abroad" for a spouse. In such instances, Chaplin, however reluctantly, not only gave his consent and allowed the slave to marry, but the ceremony was held in Chaplin's house and conducted by a white preacher.[5]

According to former slave Sam Polite, the norm in the low-country area containing some of the largest plantations in the state was to marry "off the plantation"—that is, to have "broad" wives and husbands. Polite stated that "slabe don't marry—dey jest lib togedder." He then added that although the slaves had to remain on the plantation during the workday, "w'en wuk done," the slave "kin visit wife on odder plantation."[6]

The larger the plantation on which slaves lived, the more likely was it that a significant proportion of the slave population would find partners on the home place. In 1855 there were 247 slaves on J. P. Alston's True Blue plantation in low-country Georgetown District. Alston probably did not actively forbid his slaves to marry off, but he did provide conditions conducive to the establishment and maintenance of stable, two-parent families on the home place: adequate allowances of food and clothing, an opportunity to operate under a work and garden system, and an outlet for their produce.[7] Of the forty-seven family groupings recorded by Alston, thirty-four were headed by two parents. The conditions that would have operated to keep the Alston slaves in stable families on the home place also made True Blue attractive to slaves on plantations where all or most of these features were absent.

The experience of slaves could differ considerably based on material conditions—if the material conditions on the home place were satisfactory, the chances of slaves "choosing" to marry off were reduced. Lucinda Miller's story is a case in point. Born in 1855, Lucinda had been owned by Nat Alexander and lived by the Tyger River. Her father was owned by Bob Alexander, Nat's brother, who lived "2 or 3 plantations away." The Alexander brothers were such different personalities that their slaves had completely different views of slavery. While Bob was described as a "good master," Nat is remembered for having been "mean and cruel" and for making his slaves work on Sundays, regularly using the whip, and locking his slaves in their cabins at night. In contrast, Lucinda's father's experience on Bob Alexander's place was one of ample food, infrequent whippings, and a generally benign atmosphere. The few extras Lucinda's mother and her siblings were able to enjoy were brought to them by her father. In this instance "marrying off" helped Lucinda's mother and her children. One imagines that many of her fellow slaves would have endeavored to marry off to find a master less "mean and cruel" than Nat Alexander.[8]

Discrepancies in the nature and condition of life under slavery were likely to create disruption, dissatisfaction, and pain. Several students of slavery have suggested that married slaves preferred to live separately on different plantations, that slave men were "practically unanimous in their desire to marry women from another plantation." *The American Slave* narratives for South Carolina and the other sources consulted do not support this contention. Although a slave's personal situation could be improved by marrying a man or woman who belonged to someone better situated than his or her own master, the inverse would also be true. If slaves had to travel great distances or cross dangerous creeks and risk the malevolence of wandering patrols to see their families, how many would have made such a choice given reasonable alternatives? A popular argument is that slave husbands "did not want to marry a woman from their own [plantation] and be forced to watch as she was beaten, insulted, raped, overworked, or starved without being able to protect her." This is a compelling argument, but it must be set alongside the numerous disadvantages of "broad" wives. If slave husbands were on the home place, masters may have had less compulsion to whip married slave women, who would have felt much safer having their husbands on the place, if not directly to protect them from their masters, to discourage them, or to encourage masters, sons, and overseers to pester single rather than married women. As Deborah Gray White suggests in her study of female slaves, some slave women must have found themselves "at eighteen or nineteen loving no particular male but having to find a husband in order to satisfy the whites and secure herself against abuse." In her study of piedmont Georgia, Carole Merritt observed that "women living apart from their husbands . . . were particularly vulnerable to the sexual advances of black and white men." Cruel masters, however, would probably have whipped women and children whether or not husbands were on the place. Male eligibles wishing to marry a woman from True Blue would have found access to membership in one of the Alston slave families restricted because more than 70 percent of the True Blue women of childbearing age had already found husbands on the home place.[9]

Of course, the vast majority of South Carolina's slaves lived in substantially smaller slave quarters than the True Blue slaves.[10] A smaller but still atypically large slave quarters was that of J. O. Willson's Goose Creek, Charleston District. In 1848, some 139 slaves lived on the Willson plantation. A look at the eligibles in each family at a given period will help us better understand the options available to them. Thus by using demographics we can obtain some measure of the extent to which they were able to choose their partners.[11]

Willson listed his slave families by numbers and added the number of singles or "scatterings" at the bottom of the list for each year. In 1844, the

Willson Plantation Book recorded a population of 122 slaves. By 1848, it had grown to 139, a net increase on average of between 4 and 5 per year. Willson Family Number 1 had seven male eligibles in 1848, from Isaac, the eldest at forty, to Peter, his eighteen-year-old cousin. Six female eligibles ranged from thirty-seven-year-old Bess to Mary, her seventeen-year-old niece (figure 1). Of the men, Isaac had "a wife at J.T.C." [Coles]; Yanty was married to a Rachel, who was probably the Rachel purchased in 1845. York married Becca of Family Number 9 sometime before 1850, and by 1861 they had produced four children. Peggy's son William, twenty-three years old in 1848, found himself a wife at the Coles plantation. His younger brother Nero, who was "crippled," had married a woman who lived in Charleston, and Peter, another brother, died probably when he was quite young. Caesar married Lucy from Family Number 2 sometime before 1847, and by 1862, they had produced seven children. Thus of the seven male eligibles in this family four found wives off the plantation, Yanty married Rachel, who had been purchased in, and York and Caesar married women raised on the home place.

Of the women from Family Number 1, Bess was probably a widow because there is no reference to her husband and no indication that she had any children after May 1832. Her sister Caty, the house cook and mother of three, had produced no more children after her twenty-fifth birthday. She is not listed as having a husband on the place. Edy was married to Stepney although no children were listed. Nelly, her younger sister, was married to thirty-year-old Andrew. Louisa, Bess's daughter, who was eighteen years old in 1850 when her first child was born, had married Phillis's third son, William from Family Number 6, who was seventeen years old when he became a father. Of the females of Family Number 1, then, allowing for the possibility that both Bess and Caty may have had "broad" husbands, three of the six women married men from the home place.

Family Number 2 had only a few members poised to begin their own families (figure 2). The head of the family, Lucy, had two sons, Isaac, aged thirty-one, and Andrew, aged thirty. Her daughter Nancey, aged thirty-nine, and granddaughter Lucy, aged twenty, qualify as eligibles. Although they produced eight children between June 1828 and September 1850, Nancey's husband and the father of her children, lived on another plantation. Her eldest daughter, Lucy, married Peggy's third son, Caesar, and thus linked Families 1 and 2, and by 1862, Caesar and Lucy had produced seven children. Of the two female eligibles from this family, one married off and the other married on the place. Among the male eligibles, Isaac, one of the plantation's six "plows" in 1844, was not listed with a wife on the place, but his brother, Andrew, was married to Nelly from Family Number 1. And Timmy was married to Chloe from Family Number 6.

In 1848, Family Number 3 (figure 3), Hector and Charlotte's family, had two male eligibles, George, aged twenty-three, and his younger brother Anthony, aged eighteen. Their daughter Sumitra, aged twenty-four, was the only female old enough to have seriously considered starting a family. Sometime before Christmas 1853, Willson purchased, from a Dr. Hill, Sarah and her two daughters, Charlotte and Mary. Sarah must have soon married George for in October 1854 she had the first of five children with him. It is possible that George and Sarah were already married and were reunited on the Willson place; that Sarah's firstborn shares the name of George's mother increases this possibility.[12] In 1863, Anthony was listed among the single men, along with his younger brother Robert, and thus, if he was married, it was not to someone on the home place. Sumitra married David, who was ten years her senior; he was also "deaf." Neither of these factors seems to have affected their relationship because between December 1845 and December 1860 they produced six children.

Family Number 6 had four male and seven female eligibles, eight of whom were Simon and Tirah's children (figure 4). Their daughters Phillis, Mary, Chloe, and Pheobe were mature women with children. The younger women, Benah, aged twenty-six, Kerziah, aged twenty-four, and Susan, aged nineteen, also produced children. By 1862, Benah had given birth to nine children, and Kerziah and Susan each had three children before they both succumbed to typhoid and died in 1856. There is no indication that these seven female eligibles, all of whom had children before 1850, had husbands on the home place. The absence of husbands at home probably contributed to this family's poor economic state. Although there were thirty-four members in this family, they failed to figure prominently in Willson slave accounts.

Of the men of Family Number 6, Simon and Cicero, Simon and Tirah's sons, and Robert and Peter, their eldest grandsons, Simon had a wife "at Mr. Murray's," and his brother Cicero was sold away in 1854 at age thirty. Robert had a "wife at J.H.," and Peter's situation is unclear. Compared with the above families, Simon and Tirah's situation was something of an exception. Larger even than Family Number 1 with twenty-four members in 1848, Family Number 6 boasted a total of thirty-four. The latter family had eleven eligibles to Family Number 1's thirteen and so compared unfavorably in their attempts to find spouses on the home place if, indeed, this had been their intention. Had these slaves determined to marry off, they were successful. With all their women and at least two of the four men marrying off the place, the rates differ considerably from those of Willson's other large family.

A look at Family Number 7 provides an opportunity to put the extremes of Willson's two largest families into perspective. The third largest family with nineteen members, Family Number 7 had four eligible males and five eligible females in 1848 (figure 11). Among the women were Mary's daughters Aphe, Elcey, Margarette, and Tirah and her granddaughter Sarah. Aphe had four children before she died of "serophilia" around 1843. There is no information about her husband. Elcey and Tirah are both listed with children. Elcey had ten between 1829 and 1857, and Tirah had two during the first half of the 1850s. Everything suggests that both had husbands off the place. Of Margarette, there is no clear information, but she might have been given away to a female member of the Willson family. Sarah, Mary's granddaughter, had married by 1853 and before the end of slavery had given birth to at least five children. She too seems to have married off the home place. As with Family Number 6, none of the women appear to have married Willson men. Their male counterparts, Sam, aged thirty-one, Tom, aged twenty-nine, Jerry, aged twenty-five, and Nero, aged nineteen, had similar experiences. If Sam and young Nero found wives on the place, it was not recorded, and Sam's brothers, Tom and Jerry, were sold. Both had been listed as "not sound." That Willson's third family in size had an experience closer to that of Family Number 6 than that of Family Number 1 suggests that members of the older and more economically productive families were more inclined to marry on rather than off the home place. Among these largest families on the Willson place, six of twenty-three female eligibles and five of the twenty male eligibles married on the plantation.

A jump ahead ten years offers some insight into the choices available to the next generation of eligibles in the Willson quarters. By 1858, the new eligibles in Family Number 1 included Peggy's Sarah, aged twenty-one; Bess's Louisa, aged twenty-six; Caty's Caroline, aged twenty-one, and Emma, aged nineteen; and Nelly's daughters, Ann aged twenty, Lavina aged eighteen, and Nance, aged sixteen. The lone male eligible was Peggy's nineteen-year-old son John. Thus, within the space of ten years, the number of eligibles in Family Number 1 had changed from eight males and five females in 1848 to one male and seven females in 1858. How did this generation of Willson slaves fare? In 1857, Sarah, only twenty-one years old, died from typhoid fever. She left a four-year-old daughter called Daphne who was taken into her grandmother's house. Sometime before 1850, Louisa married William, grandson of Simon and Tirah. This relationship may have been unplanned as Louisa was only in her seventeenth year when her first child was born, and the father, William, was almost a year younger. Among the factors that brought these two young people—from families with very different levels of economic productivity—together might well have been the link such a marriage would have created between Families 1 and 6.

Caty's two younger daughters, Caroline and Emma, seem to have followed both their mother and their older sister and married men off the home place. By 1858, Mary, almost seven years Caroline's senior, had five children, while the younger sisters had produced three and one, respectively. Being the plantation cook, Caty perhaps was in a position to choose a partner from a wider selection of eligibles than the Willson quarters offered.

Nelly's daughters, Ann, Nance, and Lavinia, were not house servants and may not have felt the pressures or entertained ambitions similar to those of Caty and her daughters. Sometime before 1856, Ann married Richard, Tirah's son, and had produced three children by 1862. Nancey (Nance) also married on the place. Her husband, Jim, was Mary's grandson. Aged twenty-four in 1858, Jim had five brothers aged thirteen or older, the eldest of whom, Nero, was one of the plantation "plows." Although he had two uncles who were described as "unsound," Jim would not have considered himself particularly fortunate to have succeeded in marrying into a family as economically powerful as Family Number 1. By 1862, Jim and Nancey had produced two children. There is, nonetheless, some indication that the quality of the eligible males on the home place in the mid- to late 1850s had declined and that women such as Caty and her daughters, from the better situated families and enjoying greater choice as to their marriage partners, were obliged to look farther afield.

Lavinia, eighteen years old in 1858, may have been one of those slave women constrained by a qualitative decline in the number of male eligibles. She married Aphe's son Brister from Family Number 7—one of the plantation's least economically powerful families. Of the seven female eligibles in 1858, then, two married off, Sarah died, and the remaining four married men who had been born on the Willson place. Nineteen-year-old John married Benah's second child, Pheobe. Of the eligibles in this third phase, five of eight married on compared with six of thirteen in 1848, that is 62 percent compared with 46 percent.

The Willson slave quarters appears to have gone through a three-stage process in which the first was characterized by slaves either brought onto the plantation in family groups or single people brought in for the purpose of establishing slave families.[13] During this first period the number of eligibles would have constituted a high proportion of the slave population. A rapid decline in the number of available partners then followed as couples settled into families and commenced producing and rearing the third and sizable group of eligibles. Of course, consanguinity would have reduced the number of these eligibles who could actually have married on the home place. Thus, of the three stages, the first would have encouraged slaves to marry on; the second would have severely reduced the chances of eligibles marrying on; and the third would have made marrying on either likely or very unlikely, largely dependent upon the number of unrelated families that had taken part in the earlier stages of settlement. The more of these families involved in the first stage the fewer would have been related by blood and the greater would have been the opportunities for intermarriage among the home place slave population during the third stage.[14]

When both parents were present on the home place, the chance of young eligibles "choosing" to marry off was low. When parents lived on different plantations, young eligibles (particularly females) probably felt that they could choose a spouse on either place because both places would have been viewed as home. Thus females who wanted to marry men off the plantation could select from eligibles living on their father's plantation. This practice, effectively increasing the number of "broad" wives, would have drawn the extended, multiplantation family into an ever-expanding web of familial relationships within a widening slave community consisting of several slave quarters. Furthermore, the presence of large families such as Willson Family Number 1 and Family Number 6, who between them probably linked all the other families on the plantation, would have increased the difficulty of finding eligibles not ruled out by blood ties. This would have forced an already increasing number of eligibles to look off the home place for suitable spouses. Additionally, the more slaves "married off," the more they expanded familial networks beyond the home place so that ties of blood, affinity, and fictive kinship produced an interconnectedness that continually reduced the slaves' ability as well as their need to marry on the home place. Seen in this light, the issue of slaves choosing to marry on or off the home place becomes more complex.

Although the Willson slave quarters was among the largest in the state, at no stage in the three cycles could the majority of eligibles have married on the home place. To a large extent, however, the choice the slaves had as to where, when, and who they married was linked to economic power: the more prosperity slaves enjoyed, the more choices they could make, and the more they were located in strong families the more authority heads of families would have held.[15] Slaves such as Caty, the cook, who were better situated, may well have desired greater choice in finding mates for her family. A similar situation probably existed for Mary's son John, the wheelwright, whose job would have both extended his geographical horizons and reduced his dependency on agriculture to provide his family with much needed extras. Thus, although men such as the four from Family Number 1 might have preferred to marry women on the home place (the important role women and children played in working family land alone made it desirable to have one's family at hand), men such as John and women such as Caty and her daughters may have demanded (and been permitted) a wider selection of eligibles and a higher level of choice. Furthermore, marrying on or off the home place would not have affected these women economically because they were already full members of the most powerful family on the plantation. Who they married may have been far more significant for status than for economic considerations. Blessed with a sound economic base and a strong family, some slaves would have been far more concerned with strengthening other important (noneconomic) areas of their lives.[16]

A selection from a list of slaves on the Guignard Richland District plantation compiled around 1857 presents an opportunity to examine the situation of some middle-country slaves and to assess the frequency with which eligibles there could have found partners to marry and start families on the home place. The slave population is of a size similar to that on the Willson place and therefore permits a direct comparison. Of a total of 125 slaves, twenty-seven "groupings" were identified of which twenty-two provided a clear indication of family households, that is, the several variations on the nuclear family structure.[17] Of the twenty-two groups, eight included both parents, and in all but one instance there were children. Assuming that those women with children who were not listed as having husbands on the place had married men off the plantation rather than losing their husbands through sale or death, this would have meant that, similar to the figures for the Willson quarters, only about a third had married on the home place.[18]

The slave lists of T. C. Law in Darlington District provide some additional information about middle-country slaves. Using 1859 as a reference point, we can investigate the process of spouse selection used by the seventy or eighty slaves in the Law quarters. Law's first and oldest family was that headed by Bess and Yenty (figure 5). Born in 1764, Yenty was probably imported from Africa. He must have married Bess sometime around 1810, when she was twenty years old. Between 1810 and 1834, when Yenty died, Bess gave birth to thirteen children. Of those surviving into adulthood and becoming eligible for marriage around 1850, there were six sons aged eighteen to thirty-six and four daughters aged twenty-three to thirty-eight. Venus, the eldest, died, as did Wesley, the second son. Emily, born in 1821, was sold away when she was twenty years old, along with her daughter born in 1837. The child was named Bess after her grandmother. The next surviving daughter, Dorcas, married off the plantation and had her first child, Sarah, when she was seventeen years old. Hannah, the next daughter, born in 1827, married Henry, born in 1823, and had ten children before the end of slavery. Of the surviving men, Howard, the eldest, was also the plantation driver, and he may have married off the place. The next son, Peter, born in 1816, probably married off. One of his purchases with the money earned for the 385 pounds of seed cotton he sold in 1859 was thirty-two yards of cotton, which suggests he was purchasing the cloth for a sizable family. Cyrus, his younger brother, remained closer to home. Born in 1819, he married Louisa from Lucy's family. Their first child was born in 1849 when Louisa was twenty-three years of age. The two younger men, Derry, aged thirty, and John, aged twenty-eight, had probably married off. Each of them produced and sold over 300 pounds of cotton to Law in 1859. Their purchases, however, suggest that they might not have had wives to support, on the place or elsewhere. Derry purchased a cloak for $1.75, two pairs of stockings, and two spools of thread, whereas John purchased nine yards of "bed ticking" at 10 cents, and took $5.57 in cash. These purchases are ones that might have been made by single men or men with few, if any, dependents.

Of the ten eligibles among this family, two died, one male and one female; Emily and her daughter were sold away; Dorcas married off; and Hannah married on. Howard may have had a relationship with Ritta, but he was not married to her.[19] Born in 1813, he was old enough to have been a widower, or he may have had a wife living off the place. Peter married off, and Cyrus married on. It may be assumed that the two younger men married off, although one or both of them might have been single. These ten eligibles from the largest family on the Law plantation had a greater chance of dying or being sold away than of marrying someone on the home place. Only two of the ten found spouses on the home place.

The records for the families headed by Ellec and Little Sophy and Ritta and Henry permit us to examine the second generation of eligibles in the Law slave quarters. Ellec and Little Sophy (figure 12) were born in 1820 and 1825, respectively, and the oldest of their eligibles was Randolph, who was seventeen years old in 1860, and Celia, who was almost sixteen years old. Celia married someone off the place and had her first child in 1863. Randolph was certainly still single in 1859; in his one appearance in the slave accounts, probably still working with his parents on their land, he earned some extra money by watching the "sheep and mules" for half a day. The money was spent on a "shirt bosom."

Ritta and Henry's family included Sidney, born in 1840, and Laura, born in 1848, both of whom became eligibles before the end of slavery (figure 13). Sometime before 1862, Sidney married Sarah from Bess's family, and Laura married a Riah or Ran sometime before 1864. Both of these second or third stage eligibles, one male and one female, found and married partners on the home place.

The male eligibles in the Law slave community had a one in five chance of marrying on; for the females the chance was one in four. Overall, from a total sample of twenty-four eligibles, 21 percent married on, 50 percent married off, 8.5 percent died, 8.5 percent were sold away, and the fate of 12 percent is unknown. These figures compare with those taken from the low-country Willson place, where fewer than 50 percent of the slaves married on the home place. Clearly, marrying on the home place was never simply a matter of choice. Slave men with large and productive gardens—suggesting membership in an economically strong family—who wished to benefit from the assistance of their wives and children on the home place would have been better able to compete for the few home-based female eligibles than less well-situated males on or off the plantation. Furthermore, considering that this was the reality for slaves living in quarters whose population was 80 in the Law community in 1865 and 139 in the Willson community, it is clear that neither of these sizable slave

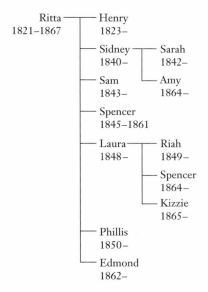

Fig. 13. Law Family—Ritta and Henry's Family

populations came close to accommodating as large a proportion of their eligibles as did the Alston True Blue plantation with its slave population of 247. The majority of South Carolina's slaves living on plantations with slave quarters significantly smaller than that of True Blue had great difficulty finding suitable partners on the home plantation.[20]

Even when a young man was lucky enough to find someone to whom he could direct his attentions, winning her affection, much less her hand, was not easy. Not only would it have been particularly difficult to find eligibles on the farms and smaller plantations of the up-country, but the fortunate young man would still have had numerous obstacles to overcome before he made his sweetheart his wife.[21] Not the least was gaining the lady's attention. Male eligibles often needed some physical prowess just to get over this first obstacle. Frank Adamson's father, who was bought by Nicolas Peay of Winnsboro, was said to have been "got . . . off de ship from Africa." His son remembered him fondly: "He sho' was a man," Adamson recalled, "he run all de other niggers 'way from my mammy and took up wid her."[22]

Courting, of course, was a game designed for two players. Louisa Davis, born in 1831, had fond memories of her courtship with her husband, Sam Davis. She recalled, "One springtime de flowers git be blowing, de hens to cackling and de guineas to patarocking . . . Sam came along when I was out in de yard wid de baby. He just talk to de baby, and I asked him if de baby wasn't pretty. He say, 'yes, but not as pretty as you is, Louisa.' I looks at Sam, and dat kind of foolishness wind up in a weddin'." Living on another plantation, Sam had to venture abroad to find Louisa and win her consent. They were married on a Sunday by a Reverend Boggs. Unfortunately, Sam "didn't get to see [Louisa] as often as he wanted to."[23]

George Fleming of Laurens District described one of the many courting games played by young slave men and women. One game, he remembered, was called "please and displease. . . . When de gal say, 'What it take to please you', de boy say, 'A kiss from dat purty gal over dar.'" On Fleming's plantation, the master seemed not to have objected to the slaves having frequent "frolics." These parties and general social gatherings were held by the "older boys and gals . . . 'specially in de fall of de year." Sometimes the frolics were on a neighboring plantation. The youngsters "sho had some awful times dancing and cutting jigs." They even drank a little liquor but only "on de side," Fleming explained. If and when the court-ships—some of which must have commenced and blossomed at these gatherings—proved successful and culminated in marriage, the couple would have married "in Marse Sam's back yard," and he "sho' fixed up fine for 'em." The slaves also played their part. The custom was for the couple to dress up in "high fashion." The man would wear a "good stripped suit, and de woman have silk and satin clothes." The couple was married by a white preacher "same as de white folks," and a dinner was "fixed in dier honor." As Fleming cautioned, not all slaves could expect this attention as Master Sam's slaves were "treated better dan any I ever know'd of."[24]

An incident recalled by Newberry District former slave Caroline Far-row reveals the importance slaves in general, and perhaps those courting in particular, placed on clothes and their personal appearances. "Once a nigger boy stole out to see his gal," she related, "all dressed up to kill. De patrollers found him at his gal's house and started to take off his coat so they could whip him, but he said, 'please don't let my gal see under my coat, 'cause I got on a bosom and no shirt.'"[25] Elijah Green of Charleston District exposed what may have been an understandable increase in the level of materialism informing the slaves' courting practices and mate se-lection.[26] A concern for material possessions was manifest in the impor-tance slaves placed on clothes and the way they dressed. Born on Christ-mas Day 1842, Green was a slave of George Jones. The youngest of seven boys and the only one of his family to work in the house, Green wore his master's cast-off clothes, which he was glad to have. The slave's footwear was of particular importance because it was often a quick and accurate way of assessing status. The shoes Green received from his master were of a very special type, and "w'en a slave had one of 'em you could't tell 'em he wasn't dress to death." Therefore, the better dressed the slave, the better would be his chances of winning the object of his desire. In Gus Feaster's world, clothes (and money) were of considerable importance. The girls' Sunday best was dyed red, and the boys "made de gals' hoops out'n grape vines." The girls would give the boys a dime, "if dey had one, for a set of hoops."[27]

These rituals of courtship were closely followed by young women seek-ing to win the affection of their beaux by charming them "wid honeysuckle and rose petals hid in dere bosoms" and drying chinaberries and painting them and wearing them on a string around their necks "to charm us." These young women were also adept at what they considered to be the highest forms of etiquette in public. They would not, for example, "eat much in public, kaise it ain' stylish fer young courting gals to let on like dey has any appetite to speak of." In this important area of their lives the young ladies, according to Feaster, followed the practice of the public world and "tried to do jes' like de young white missis do."[28]

Middle-country Clarendon District resident Gabe Lockier described another slave courting ritual. At cornshuckings, which for Lockier "won't no work times" but times that courting couples could use to their advantage, the first one to "shuck red corn had to tell who his best girl was." This ritual, followed by a public statement about and identification of one's "best girl," was surely only an early step toward a more permanent statement of commitment before a wider but no less public audience.[29]

Union District former slave Gus Feaster, who was born in 1840, left a vivid picture of young slaves and their courting rituals. "When boys and gals gits up some size," Feaster recalled, "dey feels dey selves." At this time they went "bird thrashing in de moonlight . . . and sing dis vulgar song. 'I'll give you half-dollar if you come out tonight.'" In Feaster's world of young love and courtship, money played a significant part.[30] Slaves without access to cash may have found themselves severely handicapped when it came to competing for, much less winning, a young lady's hand.

Physical strength, wit, dancing ability, an ample wardrobe, and some cash money, although important, were no guarantee of success in the courting game. Spartanburg's Govan Littlejohn had more serious matters to relate. Govan recalled that one day "when I was a young 'buck', I was setting up to a gal and there was another fellow setting up to her. I held a little bit the upper hand with the gal . . . when my left foot began to swell up and pain me." Littlejohn was confined to bed, where he remained for three months, at which time a "herb doctor came to see me and said he could cure my foot." When Littlejohn's mother found a "conjuration" in the front yard "all tied up in a bag," it became clear that the young suitor had been "conjured" by his competitor.[31]

Considering the competitive nature of their courting rituals, it is not surprising that, despite the absence of legal sanctions, slave marriages were no insignificant occurrences. The wedding ceremony might not have required any special "dressing up," but once it became known that a wedding was to take place, Gus Feaster informs us, you could expect "'bout 40 or 50 folks dar to see it." Presiding would be Tony, an elderly slave and preacher, who would "marry you for nothing"—money, then, was not needed for everything.[32]

One might assume that when both partners had made strenuous efforts to find each other, to win the other's trust and affection, and then to have their marriage performed in front of "40 or 50 folks"—relations, friends, and members of the community—the joining together in marriage was not a step taken lightly. For the slave community, these weddings, whether or not they were blessed by the church or protected by law, must have had great significance and moral force, thus warranting all the sanction that they as a group could bestow upon the union of two of their own. For the slave quarter community these would have been marriages in the fullest sense.

In the areas of the state where plantations were larger and eligibles on the home place more numerous, the slaves' response to marriage—reflected in their attitude toward courtship and the effort put into courtship rituals—did not differ considerably. The supporters of slavery (as well as some of its attackers) argued that the slaves, given their function and status in the public world, adapted themselves and their "feelings more or less to the circumstances of their class." Masters could sell slaves away from their families, separating mother and child, without the moral opprobrium, guilt, and shame that could be expected to accompany such "un-Christian acts." Part of the masters' rationalization was that the "joys and sorrows of the slave . . . are entirely dissimilar from what would make the happiness, or misery, of another class." The slaves, then, could not be expected either to set much store by romantic love or to become emotionally attached to their children.[33]

Jane Johnson's recollections add weight to this claim. "Dat courtin' stuff," she pooh-poohed, "is what white folks does." The slaves Johnson had known, including herself, "just natchedly lives together." The absence of some form of "courting" notwithstanding, and contrary to her earlier generalization, Johnson had managed to find love with Tillman Thompson, "dat man of mine," with whom she "got along right smart 'till he die." As well as attempting to distance herself from the ways of the public world of white female coquettish behavior of the kind recalled by Gus Feaster, Johnson may have been recounting a significant truism of slavery: the importance some slaves placed on the more practical aspects of the marriage union. To these slaves, finding a partner to complement their practical needs would have seemed far more important than being totally and sometimes recklessly guided by romantic impulses. This was especially likely of South Carolina slaves, who labored under the work and garden system, and of slave and precapitalist agricultural communities in general. Where the element of choice is reduced and the need of a partner remains great, romantic love may seldom have become more than a secondary (although still important) consideration. Low-country slave Ben Horry of Georgetown, however, suggests that the slaves simply allowed romantic developments to take their natural course within the parameters of the more practical requirements of slave and plantation life. Horry recalled his experiences with young women. "Fuss one I go with was name Teena," he reported, "next Candis. Candis best looking, but Teena duh largest."[34] The demands slavery placed upon these people made it imperative that considerations of physical strength, health, and technical and mental ability—the very factors that could make the difference between surviving and not surviving slavery, being sold away from one's family and being allowed to remain on the home place—be elevated above more romantic ideals. Of course, romantic love and the intrinsic worth of a person had a part to play, but it may not have been the main part. The trick was to be selective and then fall in love.

Throughout the state slaves courted one another in the hope of entering some permanent relationship. The likely degree of permanence, of course, would have varied from plantation to plantation and from couple to couple. Possible variables in assessing the level of permanence were the effort expended by the two slaves during courtship, the involvement of the slave quarters community, and, significantly, the owner's participation in the later stages of the marriage rituals.[35] Benjamin Russell, born in 1849, lived on a plantation belonging to Rebecca Nance and her husband near Chester. His father, Baker, had been bought out of a "drove of slaves" from Virginia by a Mr. Russell, who lived about three miles from the Nance place. As Benjamin explained, Baker's "attentions" were encouraged because he was "religiously inclined, dutiful and faithful as a slave."

His persistence and good grace were rewarded with marriage, but only after he had been closely scrutinized by the Nances, who were most particular about the company the slave girls kept. These slaveholders were not averse to monitoring the slaves' behavior and to interfering in the important early stages of their courting rituals. Sometimes they were warned, "If you cannot pick a mate better than that I'll do the picking for you."[36]

Without a doubt, slaveholders' attitude regarding their slaves marrying and living in stable family units could affect the permanence of these marriages. The piety of both the master and the slave and their commitment to the church would also have influenced slave marriage forms. The majority of slaves who married, however, did not do so in a church, although those who reported having done so seem to have had a certain pride not detected in the statements of those who reported having taken part in more simple ceremonies such as "jumping the broom" or those who recalled having no ceremony at all. To some slaveholders and slaves, church weddings appear to have indicated a desired (and promised) permanence not usually associated with nonchurch marriages.[37]

Having allowed their slaves a big wedding celebration, concerned masters were not likely to want to go to the expense of a repeat performance again soon, particularly without a good reason. Furthermore, when slave couples and the slave community knew that the weddings would involve both the public and the private worlds, their attitude to marriage may have acquired an added element of solemnity which otherwise might have been absent. If such rituals were to have the desired effect on the slaves involved and the significance of the marriage ceremony be transmitted to the community as a whole, the relative rarity of weddings and strong sanctions against divorce would have been essential. Middle-country planter James H. Hammond involved himself closely in this aspect of slave life, formalizing slave unions by means of a ceremony which he often conducted as part of the customary Christmas festivities. Each bride and groom would be presented with a gift of $5 for a first marriage; for a second, the sum was reduced to $3.50. Divorce, however, which could follow only after a "family court" had been convened, was accompanied by one hundred lashes. Thus those Hammond slaves whose marriages ended in divorce were punished publicly. The enormity of the punishment rendered divorce one of the plantation's most serious misdemeanors.[38]

That marriage was often a social and religious event encompassing both the public world of the master and the private world of the slave is attested to in the recollections of Richland District former slave Margaret Hughes, born late in slavery. Hughes recalled that the slaves had a "big time" when any of them got married. The couple would be married in the master's house, followed by a "big dance" at one of the slave houses. The master's family would furnish "all kinds of good things to eat and the colored peoples furnish de music for de dance."[39] This level of community involvement surely placed some additional pressure on the bride and groom to respect each other and to honor their vows.

For married slaves living on different plantations there were particular pressures. Will Cook, born a slave in 1825, lived on Thomas Cook's Bennetsville plantation in Marlboro District. Will married a woman named Maria from a neighboring plantation and was able to visit her on Wednesdays and Saturdays. Will stated that he "never had but one wife," and she still lived with him as his wife. That Cook had courted and won the consent of a woman on another plantation may well have increased the couple's chances of having a sophisticated marriage ceremony because it would have involved two slaveholders and two slave communities. Indeed, the involvement of more than one plantation may have increased the need for and frequency of such ceremonies and supplied the community sanction necessary to set an "abroad" marriage on a firmer footing. That Cook was a hardworking field hand who cared deeply for his family is attested to in his testimony before the SCC.[40]

Broad marriages probably possessed a special ingredient not experienced by couples who married and lived on the home place.[41] Priscilla Prince, born in 1823, had a husband, Carolina Prince, who lived on a plantation some "nine miles away." She had been married before in Virginia but was purchased by Peter Odom of Marlboro District in 1844 as a cook, forced to leave her husband behind. Priscilla had met and married Carolina, who worked as a field hand. He visited her every Saturday night and remained there "with his family until Monday morning." Priscilla, in turn, sometimes visited her husband's place, where he had a small garden. With Priscilla working as the Odoms' cook and Carolina belonging to another master, the chances are that the rituals that led up to their marriage were more formalized than those Washington Dozier and his fellows could have expected on Wiles Gregg's plantation. Years later, Priscilla could make the following (qualified) statement expressing her attachment to her husband: "Never had another husband except Carolina Prince since I came to Carolina."[42]

The constant worry, infrequent visits, and mental and emotional preoccupation may have helped to take the "distracted" mind of the spouse off the dull monotony of plantation labor and the sheer boredom of an existence that provided only limited opportunities for entertainment, diversion, or self-expression. Having a loved one on another plantation may have helped in bearing some of the more arduous burdens of slavery, knowing that a visit to wife and family was seldom more than two or three days away. Knowing there was something to look forward to perhaps made a seemingly ordinary situation seem extra special.[43]

Caleb Craig lived on Ed Mobley's Blackstock plantation. As Craig explained: "A man dat had a wife off de place, see little peace or happiness. He could see de wife once a week on a pass, and jealousy keep him 'stracted de balance of de week, if he love her very much."[44] Louisa Davis worked as a housemaid for her master, Jim Lemon, who in 1850 owned sixty-three slaves.[45] Her husband, Sam, belonged to the Sloans, and he "didn't get to see me as often as he wanted to." Because she worked in the house, there were times when Louisa "couldn't meet him clandestine like he want me." We had "some grief over dat," she recalled, "but he got a pass twice a week from his master."[46] The ability to leave one's home place and visit another would have been an exciting event in an otherwise dull week.

On the other side of the equation, there was the likelihood of pain and hurt being caused when one master or the other died, migrated, or, worse, ran into financial difficulties that led to the selling off and dispersal of slaves. Millie Barber's parents, Tom and Nicie, lived in Fairfield District on a plantation some four or five miles apart, which, she recalled, "caused some confusion, mix up, and heart aches." Some years later, when Nicie's young mistress, Janie Wier, married and moved to Texas, Nicie and her young baby, Isiah, accompanied her and were never seen again by the rest of her family.[47]

The amount of attention given to wedding ceremonies both influenced and reflected the level of the community's commitment to marriage. Hence, the slave quarters community's sanction of a wedding might serve as a measure of the likely stability of the union. Morgan Scurry, born on Dr. Scurry's plantation near Laurens District, recalled that the slaves had "feasts at their marriages" and the master and his family took part in the ceremonies. Mary Veals had been a slave of Judge J. B. O'Neall and lived near Newberry. A young girl under slavery, she had often heard her parents, Washington and Polly Holloway, talk about "slavery times." She recalled that weddings were usually accompanied by "frolics and big dinners." Emoline Wilson lived near Dutch Fork. Born in 1847, she could rely on her own recollections of "slavery times." When she married on her master Lemuel Lane's plantation, she had "a good hot supper," although Lane was described as mean to most of his slaves. Nellie Loyd of Union District, who was born a year later, recalled that at weddings on her master George Buchanan's place, everybody would "eat and frolic." Albert Means, born the same year as Loyd, recalled that his first wife, Jane, had belonged to Jim Ellis. He had been married to Jane there by the plantation preacher. Those were good times, Means reported, because they were given plenty to eat, good clothes to wear, and a new log house to live in. Albert and Jane were given a memorable day and a new house in which to begin their life as a married couple.[48]

It cannot be stated categorically that any positive correlation existed between the level of sophistication of the courting and marriage rituals and the likelihood of a slave marriage's permanence, but some evidence seems to support this contention. Because involvement in these rituals usually revealed community attitudes toward marriage, a wedding ceremony should not be seen in isolation. It reflected a generally favorable and respectful attitude among the slaves toward marriage and the family. Where rewards and punishments for marriage and divorce were institutionalized, a lower level of unforced marriage breakup could be expected. And where slaves and the wider community worked hard in productive and stable family units, marriage and family received additional protection.

A high level of community involvement in the rituals leading to a slave marriage increased the weight of sanctions against marital breakup, and continued community involvement encouraged the couple to remain together and to become valuable members of the community. Slave men and women who met, courted, married, and lived on the home place may have been better served in this regard. When slaves married abroad, particularly when they were separated by considerable distances, they were more likely to have been parted from the very people—relatives and friends—who provided first the sanctions then the much needed support at times when the marriage and family stability came under attack. A community valuing hard work, industry, and good order would use its collective strength to protect the family unit by encouraging stable marriages and censuring divorce.[49]

The trial of a member of a low-country Ladies Island slave community and the actions of the key players provide an example of a slave quarters community attempting to regulate the behavior of individual rule breakers. In the case, tried before a military commission in Beaufort District in July–August 1862, one Moses, a slave, was found guilty of second degree murder, having struck one June, a slave, a mortal blow on the back of the head. The evidence reveals that the crime was the result of tensions created by a triangular relationship between Moses, his wife, Maria, and June. For some time, June had been having an affair with Maria, much to the chagrin of Moses, who had tried to dissuade his wife from continuing the affair. On several occasions Moses was alleged to have beaten Maria in an attempt to control her behavior. Once it had become public knowledge that one of Maria's children had been fathered by June, an attempt at a reconciliation had been made. The distraught Moses had accepted an apology from June, who, in turn, had encouraged Maria to apologize to her husband.[50]

June was already married to a woman by the name of Jermina, who was described by her uncle Charles, deacon and former plantation driver, as a "good quiet woman, [who] don't know much—[who] is weak," and by other witness as a "weak woman in body and mind." June may have been attracted to Maria because of the clear differences between the two women: Maria was described as a "passionate woman." It becomes clear, however, that neither June nor Moses had much respect for the sanctity of marriage. Deacon Charles, June's relative by marriage, testified that when as a driver he had caught June "with Moses' sister," he had cast him out of the church. The deacon had also had cause to flog Moses three times "for being with another man's wife." On one occasion Moses was caught with "a strange black man's wife" by her husband. The deacon-driver had flogged Moses and "the woman too . . . [who] did not deny it."

To complicate matters further, both Moses and June had reputations for being violent men, and, consequently, they were objects of terror to Charles, who had declined to continue as driver on the place. In this and other slave quarters, violence, brute force, and the willingness to use both could bring the perpetrator a good deal of power, even respect. June's bravado, recklessness, and seeming indifference to community sanctions probably were related to the fact that he was the only black man on the place who possessed a pistol. Although the weapon was supposed to be used to shoot squirrels in the corn fields, June used it both for protection and self-aggrandizement in a way that the unarmed Moses could not have matched. June's disavowal of the community's sanctions on marital infidelity was probably part and parcel of his braggadocio and disrespect for authority figures.

The members of the Gibbs slave community generally were publicly silent about the events surrounding the murder. When asked by Deacon Charles (surely a representative of both the public and the private worlds) if they knew that Moses had caught June and Maria together, they all said no. Those most willing to testify as to what had taken place in the quarters were either full members of the public world (i.e., white people) or those with a significant involvement in it such as Deacon Charles. The instinct of the community, it seems, was to keep the matter private. This should not, however, suggest that the community condoned the crime or the behavior that led to it. On the contrary, senior members of the quarters had been quick to make Maria aware of the dangers inherent in her behavior and to advise her against any action that would constitute a public statement that all was not well with her marriage. Old Rose, for example, had warned her not to take her corn to June to grind but to have Moses perform this service because, as her husband, it was his responsibility. Maria was fully aware of the community norms and of her infidelity, and, fearing the consequences of a public admission of guilt, she denied her involvement with June to the very end. "I never slept with June," she insisted, and "I never had any corn ground for me, Moses ground my corn . . . never done anything with June . . . know I should be punished if I did." Clearly, Maria's punishment would not have been inflicted so much by the public world as by the members of her own world—the slave quarters.[51]

Another figure from the public world, Jack Sills, the overseer, perhaps reflecting his own values rather than those of the cuckolded husband, observed that Moses must have "loved his wife very much or he would not have put up with her so long." Although this may well have been an accurate reflection of Moses' feelings for his wife, his decision to act was reached suddenly. A reading of the records for slave crime suggests that violent acts were seldom premeditated but resulted from a final explosion of emotional energy when, for one reason or another, slaves were pushed to a point at which matters became unbearable. The day before Moses struck June, the three main characters had exchanged heated words. Earlier that day, Moses and Maria had quarreled; Moses had "barred" her from their house and thrown out her things. Maria had been obliged to move in with her mother. In the middle of the altercation between the two men, Moses told June that he would not fight him with a stick and threw down his stick. He then asked June to come and "fight him like a gentleman with his fists." June, however, pulled out his pistol, called Moses an "infernal rascal," and threatened to "blow his brains out." Despite this heated argument, it was not until Moses actually caught his wife and June together in the woods and had begun to wreak his vengeance upon her by flogging her and June had come to her rescue that Moses struck the fatal blow. For his crime Moses was sentenced to ten years' imprisonment. And so the Gibbs slave quarters was rid of two of the "wickedest men on the plantation." But despite their desire and collective will, they had failed to control these men, even with the help of both the black and the white churches. The Gibbs slaves had also been given an unnecessary and unwelcome reminder of the potential dangers of infidelity and the consequences of violence. Breaking their own community rules had created a level of tension and disharmony that, unresolved, had finally exploded in an act of murder. In this particular instance, the Gibbs slaves were probably not overly sorry to have the outside world intrude and remove from their midst two very unsavory characters.

Why should slaves have taken the risks of marrying and organizing themselves into stable families when such families were likely to be destroyed at any moment?[52] Two crucial factors need to be considered. The first, the economic benefits to the family unit, has already been suggested as a major element in any marriage arrangement. As important as were the feelings that existed between these men and women, they present a different set of problems. Although the economic and social arrangements are easily described and identified, examples of the slave couple's personal feelings toward each other and family members are not. In the narratives, however, some slaves describe the affection husbands and wives and parents and children had for one other, which went a long way toward ensuring that their union, in spite of the ceremonial recognition it might have received, had a good chance of surviving all but the very worst attacks slavery hurled its way.

How can the affectional ties that existed between slaves be examined given their tendency to camouflage their personal feelings when functioning in the public world? The dearth of evidence demands that other means be used in the hope of better understanding this most intimate area of slave life. In this endeavor, examples of slaves taking steps to protect spouses and children economically and physically and their attempts to safeguard the integrity of their marriages and to protect them from external attacks prove more fruitful.[53] Charlie Davis's parents had not married until "after freedom" although they "called deirselves man and wife a long time befo dey was really married"; what seems to have been important for Davis, and no doubt for his parents, was that "they never did want anybody 'cept each other." Such stories that open windows to the slaves' most private feelings are all too rare. Hence the scarcity of accounts that directly attest to the affection between slave couples and between parents and children should be viewed more as a reflection of the slaves' reluctance to behave openly in the public world than as an indication of an absence of such affection. It was not until slaves were safely in the private world of the slave quarters that they felt sufficiently uninhibited to display their affection for each other. John Collins grew up on Nick Collins's Chester District plantation. He could not recall whether his parents, Steve and Nancey, had married under slavery, but his father, who had died during the Civil War, remained strong in the son's memory. "I 'members him well," Collins reported, "he was a tall black man, over six feet high, wid broad shoulders," an affectionate man who used to "play wid mammy just lak she was a child. He'd ketch her under de arm pits and jump her up mighty nigh to the rafters in de little house us lived in."[54] It is likely that Steve and Nancey did not enjoy a solemnized wedding or any special privileges that they thought worth relating to their son John, but their marriage may have been built on a solid foundation of love and mutual affection and, like that of Charlie Davis's parents, did not depend on community sanctions to keep it intact. Of course, not all households in the slave quarters experienced this level of love and demonstrative affection, but this is not to say that affection and respect between family members were not present and demonstrated in other, less overt ways.

Because they reveal attempts by husbands and wives to protect their relationships from external intrusion, many of the accounts summarized below may not appear to be positive and conclusive evidence of affection. They do, however, reveal some of the methods used by slave men and women to control these important areas of their lives. For example, Henry Gladney of Fairfield District had a father who was known as "Bill de Giant" because he was "so big and strong." Bill did not allow other slave men to look at Lucy, his wife. On one occasion Bill had grabbed "Uncle Phil" and thrown him down on the floor, "and when he quit stompin' Uncle Phil they have to send for Dr. Newton, 'cause pappy done broke Uncle Phil's right leg." The other side of the coin was Tom Rosoboro's account of his parents, Tom and Sarah. They belonged to different masters, and Tom was usually allowed a general pass—one good for the year—to visit his wife on John Propst's plantation. As Rosoboro explained, his mother had only three children "'cause she was a good woman and would never pay any attention to the men slaves on the Propst place." Inasmuch as fidelity can be seen as both a cause and a result of lasting affection among two people, Sarah was full of affection because she "was faithful to pappy through thick and thin, whichever it be."[55]

The complicated story of his parents told by Emanuel Elmore attests both to deep affection between slaves and to the extraordinary lengths some were willing to go to protect the integrity of their families. One of sixteen children born to Emanuel and Dorcas, slaves belonging to Colonel Elmore of Spartanburg District, Emanuel told how his father, also called Emanuel, was sold four times while a slave. Born in Alabama, he was sold to someone in Virginia and then to Colonel Elmore in Spartanburg, where he married a slave woman by the name of Jenny. Perhaps because Jenny failed to produce any children or because Elmore permitted his slave men a good deal of laxity, Emanuel seems to have been married to Dorcas "around the same time." Homesick for Alabama, Emanuel managed to persuade the colonel to sell him back to his home state, and Dorcas was sold with him. After several years, Emanuel became homesick for South Carolina, but, unable to persuade his new master to sell him to someone there, "he just 'refugeed' back to Colonel Elmore who took him back and wouldn't let anybody have him." Left alone in Alabama, and perhaps pining for Emanuel and her children, Dorcas was sold by her master to a slave trader from whom she managed to escape and then spent months making her way back to South Carolina. She said that she stayed in the woods at night, slaves along the way gave her bread, and she killed rabbits and squirrels and cooked and ate in the woods. She would get drunk and beat anyone who tried to stop her from coming back. When she finally arrived at the colonel's, she was "lanky, ragged and poor." Happy to see her, the colonel told her he would not "let anybody take her off." While Emanuel and Dorcas had been on their travels, Jenny, Emanuel's first wife, had been taking care of Dorcas's children. She "had cared so well for them while she was off," young Emanuel recalled, that Dorcas "liked her," and all three adults set up a home together and lived in the same house until Dorcas died.[56] The affection, love for spouse, and determination to be together demonstrated by Dorcas and Emanuel and Jenny's loyalty—playing the role of both substitute wife and substitute mother and responding to her situation in a loving way—belies any suspicion that slaves generally lacked affection for those they were close to. Were there no genuine affection, it would be difficult to imagine Jenny caring for Dorcas's children and then welcoming their real mother back into her home.

The level of affection in some slave families adds a special bite to one of the most cruel realities of slavery: the sale and separation of loved ones. A common tactic used by planters to control their labor force was the threat of sale.[57] The exact number of slave marriages that were broken through sale and gift giving is not known, but the possibility of marriage and family breakup through sale was a stark reality for all slaves. Economic prowess and organization in strong, productive families could offer slaves some protection against sale, but it was certainly no guarantee. All too often slaves saw neighboring planters forced to sell their property or risk bankruptcy or criminal proceedings. However much slave owners might have wished to retain their slave labor force intact and on the home place, death or financial demands could take the matter out of their hands. The slaves had to cope with psychological and physical attacks on their persons and on the integrity of their families. They lived with the ever-present threat of sale, and for some, when the dreaded morning came, those among them who had time to say good-bye to their loved ones considered themselves fortunate.

There are numerous examples of slave owners who appeared to have little or no regard for their slave families. One particularly revealing example of a level of callousness that was neither common nor unknown in the state was reported by Susan Hamlin of Charleston. Born in 1833, Hamlin was acutely aware of the proscription placed upon white church ministers who, though they could marry slaves in their churches, could not use the words "let no man put asunder" because masters had ultimate control over whether slaves would be sold. She recounted the experience of one slave couple: "One night a couple married an' de next mornin' de boss sell de wife. De gal ma got in de street an' cursed de white woman fur all she could find. She said 'dat damn white, pale face bastard sell my daughter who jus' married las' night.'" The girl's mother, understandably distraught, made it clear that she would "redder die dan to stan' dis any longer." Her protest was futile, however, as she soon found herself locked up in the city workhouse. Hamlin's master, Edward Fuller, had little compunction about separating slave families. He was reported as having been in the habit of selling children "away from dey parents." Sylvia Cannon of Florence District had also experienced sale and separation from her mother, who had been Bill Gregg's cook. Her high-status position in the public world notwithstanding, Sylvia and her twelve brothers were sold away from their mother. Perhaps because she was aware of this possibility, Sylvia recalled that her mother "didn't talk much to we chillin'." Sold away but not so far away that she could not return to visit her mother and her grandparents on the Gregg place, Sylvia would visit "every two weeks," getting a "note" on a Sunday evening and returning to her new owner on Monday. Sylvia Chisholm was born in June 1849 in Hampton District. Her owner, Joe Bostick, separated her from her parents when she was eight years old. Bostick took her from his Pipe Creek place to Black Swamp, some forty-two miles away, to work for the overseer. Although Chisholm was probably still legally owned by Bostick, the distance proved insurmountable for this slave family. As she recalled, "I never see my mother and father anymore. . . . Not 'til after freedom."[58]

Even when slaves were not victims of sales, there were slave owners like Bigger Mobley of Kershaw/Camden District who were not reluctant to threaten a sale to keep their slaves in order. Peter Clifton was born a slave on his plantation in 1848 and confirmed the effect the threat of sale could have on slaves. Mobley, Clifton recalled, "believed in whippin' and workin' his slaves long and hard," and they seemed to have responded because "then a man was scared all de time of being sold away from his wife and chillin'." Even though it had become common knowledge that Mobley's "bark was worse than his bite . . . for I never knowed him to do a wicked thing like dat," Mobley had sold one slave (about whom there had been a certain "uneasiness") so the slaves had reason to be constantly on their guard. When Clifton's mother and sister Lizzie were put on the block at Chester Court House and about to be sold away from his father, their tears had persuaded Mobley to buy them all, but the memory must have lingered in the minds of Clifton's parents, giving an extra edge to any threat by Mobley to return them to the block. On that occasion, the slaves had been able to influence their master to alter his plans and keep a family together; however, not all slaves were so fortunate. Lizzie Davis, born in Marion District, remembered hearing her father talk about how his mother was sold at public auction and carried away. The experience had made his "heart swell in his breast," but he could do nothing to prevent the separation. Silva Durant, who was born in the same district, recalled her father recounting how his brother Elic's wife was sold away "wid the onlyest child dey hab." They were never seen again. A single man again, Elic would have had to begin the process of finding a wife all over again.[59]

For all too many slaves, the threat of sale and family separation became a reality. As a slave in Richland District, Samuel Boulware was owned by a Dr. Hunter. He was one of twelve children, and his father lived two miles away, which was perhaps a good thing for him because Hunter seems to have been indifferent to the slave family. Boulware recalled that there were some twenty "grown slaves all de time" on the plantation. Hunter "bought and sold them whenever he wanted to." Boulware spoke of the "sad times to see mother and children separated" and of the little children, who would "cry and run after de wagon dat was takin' their mammies away."

Perhaps the Boulware family escaped the horrors of sale and separation because his mother "worked hard in the field" and had sufficient gumption to "talk back to de overseer."[60]

It is all too clear that there was no guarantee that however exemplary the behavior of individual slaves or whole slave quarter communities was, they would not be protected against sale. Although sensible masters endeavored to hold on to their most productive workers, few would have thought twice about ridding themselves, their plantation, and their neighborhood of troublesome slaves. If a slave was recalcitrant and a hindrance to the smooth running of the place, he or she was likely to be sold away. George Fleming of Laurens District recalled that his master would say, "If dat nigger didn't walk de chalk he would put him on de block and settle him." Slaves who were particularly marketable but unattached were also likely to find themselves sold away if masters needed cash quickly. As Isaiah Butler of Hampton District put it, "Every slave know what 'I'll put you in my pocket, sir', mean."[61]

The test of a slave family's strength did not end with its ability to prevent sale and separation. A family's ability to rebound economically and emotionally from untimely death and other misfortune and "reunite or rebuild despite the pain associated with such efforts and adjustments" was a crucial factor.[62] The records of low country's J. R. Motte provide a fuller picture of slave sales and of mechanisms slaves used to reorganize following family disruption through sales. In 1848 Motte purchased Frederick, a young carpenter born about 1830, and Silvia, born about 1826. Eight years later, however, Silvia was still without a child, and, probably for that reason, she was sold away in 1856 for $500. Frederick, now without a wife or children, married Cambrick, daughter of Sam and Die, a family purchased in 1852. Frederick and Cambrick had their first child in 1861 (figure 9). Although masters may not have practiced slave breeding, many, particularly those operating new plantations, may have discouraged and actively attempted to prevent extended periods of infertility. Silvia may have been a willing or unwilling victim of Motte's determination to have his slave families expand as rapidly as possible.

The case of Tommy reveals an additional dimension in the realities of slave family life and the effects of separation through sale. In 1848, Tommy, a carpenter by trade, was purchased for $800. The following

TO HAVE AND TO HOLD

year his wife, Betsey, and their children were given to Mrs. J. R. Motte by Mrs. C. G. Morris—these women were probably sisters—reuniting the family. Thus a sale may have separated Tommy from his family, but because the sale took place within the slave master's extended family and locally, the reunion was possible through a gift from one family member to another. When twenty-six-year-old Betsey arrived in 1849, she already had two children, six-year-old Cornelia and three-year-old Affy, who died soon after arriving at Exeter. Affy's death may have had some bearing on Betsey's failure to have another child until February 1853. Another explanation, of course, might be that the work necessary in ordering a plantation whose condition was described as being "very poor" may have placed additional burdens on young women whose children were not past the suckling stage. After Betsey and Tommy resumed having children in 1853, they had six in a little over ten years.

House slaves were not immune to sale and separation. Purchased as a unit in 1846 were Clarissa, aged twenty, a cook, and Cornelia, aged eighteen, a seamstress. Motte paid $1,000 for these two house servants, and perhaps because he was overstaffed, or perhaps because her conduct was unsatisfactory, Cornelia was sold in 1850 for $700. The profit of some $200 may have been a primary consideration. In 1859 and 1865, Clarissa is listed alone, unmarried, and childless. Her position as a cook may have protected her from the treatment experienced by Cornelia.

It would seem that Motte had few qualms about selling his slaves when he considered it necessary. Quash was purchased in 1848 for $730, and in 1854 he was sold for $740. In 1852 Motte purchased two plantation workers, Simon, aged fifty, and Prince, aged twenty-two, for $1,060, only to sell them three years later for $1,075. Slaves sold so soon after being purchased and for only a small profit may have proved unmanageable or failed to adjust well, perhaps as a consequence of having been purchased away from family and loved ones.[63]

For many slaves the threat of sale caused great fear, given the precarious nature of family life in a slave economy dependent on a credit-based agricultural system. Slave men and women had a better chance of avoiding sale if they were productive both economically and biologically. All too often, however, even these abilities proved insufficient protection against sale and family separation. Thomas Chaplin of Beaufort District, for example, agonized over the impending sale of some of his slaves and displayed the shame some masters felt when faced with an enforced sale. In his journal for May 3, 1845, Chaplin recorded that he was "compelled to send about ten prime negroes to town." Some ten days earlier, Chaplin had received a sheriff's judgment against him for $2,500; he was thus "obliged to sell negroes." He was both shocked and surprised. "I never thought I would be driven to this extremity," he wrote. He was particularly troubled by the realization that he would have to "select out some negroes to be sold" and not knowing "to whom, or how they will be treated by their new owners." Furthermore, these slaves would be "negroes that you find no fault with." And it would be necessary "to separate families, mothers and daughters, brothers and sisters—all to pay for your extravagances."[64] Given a choice, Chaplin would not have sold these slaves. He probably would have done as did Richland District planter John Kinsler, whose former slave, Gracie Gibson, recalled that Kinsler "wouldn't sell his niggers and part de members of de family." He had purchased Gracie's whole family, "Daddy George, Mammy Martha, Gran'dad Jesse, Gran'mammy Nancey, and my two brothers, Flanders and Henry."[65]

Jake McLeod's Sumter District master, Frank McLeod, was able to keep only part of his slave family together. Jake's grandparents had been born on the McLeod place. The McLeods enjoyed a reputation for neither buying nor selling slaves, but, in a division, Jake's grandfather Riley fell to Frank McLeod and his grandmother fell to McLeod's sister, Mrs. MacRae. To avoid separating them, McLeod gave Riley to his sister, who took them with her to Florida along with Jake's aunt and uncles.[66]

Slaves separated through sale would have had the difficult and often troublesome task of reconstructing important elements of their lives. As we have seen, marriage and remarriage as a result of sale, separation, or death were frequent experiences for slaves. Marriage the second time around was often complicated by the presence of children from previous marriages. Isiah Jefferies, born in 1849 in Cherokee District, had first-hand experience with some of the complications which second marriages could cause. Jefferies described himself as an "outside child." His mother, Jane, née Davis, was sold to Henry Jefferies of Wilkensville. Her first husband and Isiah's father was named Harry. When Ned Jefferies married Jane, he became stepfather to her three "outside chillins." Ned was described "as good to me as he was to his own chillin," of which he had four with Jane. "He jest came to be our Pa," reported Isiah. Jane's first three children had each "had a different father." [67]

Sales were not the only major source of family disruption. Frequently, slaves were given to white family members as wedding gifts or as parting gifts when young members of the family left their parents' home to begin a life of their own. Millie Barber of Fairfield District lost her mother, Nicie, when Janie Weir, the young mistress, received Nicie as a gift on leaving for Texas. Nicie was allowed to take only her baby son, Isiah, and Millie never "seen or heard tell of them from dat day to dis." Her father lived on another plantation some four or five miles away from the Weir place, and it is not known how his wife's departure affected his relationship with his daughter. Caleb Craig, also of Fairfield, suffered a similar fate. Caleb was born in 1851 on his master Ed Mobley's place. Caleb's mother was given to one daughter and her children to another. While the children were to be looked after by their master and mistress, Martha, their mother was off with the sister, who had "married a hoss driver from Kentucky." [68]

Savilla Burrell recounted a tale of separation of a slave family and their inability to alter their fate. One of five children, Savilla had a sibling sold away. When "she take on and cry 'bout it Marse (Tom Still) say 'stop dat sniffin' . . . if you don't want to git a whippin'." In this case, public demonstration and grief were to no avail. Savilla's mother, Mary, had to grieve in private, which she did. "She grieve and cry at night 'bout it." [69]

Masters who permitted their slaves to be taken from their plantations either through sale or gift, thereby breaking up marriages and families, probably had a far more pragmatic attitude to the subsequent problems than did their victims. Sena Moore, a slave belonging to Jim Gladney of Fairfield District, perhaps genuinely felt he was giving some comfort to Sena's mother, Phillis, when her husband, George, was sold away to Arkansas by his owner, George Stitt. While Phillis wept, "old master 'low; Plenty good fish in de sea, Phillis. Look 'round, set your cap and maybe you'll 'tract one dat'll give your heart comfort bye and bye." Perhaps Phillis took her master's advice, or maybe the neighborhood was short on attractive male eligibles, because she soon married someone who was described as a "no 'count nigger man name Bill." [70]

Keeping all the members of a family together would in most instances have been a difficult task for slaves. In this area of slave life, masters held the upper hand. Often, slaves had little or no control over the forces that brought about the sale and disruption of the slave quarters. Yet, as the antebellum period wore on, it was clear that slave masters in South Carolina were making efforts to keep slave families together. As masters increasingly sought to sell and purchase slave families intact, slave traders adjusted to the new demands.[71] Although the arbitrary breakup of slave families continued, evidence suggests that the practice was declining. This, of course, did not decrease the potency of the master's threat of sale. Furthermore, although sensible masters sought every alternative to, first, selling their slaves, and, second, separating a slave family, only the foolish or the weak-minded would allow unruly and rebellious slaves to remain on the home place, a constant threat to the general peace and welfare of slave and free alike. Cases of slaves deliberately misbehaving in order to be sold are few, but they do exist.[72] And it might have been deemed bad practice to have kept an unhappy slave when he or she would have preferred to be elsewhere even if it did cause marriage and family breakup.

Given a modicum of economic stability on the part of one's owner—a productive labor force and a well-behaved quarters—a good chance existed that the slave's world would remain stable, dynamic, and protective of the family. Alas, the vast majority of South Carolina slaves did not live on farms and plantations with such high levels of stability that the more protective features of the family group were rendered unnecessary. Slaves organized in strong and stable families would always be in a position to provide a buffer between themselves and the forces that might lead to sale and its economic and emotional consequences. Those slaves who found themselves outside of such families risked finding themselves unprotected from the harsh and cruel winds of slavery.

Whether family members lived on the same plantation or abroad, the stability of the family unit was not necessarily weakened. Although the simple nuclear family structure wherein all members lived under the same roof did not always exist, slave families with members on different plantations were able to (and often did) form economically and emotionally strong, stable households.[73] When family members lived on different plantations, they had to make an effort to spend time together, probably rendering this time all the more special for its scarcity. Of course, the financial risks slaveholders undertook constituted a constant threat to the stability and integrity of slave families, particularly when planters were economically unsuccessful. When slaves married off the place, the situation became doubly precarious. Unless they married a slave from a "rich man plantation" like True Blue, where their personal security—opportunity to live and work within a stable family—would have increased, most slaves were taking a real chance on their family's future by marrying off the home place. Many, however, had little choice.[74] The premium slaves placed on the institution of the family outweighed the risks. Although no slave family was sufficiently powerful and economically strong to guarantee its protection against sale, illness, untimely death, and the many other attacks upon its integrity, strong families provided their members with some much needed insurance. The work and garden system facilitated the development of an economic and social space under slavery; the family offered the slaves the primary means by which they could organize this space and best use it to make lives of their own that would render slavery a little more bearable while preparing them for a life free from the demands and restrictions of slavery.

Conclusion:
To Have and to Hold

Even when slave families succeeded in creating an economic and social space for themselves, the public world of the master could still intrude with devastating force. Slaves could organize themselves in family units and become models of good conduct and discipline yet still be at the mercy of masters, mistresses, the wider white community, other members of the slave quarters community, and, of course, the vicissitudes of economic fortune. It would seem that what was most difficult and troubling for South Carolina slaves was not their inability to acquire the goods and services that improved their chances of making a life of their own. The most pernicious reality of their lives as slaves was their inability to safeguard their finest achievements—to have and to hold what they considered most dear.

The case of Andrew, a slave tried before the Magistrates and Freeholders Court, provides a stark reminder of the essential vulnerability of all slaves and the obstacles that even the most hardworking and industrious among them may have encountered trying to maintain some semblance of family life. On December 29, 1841, a slave house on the plantation of Andrew Oliver was broken into by Thomas Duckworth's Andrew. Some clothing, washing apparel, a bonnet, and other goods were thrown out; a chest was broken into and its contents were also taken. The house belonged to Candy, Andrew's wife. There had been a "falling out between the two," and they had separated. Oliver had forbidden Andrew to come to the place, one time threatening that he would "whip and kill him" if he found him there again. Sometime after this and before the house was broken into, Oliver again found Andrew on his property and drove him off.

Andrew, in turn, swore to Oliver that he would have satisfaction "if it took him five or ten years." In testimony before the court, Oliver reported that he had always treated Andrew well until he and his wife "fell out and separated, but when that happened . . . I forbidded him from coming there." Sometime later, he had overheard Andrew swear that he would go to Oliver's "when he pleased; would take his young master and break open the house and take off his things in spite of him." Andrew did not deny having broken into his wife's house but explained that "he had things there which he had given to his wife" and that she had "taken up with another" man and he refused to "let him wallow on the things he had bought." He had, therefore, taken away some "bed clothes, spread and such, that had been bought with his money." He gave the court some idea of the emotional torment he had been suffering when he described the action of his wife in taking up with another man, concluding that "no man could submit to such treatment."[1]

The goods Andrew had accumulated and given to his wife had been purchased with his own money acquired by "knocking about, by buying and selling things." Andrew, his wife, Candy, and other witnesses acknowledged the nature and quality of the goods that had been thrown out of the house. Their presence in Candy's house testifies to the amount of property ordinary slaves could accumulate. The goods, according to Oliver's testimony, included a pitcher, which Andrew broke, some plates, three shirts, four cotton frocks, two or three calico frocks, two of which "he knew belonged to Candy," and some clothing that "belonged to a young child." Candy claimed that two quilts she had made had also been taken and that she had spun the shirts and the frocks and that Andrew had taken a bonnet that was "nearly new and cost $3." Candy also owned "a stear . . . valued at $6 or $7." Andrew was clearly in a position to provide these goods, and Candy was useful in working with cloth and looking after the livestock—doing her share in what had been a harmonious relationship based on complementary roles.[2]

Andrew's relationship with Oliver was described as "friendly as brothers previous to them falling out." Andrew's familiarity and intimacy with his wife's owner might have given Andrew a strong sense of his own worth and enhanced his feelings of equality with Oliver. When they fell out, each threatened the other's life. Oliver, however, had the power to act decisively. At one point, Andrew had considered trying to even the odds by taking along his young master when he went to retrieve his belongings from his wife's house.

The economic and social space that Andrew worked hard to carve out for himself had proved insufficient to secure permanently the creature comforts he desired for himself and his wife. Andrew's commercial activities had enabled him to have a life under slavery. In the absence of a falling-out with his wife's owner, Andrew had good reason to expect that he would remain the de facto head of his family. There was little even the strongest family could do to provide adequate protection against a white world turned hostile. For once the white world decided that the slaves had gone beyond the boundaries of their "space," it was seldom slow in firmly pushing them back into place. That most slaves did not step too far out of the economic and social space they had helped create suggests a level of social dexterity that enabled the vast majority of them to expand their sphere of influence within the slave quarter community without appearing seriously to challenge the structure and viability of the master's public world.

Throughout the state, to a greater or lesser degree, masters employed a work and garden system that allowed the slaves a small plot of land to plant for their own use. At its most successful, the work and garden system came to represent an acceptance on the part of both master and slave of a degree of trust and mutual responsibility, encouraging both parties to maintain their part of the bargain. Slaves residing in the low country, where landholdings were larger, had a marked advantage over their counterparts in other regions of the state, particularly the up-country, where the size of the labor force and the amount of land typically under cultivation reduced the number of jobs that could be usefully tasked, as well as the land available for slave gardens. Because up-country farms and plantations tended to be smaller and to have fewer hands, it was not always possible to set tasks that would provide slaves the necessary incentive to work hard and complete their assignments before day's end. These factors denied up-country slaves some of the financial and psychological benefits of working under the task system. For example, as unusual as it was to find slaves working gardens as large as twelve or fifteen acres, such slaves could be found in the low country, and there were numerous ordinary slaves who worked gardens of two or three acres. Middle-country slaves had a similar experience. In the up-country, however, the relative scarcity of improved land reduced the amount available for slave gardens. Former slave Mary Jane Kelly may have had a typical up-country experience. On Bill Jeter's Santuc plantation the slaves were allowed only a small piece of land, which was restricted to family groups and used only to plant watermelons.[3]

In encouraging slaves to work land for their own use, masters were motivated by a curious mixture of duty, discipline, and a desire to encourage in their slaves a commitment to a stable and productive family lifestyle. When a sense of industry was instilled in the slave, the master was sure to benefit because each slave would have a stake in the plantation. Slave owners calculated that hardworking and well-behaved slaves would have an increased attachment to the home place, which would increase the harmony and improve morale on the plantation. The benefits to the slaves were not always immediately apparent, and a system that served the slave owners' financial interests was typically viewed with some suspicion. Not a few slaves must have wondered why they should labor extra hard only to accommodate the wishes of the owner. Whatever dilemmas their involvement in these work systems presented, once the material and social benefits of the work and garden system became clear to them, South Carolina's slaves used the system for their own ends.[4] The exploitation of their garden opportunities and the resulting expansion of their commercial activities ensured that the values of the marketplace characteristic of the public world of the masters would slowly begin to influence the more traditional values of the quarters. Whether the slaves liked it or not, the work arrangements that operated in the public world of the masters would have a profound, if sometimes unwelcome, impact on the structure of the slave family and the slave quarter community.[5]

Given the opportunity to work a piece of land, slaves were not slow to exploit the benefits of cooperative family labor. They organized their work and economic activities around the family, and family landholdings, and the dispensing of the products thereof were probably controlled by the senior members of the family. This factor alone would have encouraged a high level of family cohesion and interdependency among younger and older members—particularly older members who had property to bequeath and the next generation. These arrangements would also have helped cement and stabilize conjugal relationships.[6] In this and in other ways, the slaves' work and economic enterprise, which in the public world might only have resulted in a reduction of the master's responsibility for his slaves' welfare, echoed far more loudly in the quarters, where it had a profound impact on slave family and community structure.

There is evidence of some correlation between the nature of the slave's work on the plantation and the amount of land he or she was deemed capable of tending and, by extension, the amount of crops particular slaves and slave families could expect to produce. Those slaves who controlled the larger pieces of land and had more time to work their gardens were more likely to accumulate substantial property. As a result, the income of slaves in low-country and middle-country slave communities varied a good deal more than that of slaves in the up-country. Few up-country slaves accumulated as much property as Marlboro's Silas Cook or Beaufort's Henry Newton.[7]

One result of the wide range of income among slaves was the development of clear social distinctions based on property accumulation between slave families, with the richer, more powerful slave families tending to dominate both the weaker families and the wider slave quarter community. Groups such as single women without close family attachments on or near the home place risked being totally dependent on their masters or others for their needs.[8] Without an economically supportive family, single women could find themselves as badly off as the traditionally dependent groups—the aged, infirm, and sick.

Yet simply to begin the process of family formation presented most slaves with an overwhelming set of problems. Demographics alone would have increased the chances of low-country slaves finding suitable eligibles on the home place. In 1860, low-country districts were home to some 127,800 slaves, the middle country to 138,000, and the up-country to 125,800, with 6,189, 9,190, and 11,619 slave owners, respectively. The stark reality for the majority of South Carolina's slaves, therefore, was that they had great difficulty finding suitable partners on the home place with whom to begin the arduous process of building and maintaining the desired family unit. This was a fact of life for the majority of slaves living on farms and plantations with a slave population smaller than that of T. P. Alston's True Blue with its 247 slaves. Furthermore, the greater the number of slaves "marrying off," the more the familial networks extended beyond the home place and a growing interconnectedness of blood-related family members extended the young slaves' catchment area while reducing the number of suitable mates. These familial links between farms and plantations in the area render the vexing issues of slaves being sold away and slave men choosing to marry someone from another plantation not only more complex but perhaps less important. What remains significant, however, is the suggestion that the amount of choice the slaves had as to where, when, and to whom they married, to a large extent, depended on their economic power: the more the slave enjoyed, the more choices he or she could make about marrying or not marrying, when, and to whom.

A major force that could not always be ensured against, foreseen, or prevented, but which often had dire consequences for the slave family, was the frequency of sickness, disease, and untimely death. The economic advantages that low-country and middle-country slaves had over their up-country counterparts were largely offset by the healthier climate of the more mountainous regions of the state and by the prevalence there of self-sufficient farms and plantations. Although most up-country slaves lacked the opportunity to fish in the sea or in nearby rivers to supplement their diets, most had access to a wide variety of food, vegetables, and wildlife. Thus, though slaves in the up-country may have enjoyed a climate more conducive to maintaining good health, they were less able to increase their income and add variety to their diet through their own efforts than were slaves in the middle and lower regions of the state. When disease or untimely death did strike, the family's material and emotional resources were severely tested. The important role the family played on these occasions should not be underestimated because it was at times of most difficulty that the family—the larger and stronger, the better—was severely tested.

Once a slave had found, courted, and won a partner, some form of marriage ceremony would have followed, but there could be no guarantee that the marriage would last, although a correlation does seem to have existed between the level of sophistication of the courting and marriage rituals. Widespread community involvement in these procedures increased the likelihood of permanence of a slave marriage. The slaves' wedding ceremonies should not be seen in isolation because involvement in these rituals usually revealed community attitudes toward marriage, and thus they provide an accurate reflection of the public and private worlds' attitudes toward marriage and family.[9]

Although slave owners continued to break up slave families, evidence suggests that the practice was on the decline as masters, encouraged by the church and in part as a response to the growing abolitionist attacks and the movement to reform the institution of slavery, made greater efforts to keep families together.[10] The slaves' willingness and ability to organize in stable, productive, and mutually supportive family groups also weighed against their chances of being arbitrarily sold and separated from family members.

In sum, the family unit was of crucial importance to South Carolina's slaves as it was to all slave communities. Whenever possible, young people, having reached a certain maturity, found themselves moving unwaveringly toward marriage and a family of their own. Who a slave was, what he or she did to earn a living, whether she or he lived on a small farm or a large plantation, on the Sea Islands or in the more mountainous regions of the state, affected the nature of the choice of partner and, indeed, whether there was any choice. These factors, of course, had a profound bearing on most aspects of slave life. Once organized in a family, particularly a large, able-bodied, hardworking, and skilled family group, slaves were in a good position to control some of the many forces that affected the quality of their lives.

Working and living together, these people were able to make a world of their own under slavery. Although their private world was never immune to intervention from the white world, the slaves' economic activities did facilitate the creation of a "space" wherein they could live out their own lives and participate in the wider black community composed of slaves and free black men and women. In the slave community, linking several slave quarters into a single economic and social unit, the family was predominant. It was the family group, functioning in this private world, that most powerfully influenced the personalities of the slaves; it was there that enslaved African Americans, young and old, were nurtured and socialized. It was in the quarters that they established the foundations of an African American culture.

Where the slaves had some control over their work and nonwork time, where they were allowed the opportunity to plant some land for their own use, and where they were provided with an outlet for their surplus products, they were most likely to find themselves in a position to begin to make a life of their own. To reap the full benefits of their opportunities, slaves organized themselves into mutually supportive and productive family units. Denied any of these advantages, the slave family would have struggled to maintain any sense of unity and cohesion and would have little hope of determining the quality or direction of their lives. At best, they would have been little more than the child-producing machines with which some masters, but no slaves, would have been satisfied. The slaves needed, wanted, and took much more from their families. The opportunity to work with and for the benefit of the family allowed slaves the economic space to shape the structure of their families and communities and to go a long way toward controlling significant areas of their lives. The more property families were able to produce, the better were their chances to have and to hold what was most dear to them—their families. Indeed, the family provided both a rationale for their lives as slaves and a means of measuring their progress toward freedom. An appreciation of the links between garden plot, surplus, family structure, and a level of material and spiritual well-being was an important item in the cultural baggage that the slaves carried with them into freedom.

Notes

The American Slave   George P. Rawick, ed., *The American Slave: A Composite Auto-*
                             biography, South Carolina Narratives, 19 vols. (Westport, Conn.:
                             Greenwood Press, 1972)

SCC   Southern Claims Commission

SCL   South Caroliniana Library, University of South Carolina,
                             Columbia

SHC   Southern Historical Collection, University of North Car-
                             olina, Chapel Hill

Preface

1. W. E. B. Du Bois, *The Negro American Family* (1908; rpt. New York: Negro Universities Press, 1969), 9.

2. Justin Labinjoh, "The Sexual Life of the Oppressed: An Examination of the Family Life of Antebellum Slaves," *Phylon* 35 (1974): 383.

3. Although wide-scale property ownership did exist, slaves were often placed in the awkward position of having to prove ownership of the goods in their posses-sion: the onus of proof, resting with the slaves, always put their hard-earned prop-erty at risk. Helen Catterall reported a South Carolina case in 1848 in which a white man came onto the plaintiff's plantation and took five hogs from pens near the "negro house" and hauled them away in a wagon, saying, "It is negro property and I intend to take it away." The lawmakers were not inclined to leave the slave entirely at the mercy of such unscrupulous persons. The South Carolina Court of Appeals in reviewing the Case of *Richardson v. Broughton* in May 1848 held that the act of 1740 did not confer the right to enter the enclosure of the owner of the slave for the purpose of seizing Negro property.

The absence of legal title to their own property sometimes made it difficult for slaves to safeguard the privacy of their home and family life. Indeed, despite the informal rights of slaves to hold property and to organize in stable family groups, these rights were never legally protected. Nonetheless, property ownership, marriage, and stable family life were commonplace and highly valued among South Carolina's slaves. See Helen Tunnicliff Catterall, ed., *Judicial Cases Concerning American Slavery and the Negro*, 4 vols. (Washington D.C.: Carnegie Institute of Washington, 1929), 2:408.

4. On the significance of naming practices and family structure see Cheryl Ann Cody, "Naming, Kinship and Estate Dispersal: Notes on Slave Family Life on a South Carolina Plantation, 1786–1833," *William and Mary Quarterly* 39 (1982): 192–211; Herbert G. Gutman, *The Black Family in Slavery and Freedom, 1750–1925* (New York: Pantheon Books, 1976), chap. 5.

Introduction

1. Among the most recent publications see the two works edited by Ira Berlin and Philip D. Morgan, *The Slaves' Economy: Independent Production by Slaves in the Americas* (London: Frank Cass, 1991), and *Cultivation and Culture: Labor and the Shaping of Slave Life in the Americas* (Charlottesville: University Press of Virginia, 1993); Joseph P. Reidy, *From Slavery to Agrarian Capitalism in the Cotton Plantation South: Central Georgia, 1800–1880* (Chapel Hill: University of North Carolina Press, 1992); Charles B. Dew, *Bond of Iron: Master and Slave at Buffalo Forge* (New York: Norton, 1994); Julie Saville, *The Work of Reconstruction: From Slave to Wage Laborer in South Carolina, 1860–1870* (Cambridge: Cambridge University Press, 1994); Larry E. Hudson Jr., ed., *Working Toward Freedom: Slave Society and Domestic Economy in the American South* (Rochester: University of Rochester Press, 1994); Betty Wood, *Women's Work, Men's Work: The Informal Slave Economies of Lowcountry Georgia* (Athens: University of Georgia Press, 1995). Although this approach to slave life is comparatively new to the United States, students of West Indian slavery have used it for over three decades. See the Berlin and Morgan collections and, for a comparative study, Roderick A. McDonald, *The Economy and Material Culture of Slaves: Goods and Chattels on the Sugar Plantations of Jamaica and Louisiana* (Baton Rouge: Louisiana State University Press, 1993).

2. For a recent discussion of slave masters' use of certain work systems as a sophisticated means of controlling their labor force, see Norrece T. Jones, Jr., *Born a Child of Freedom Yet a Slave: Mechanisms of Control and Strategies of Resistance in Antebellum South Carolina* (Hanover: Wesleyan University Press, 1990), chap. 3.

3. James King sees the family as a "basic unit in most societies," and Ann Patton

Malone speaks of the "natural tendency among enslaved folk to form stable families, households, and communities." Although the "natural tendency" of humans toward family formation was a significant element in the successful drive toward stable slave families that approached its apogee in the late antebellum period, it remains an unsatisfactory foundation on which to construct a picture of the resilient and highly functional black family life that developed under slavery.

As King points out, the argument of African family structural retentions produces its own problems. For example, West African family forms often constituted polygamous relationships which "were based upon the husband being able and needing to support his wives economically—indeed, his wives were a reflection of his wealth and power as well as a source of increasing said wealth and power." See James R. King, "African Survivals in the Black American Family," *Journal of Afro-American Issues* 4 (Spring 1976): 153, 157; Ann Patton Malone, *Sweet Chariot: Slave Family and Household Structure in Nineteenth-Century Louisiana* (Chapel Hill: University of North Carolina Press, 1992), 2. See also Russell R. Menard, "The Maryland Slave Population, 1658 to 1730: A Demographic Profile of Blacks in Four Counties," *William and Mary Quarterly* 32 (1975): 29–54; Allan Kulikoff, *Tobacco and Slaves: The Development of Southern Cultures in the Chesapeake, 1680–1800* (Chapel Hill: University of North Carolina Press, 1986).

4. Charles Joyner, *Down by the Riverside: A South Carolina Slave Community* (Urbana: University of Illinois Press, 1984), xvii.

Chapter One. For Better for Worse: The Slaves' World of Work

1. See especially Ulrich B. Phillips, *American Negro Slavery: A Survey of the Supply, Employment and Control of Negro Labor as Determined by the Plantation Regime* (New York: D. Appleton-Century, 1918); E. Franklin Frazier, *The Negro Family in the United States* (1939; rpt. Chicago: University of Chicago Press, 1966); Stanley M. Elkins, *Slavery: A Problem in American Institutional and Intellectual Life* (Chicago: University of Chicago Press, 1959); Kenneth M. Stampp, *The Peculiar Institution: Slavery in the Antebellum South* (New York: Vintage Books, 1956). For a more recent expression see Jones, *Born a Child of Freedom.*

2. "Despite all that historians have written in the past, slaves reserved the top rung of the social ladder for those blacks who performed services for other slaves rather than for whites" (John W. Blassingame, "Status and Social Structure in the Slave Community: Evidence from New Sources," in *Perspectives and Irony in American Slavery*, ed. Harry P. Owens [Jackson: University Press of Mississippi, 1976], 142).

3. See H. M. Henry, *The Police Control of the Slave in South Carolina* (1914; rpt. New York: Negro Universities Press, 1968), 192.

4. Philip D. Morgan, "Work and Culture: The Task System and the World of Low Country Blacks, 1700 to 1860," *William and Mary Quarterly* 39 (1982): 566, 575.

5. James R. Sparkman to Benjamin Allston, March 10, 1858, in J. H. Easterby, ed., *The South Carolina Rice Plantation as Revealed in the Papers of Robert F. W. Allston* (Chicago: University of Chicago Press, 1945), 346.

6. Philip D. Morgan, "The Ownership of Property by Slaves in the Mid-Nineteenth Century Low Country," *Journal of Southern History* 49 (1983): 401.

7. James O. Breeden, ed., *Advice Among Masters: The Ideal in Slave Management in the Old South* (Westport, Conn.: Greenwood Press, 1980), 62.

8. "Only under the most urgent necessity would the driver be allowed to require work beyond the assigned task, and then . . . the excess labor . . . was to be compensated" (James M. Clifton, "The Rice Driver: His Role in Slave Management," *South Carolina Historical Magazine* 82 [1981]: 337).

9. James R. Sparkman to Benjamin Allston, March 10, 1858, in Easterby, ed., *The South Carolina Rice Plantation*. The "trash gang" was assigned such tasks as raking stubble, pulling weeds, or doing light hoeing. At harvest time on cotton plantations they usually picked cotton. Most often this group would be made up of pregnant women, women with nursing infants, young teenagers, and old and ailing slaves. See Deborah Gray White, *"Ar'n't I a Woman?": Female Slaves in the Plantation South* (New York: Norton, 1985), 94.

10. Lewis Cecil Gray, *History of Agriculture in the Southern United States to 1860* (Washington, D.C.: Carnegie Institution, 1933), 1:553.

11. Prince Smith in George P. Rawick, ed., *The American Slave: A Composite Autobiography*, 19 vols. (Westport, Conn.: Greenwood, 1972), vol. 3, pt. 4, 117. Hereafter vol. 2 with parts 1 and 2, and vol. 3 with parts 3 and 4, concerning the state of South Carolina, will be cited as *The American Slave* with the part and page number. Also Rawick, *The American Slave*, Supplement, Ser. 1, 12 vols. (Westport, Conn.: Greenwood Press, 1977).

12. Sam Polite in *The American Slave*, pt. 3, 271–72. "Between the last hoeing and the first picking, the hands were assigned to digging marsh mud and hauling it directly to the fields . . . where it would sit until it was turned under in winter" (Theodore Rosengarten, *Tombee: Portrait of a Cotton Planter* [New York: William Morrow, 1986], 71).

13. Gabe Lance in *The American Slave*, pt. 3, 92–93.

14. Quoted in Morgan, "Work and Culture," 578.

15. Ibid., 578–79; Clifton, "Rice Driver," 337.

16. Morgan, "Work and Culture," 576; Gray, *History of Agriculture*, 550–56.

17. John M. DeSaussure Plantation Book, 1861, SHC.

18. Jayne Morris-Crowther, "An Economic Study of the Substantial Slave-holders of Orangeburg County, 1860–1880," *South Carolina Historical Quarterly* 86 (1985): 296–97. On farms or plantations with fifteen slaves, as many as eight or ten might have been young children. A starting point of fifteen slaves, therefore, includes fairly small labor forces and perhaps also quite small landholdings. Population figures for 1840 show a roughly similar ratio of two slaves to each white inhabitant. Average slaveholding for Spartanburg in 1860 was eight. There were some one thousand slaveholders. See Joseph C. G. Kennedy, *Population of the United States, Compiled from the Original Return of the Eighth Census* (Washington, D.C.: U.S. Government Printing Office, 1864).

19. Michael Gramling Plantation Journal, 1839–58, SCL.

20. John Glover in *The American Slave*, pt. 2, 138; Louisa Gause, ibid., 107; Agnes James, ibid., pt. 3, 10; Jake McLeod, ibid., 157.

21. See Drew Gilpin Faust, *James Henry Hammond and the Old South: A Design for Mastery* (Baton Rouge: Louisiana State University Press, 1982), 75, 92.

22. Gabe Lockier in *The American Slave*, pt. 3, 113; Richard Mack, ibid., 151.

23. Sylvia Cannon, ibid., pt. 1, 185. The word *evening* was often used when afternoon was meant. This becomes significant when interpreting accounts that indicate the time slaves ended their working day.

24. Alfred G. Smith suggested that the transport difficulties were caused by a thick belt of swamps, which made connections with the coastal areas extremely difficult (*Economic Readjustment of an Old Cotton State: South Carolina, 1820–1860* [Columbia: University of South Carolina Press, 1958], 2).

25. David Duncan Wallace, *South Carolina: A Short History* (Chapel Hill: University of North Carolina Press, 1951); 1850 U.S. Census; Smith, *Economic Readjustment of an Old Cotton State*, 71.

26. William J. Connors Plantation Journal, 1841–43, SCL.

27. Isiah Jefferies in *The American Slave*, pt. 3, 18; William Pratt, ibid., 277; Benjamin Russell, ibid., pt. 4, 51; Victoria Adams, ibid., pt. 1, 10; George Fleming, ibid., pt. 2, 135. Under a gang system slaves were encouraged to work in a group executing the same activity—hoeing or weeding, for example. The performance of each worker was dependent upon the work of the others. Few if any of the psychological benefits associated with the task system were likely to come to slaves working under the gang system, but slaves could still be allowed time to work for themselves. See Robert William Fogel, *Without Consent or Contract: The Rise and Fall of American Slavery* (New York: Norton, 1989), 25–27.

28. For a discussion of the experience of up-country slaves in the internal

economy, see John Campbell, "As 'A Kind of Freeman'?: Slaves' Market-Related Activities in the South Carolina Upcountry, 1800–1860," in *The Slaves' Economy: Independent Production by Slaves in the Americas*, eds. Ira Berlin and Philip D. Morgan (London: Frank Cass, 1991), 131–69.

29. Morgan, "Work and Culture," 581; Breeden, ed., *Advice Among Masters*, 266, 267.

30. See Sidney W. Mintz, *Caribbean Transformations* (Chicago: Aldine, 1974), 192. For a discussion of the development of a work ethic among the enslaved, see Eugene D. Genovese, *Roll, Jordan, Roll: The World the Slaves Made* (New York: Pantheon Books, 1974), 286–87.

31. In his discussion of the Caribbean, Mintz rightly points out that as there was neither an ethical nor economic basis for the development of any "happy coalition of interests" between master and slave, wise slave owners had to try to introduce and stimulate it. See *Caribbean Transformations*, 192. On the relative success of antebellum slave masters in disciplining the work habits of their slaves, see Genovese, *Roll, Jordan, Roll*, 285–88.

32. McBride in Breeden, ed., *Advice Among Masters*, 267–68; Roswell King Jr., ibid., 266–67.

33. The Southern Claims Commission "was a sincere, well-meaning attempt to reimburse claimants throughout the former Confederacy whose property had been seized for the use of the United States Army during the Civil War." See John Hammond Moore, "Getting Uncle Sam's Dollars: South Carolinians and the Southern Claims Commission, 1871–1880," *South Carolina Historical Magazine* 82 (1981): 248–62. See also Moore's unpublished manuscript, "South Carolina and the Southern Claims Commission, 1871–1880," in the State Archives, Columbia, South Carolina. The claims of A. Jackson, No. 11199, and others are in Boxes 236 to 244.

34. SCC Claim 6654.

35. Prince Smith, in *The American Slave*, pt. 4, 117; Sam Mitchell, ibid., pt. 3, 200; Sam Polite, ibid., 272; Henry Brown, ibid., pt. 1, 119.

36. Letter of J. B. Miller dated 1855 in the Miller-Furman-Dabbs Family Papers, SCL.

37. Jake McLeod in *The American Slave*, pt. 3, 158–59.

38. SCC Claim 268.

39. See Moore, "South Carolina and the Southern Claims Commission," 184.

40. SCC Claim 882.

41. Agnes James in *The American Slave*, pt. 3, 9; Hector Smith, ibid., pt. 4, 101; Genia Woodberry, ibid., 218.

42. In the twelve districts of the up-country, the average number of farms per district was 1,210 compared with the middle country's 1,027 and the low country's 691. The up-country's more numerous farm holdings were on average some 30 percent smaller than middle-country farms and some 60 percent smaller than those in the low country. Slaveholding in 1860 shows a similar spread, with the low country averaging some 21.5 slaves per holding and the middle and up-country 15 and 11, respectively. See the 1850 and 1860 U.S. Censuses.

43. Rev. Thomas Harper in *The American Slave*, pt. 2, 240; John Davenport, ibid., pt. 1, 240; Albert Oxner, ibid., pt. 3, 112.

44. Lila Rutherford, ibid., pt. 4, 58; Emoline Glasgow, ibid., pt. 2, 134. Slave holdings for Pettus Gilliam in 1860 from the Slave Schedules, Eighth Census of the United States, 1860. Nellie Loyd in *The American Slave*, pt. 3, 127.

45. Mary Jane Kelly in *The American Slave*, pt. 3, 89; Andy Marion, ibid., 167.

46. Isiah Jefferies, ibid., 18.

47. Letter from C.P.W., November 16, 1862, in Elizabeth Ware Pearson, *Letters From Port Royal: Written at the Time of the Civil War* (Boston: W. B. Clarke, 1906), 112. See also Genovese, *Roll, Jordan, Roll*, 537.

48. Mary Scott in *The American Slave*, pt. 4, 84.

49. See the account of Victoria Adams, ibid., pt. 1, 10.

50. See Mintz, *Caribbean Transformations*, chap. 7; Orlando Patterson, *The Sociology of Slavery: An Analysis of the Origins, Development and Structure of Negro Slave Society in Jamaica* (London: McGibbon & Kee, 1967), chap. 8; Mary C. Karasch, *Slave Life in Rio de Janeiro, 1808–1850* (Princeton: Princeton University Press, 1987), chap. 7; McDonald, *The Economy and Material Culture of Slaves*. For slave market activities in the eighteenth century see Robert Olwell, "Loose, Idle and Disorderly: Slave Women in the Eighteenth-Century Charleston Marketplace," in *More than Chattel: Black Women and Slavery in the Americas*, ed. David Barry Gaspar and Darlene Clark Hine (Bloomington: Indiana University Press, 1996), 97–110.

51. Genovese, *Roll, Jordan, Roll*, 539. See also Patterson, *Sociology of Slavery*, chap. 8; Karasch, *Slave Life*, passim. Roderick A. McDonald suggests that Louisiana slaves "bypassed the plantation and sold their commodities elsewhere. Some were even involved in marketing at major ports on the Mississippi River, as well as at local markets and in the neighborhood of the plantation." See McDonald, "Independent Economic Production by Slaves on Antebellum Louisiana Sugar Plantations," in *Slaves' Economy*, ed. Berlin and Morgan, 192.

52. For a discussion of the impact of the growing presence of cash money on the values of the slave quarter community see Larry E. Hudson, "'All That Cash':

Work and Status in the Slave Quarters," in *Working Toward Freedom: Slave Society and Domestic Economy in the American South*, ed. Larry E. Hudson (Rochester: University of Rochester Press, 1994), 77–94.

53. Breeden, ed., *Advice Among Masters*, 271.

54. Ibid., 268.

55. See Faust, *James Henry Hammond*, 72; James Henry Hammond, "Notes to Overseer," Hammond Papers, SCL.

56. Breeden, ed., *Advice Among Masters*, 269.

57. See Mintz, *Caribbean Transformations*, chap. 7; Patterson, *Sociology of Slavery*, chap. 8; Karasch, *Slave Life*, chap. 7; and Michael Mullin, *Africa in America: Slave Acculturation in the American South and the British Caribbean, 1736–1831* (Urbana: University of Illinois Press, 1993); McDonald, *The Economy and Material Culture of Slaves*.

58. Whereas in 1711 Jamaican slaves were forbidden to sell items such as beef, veal, mutton, and salt fish, by 1735 they were permitted to trade in "fresh fish, milk, poultry, and other small stock of all kinds" (Mintz, *Caribbean Transformations*, 198).

59. Henry, *Police Control of the Slave*, 85.

60. Breeden, ed., *Advice Among Masters*, 270. On balance, writes John Campbell, "slaves failed to receive Charleston market prices and thus were underpaid for their cotton" ("As 'A Kind of Freeman'?," 145).

61. See Genovese, *Roll, Jordan, Roll*, 535.

62. Hammond, "Notes," 25.

63. Breeden, ed., *Advice Among Masters*, 268; Sparkman to Benjamin Allston, March 10, 1858, in Easterby, ed., *South Carolina Rice Planter*, 349, 350.

64. Bryan Edwards, *The History, Civil and Commercial, of the British West Indies*, 5 vols. (1819; rpt. London: AMS Press, 1966), 2:161.

65. Sparkman to Benjamin Allston, March 10, 1858, in Easterby, ed., *South Carolina Rice Planter*, 350.

66. For an interesting discussion of the implications for masters and slaves of the latter's engagement in the marketplace, see Lawrence T. McDonnell, "Money Knows No Master: Market Relations and the American Slave Community," in *Developing Dixie: Modernization in a Traditional Society*, ed. Winfred B. Moore Jr., Joseph F. Tripp, and Lyon G. Tyler Jr. (Westport, Conn: Greenwood Press, 1988), 31–44; Hudson, "All That Cash."

67. Genovese, for example, places far more emphasis on the role of religion. See *Roll, Jordan, Roll*, esp. Book 2; also his *From Rebellion to Revolution: Afro-American Slave Revolts in the Making of the New World* (New York: Vintage Books, 1981), chap. 1, esp. 6–8. On the developing African American culture see Sterling

Stuckey, *Slave Culture: Nationalist Theory and the Foundations of Black America* (New York: Oxford University Press, 1987); and Lawrence W. Levine, *Black Culture and Black Consciousness: Afro-American Folk Thought from Slavery to Freedom* (New York: Oxford University Press, 1977).

68. As hard a time as Charles Ball and his fellow slaves had on their plantation near Columbia, those who were able and willing managed to add substantially to their income. See Ball, *Fifty Years in Chains* (1837; rpt. New York: Dover, 1970), 276. See also Genovese, *Roll, Jordan, Roll*, 537.

69. Testimony of Eliza Peeples (formerly Goethe), SCC Claim 6654; Testimony of Rose Goethe, ibid.; Testimony of Ann Goethe, SCC Claim 6653.91.

70. Testimony of Andrew Jackson and Oliver Bostick, SCC Claim 11199; see also Moore, "South Carolina and the Southern Claims Commission," 51.

71. Testimony of Andrew Gaurin and James W. Dupees, SCC Claim 11199. They were allowed $120.

72. Testimony of David Harvey, SCC Claim 8003; he was allowed $153.50.

73. Testimony of Henry Newton and his former owner, James B. Smith, SCC Claim 9586; he was allowed $125. The reference to "rebel money" probably indicates paper money drawn upon the Confederate bank, and "state" money was paper currency drawn upon a state bank.

74. Testimony of Pompey Smith and James Smith, SCC Claim 8018; he was allowed $250. See also Moore, "South Carolina and the Southern Claims Commission," 72.

75. Testimony of Benjamin Platts and Frank Davis, SCC Claim 10088; he was allowed $166.

76. Testimony of Aleck Bryant and Virgil A. Chisholm, SCC Claim 10081; he was allowed $166.

77. Testimony of Philip Ried and Julia Speakes, SCC Claim 6660; he was allowed $110. Although some time after slavery, Nate Shaw's attachment to and uses of the horses and mules with which he came into contact sheds light on the important role these creatures played in the world of the slave. See Theodore Rosengarten, *All God's Children: The Life of Nate Shaw* (London: Jonathan Cape, 1975), 113, 450, and passim.

78. Testimony of Benjamin Tyson and Julia Speakes, SCC Claim 8019, for which he was allowed $210; Testimony of Nero Williams and Pierson Peeples, SCC Claim 5678, for which he was allowed $150.

79. Testimony of Harriet Smith, SCC Claim 10087; she was allowed $106.

80. Testimony of Mooney Sinclair and Pierson Peeples, SCC Claim 5674; he was allowed $70.

81. Testimony of Jane Ruth, Joseph Rozier, and Adam Ruth, SCC Claim 8016; he was allowed $47.50.

82. United States Census figures for 1850 and 1860. See J. D. B. De Bow, *The Statistical View of the United States: Compendium of the Seventh Census* (Washington, D.C.: Beverly Tucker, 1854); Kennedy, *Population of the United States*.

83. Testimony of Alexander Quick, SCC Claim 4084.

84. Testimony of Emily Bass and Silas Cook, SCC Claim 591; $93.80 was allowed.

85. Testimony of William Cook, SCC Claim 591; he was allowed $93.80. See also Moore, "South Carolina and the Southern Claims Commission," 184.

86. Testimony of Pompey Lewis, SCC Claim 882; he was allowed $40.

87. Testimony of Priscilla Prince, SCC Claim 268; she was allowed $60.

88. The Introduction and chapters by Roderick A. McDonald, John T. Schlotterbeck, and John Campbell in *The Slaves' Economy*, ed. Berlin and Morgan, should further alert us to these crucial aspects of slave life.

89. Henry Ryan in *The American Slave*, pt. 4, 71; Sylvia Cannon, ibid., pt. 1, 185.

90. Benjamin Russell, ibid., pt. 4, 51.

91. Richard Jones, ibid., pt. 3, 66.

Chapter Two. For Richer for Poorer: The Family as an Economic Unit

1. See Genovese, *Roll, Jordan, Roll*, 311. Charles Joyner suggests that slaves in All Saints Parish successfully imposed a cooperative work ethos, adapted the master's labor system to their own sense of appropriateness, and "imposed a group consciousness on their field work" (*Down by the Riverside*, 58–59). Norrece Jones believes masters deliberately used the task system to "hamper the annoyingly cooperative spirit among the enslaved" (*Born a Child of Freedom*, 104). For recent discussions of slave owners' willingness to use violence in their slave management strategies, see ibid., and William Dusinberre, *"Them Dark Days": Slavery in the American Rice Swamps* (New York: Oxford University Press, 1995).

2. Testimony of the two David Harveys, SCC Claim 8003; he was allowed $153.50. See also Moore, "South Carolina and the Southern Claims Commission." On the work of the elderly in slave provision grounds, see Roderick A. McDonald, *The Economy and Material Culture of Slaves*, 50–51.

3. Testimony of Silas Cook and Emily Bass, SCC Claim 591, for which $93.80 was allowed; Moore, "South Carolina and the Southern Claims Commission," 184. For a brief discussion of the important contribution of aged family members

to the family economy see McDonald, *The Economy and Material Culture of Slaves*, 51, 147–48.

4. Margaret Hughes in *The American Slave*, pt. 2, 327, 328; Jessie Williams, ibid., pt. 4, 202; Henry Gladney, ibid., pt. 2, 129.

5. Testimony of Peter Stanton, SCC Claim 892; Sylvia Cannon in *The American Slave*, pt. 4, 219, pt. 1, 185–91.

6. Ball, *Fifty Years in Chains*, 275. Of course, the argument that slaves preferred to "marry off" so as not to be around when their spouses were punished or mistreated would weaken this argument: able-bodied slaves—those best able to master the tasks assigned—would probably not have complained about working alongside equally able workers who happened to be family members and (perhaps) more reliable.

7. J. O. Willson Plantation Book, SCL, entry for March 21, 1844.

8. Gramling Plantation Journal, entry for April 22, 1842; Henry Ryan in *The American Slave*, pt. 4, 72.

9. Ball, *Fifty Years in Chains*, 272.

10. The number designations used by Willson generally reflected the seniority of family heads by age.

11. Willson Plantation Book. See slave accounts for October and December 1847.

12. In 1844, Willson had planted a total of 205 acres—115 in corn, 82 in cotton, 5.5 in peas, and 3 in rice. In 1849, his cotton production brought him $1,539.83. This income was supplemented by $975 earned from hiring out some of his slaves.

13. Ball, *Fifty Years in Chains*, 166, 187, 272.

14. Edwards, *History*, 2:163.

15. Mintz, *Caribbean Transformations*, 207.

16. Much of this is speculation and difficult to support with hard evidence. Clearly, if masters chose to leave these arrangements with family members, they would not have found it necessary to record the transfer of what to them would have constituted small pieces of property. There is, however, evidence for South Carolina (and elsewhere) that slaves were able to pass on their property to next of kin—one example being the Draytons of Beaufort. See testimony of William Izzard, SCC Claim 10096, and that of E. Brown, Claim 21768. See also Ira Berlin, Barbara J. Fields, Thavolia Glymph, Joseph P. Reidy, and Leslie S. Rowland, *Freedom: A Documentary History of Emancipation, 1861–1867*, Ser. 1, Vol. 1 (Cambridge: Cambridge University Press, 1985), 140–41.

17. A similar situation may have existed for some of the Gramling slaves discussed below.

18. This family provides an example of slave families who would have had a special need to "marry well," that is, to unite with an economically strong family. Had Simon and Tirah's daughters married men who were unable to provide the much needed extras, Family Number 6 might have found itself completely dependent on the master and others in the quarters.

19. Thomas Cassels Law Papers, 1811–88, SCL. See his Planting Book for 1841–42, January 12, 1841.

20. Law's Negro Book, 1859. For cotton prices see Smith, *Economic Readjustment of an Old Cotton State*, 220–23. One study of South Carolina planters suggests that slaves would have received a higher price for their goods from the factor in Charleston than they actually received from the planter or local merchant even after deducting the expenses the slave was likely to have incurred for transport, insurance, and so on in dealing directly with the factor. See Campbell, "As 'A Kind of Freeman'?," 144–45.

21. Law's Negro Book, 1859.

22. Unless date of marriage is confirmed, it will be assumed that some kind of a marriage agreement was entered into around the time of the birth of the first child. See discussion of marriage ceremonies in Chapter 4.

23. Clifton, "Rice Driver," 336; see the section headed "Slave Drivers: The Case of Robert" in Rosengarten, *Tombee*, 162–64. See also the observation of former slave Sam Mitchell that "Maussa would sometime tek field hand and mek him driver and put driver in field" in *The American Slave*, pt. 3, 201. Discussing an earlier period, Philip Morgan suggests that drivers "might even have had a hand in appointing their fellow drivers." See "Black Society in the Lowcountry, 1760–1810," in *Slavery and Freedom in the Age of the Revolution*, ed. Ira Berlin and Ronald Hoffman (Charlottesville: University Press of Virginia, 1983), 118.

24. Ball, *Fifty Years in Chains*, 215.

25. Letter to William Winningham, March 22, 1855, Harriott Pinckney Letters, SCL.

26. See Law's Negro Book, 1859.

27. Ball, *Fifty Years in Chains*, 194.

28. Of course, Serena may have successfully practiced some form of birth control. Slave women were aware of a variety of ways of avoiding pregnancy and childbirth. See Gutman, *Black Family*, 80–82; Sally McMillen, *Motherhood in the Old South: Pregnancy, Childbirth, and Infant Rearing* (Baton Rouge: Louisiana State University Press, 1990).

29. Law's Negro Book, 1859. On the quality of Charlotte's land and assistance she might have received from her young children, two references from Charles Ball may be pertinent. Slave gardens, suggests Ball, were usually found "in some

remote and unprofitable part of the estate, generally in the woods" (*Fifty Years in Chains*, 166). He also states: "When the weather was mild and pleasant, some of the children, who were not required to go to the field, to do a days work, would go out, in the warmest part of the day, and pick a few pounds of cotton, for which their parents received pay" (ibid., 272).

30. See White, *"Ar'n't I a Woman?"*, 99–100.

31. Keziah Goodwyn Hopkins Brevard Diary, SCL, entries for July 22, October 10, 1860, April 13, 1861. See also John Hammond Moore, ed., *A Plantation Mistress on the Eve of the Civil War: The Diary of Keziah Goodwyn Hopkins Brevard, 1860–1861* (Columbia: University of South Carolina Press, 1993).

32. Brevard Diary, February 5, 1861, November 10, December 23, 1860, January 23, 1861.

33. Brevard Diary, March 10, 18, 1861, December 8, 1860, January 3, 1861.

34. Ibid., February 3, 1861.

35. In their study of African slavery, Suzanne Miers and Igor Kopytoff identified a crucial difference when comparing African with New World slavery. As they point out: "In African societies 'freedom' lay not in a withdrawal into a meaningless and dangerous autonomy, but in attachment to a kin group, to a patron, to power. . . . It was in this direction that the acquired outsider had to move if he was to reduce his initial marginality." See Miers and Kopytoff, eds., *Slavery in Africa: Historical and Anthropological Perspectives* (Madison: University of Wisconsin Press, 1977), 17.

36. Case 82, January 15, 1847, Spartanburg Magistrates and Freeholders Court Trial Papers, State Archives, Columbia, South Carolina.

37. John W. Blassingame contends: "However much personal gratification a bondsman obtained from a job, occupations translated into high social standing in the [slaves' world] only if they combined some of the following features: (1) mobility, which allowed the slave to leave the plantation frequently, (2) freedom from constant supervision from whites, (3) opportunity to earn money and (4) provision of direct a service to other blacks" ("Status and Social Structure," 142).

38. Of course, family forms differ from society to society; the slave family, with only a few exceptions, has been presented, on the one hand, as an imitation of white families from which they drew their models, and on the other, as loosely organized, usually female-headed structures. The more economic responsibility that accrued to slave families the more they would have developed something approximating corporate families functioning in communities where the generations were increasingly tied together by economic bonds. This, as Geoffrey Hurd points out, was usually the case in agricultural economies with peasant cultivation where family landholding and the need for organized cooperation hold the generations

together around economic production and consumption. With certain important qualifications, the work and garden system created situations not dissimilar to those described by Hurd. See his *Human Societies: An Introduction to Sociology* (London: Routledge & Kegan Paul, 1977), 81.

39. The relative disadvantage of the poorer, disease-producing environment, offsetting the benefits of the regions' widespread use of the task system, may well have reduced any overt discrepancies in the overall quality of life in low- and up-country slave quarters. See discussion in Chapter 3.

40. Sam, perhaps with better understanding of the work system under slavery, recalled, as did many other former slaves interviewed in the 1930s who had been young children under slavery, that his father "had to do his work at night 'cause in day time he have to do his task." Reports from people who were children under slavery that their parents worked all day from "sun to sun" probably made no distinction between work for the master and that for the slaves. See Sam Mitchell in *The American Slave*, pt. 3, 200.

41. Sam Polite, ibid., 271–76; see also Paul D. Escott, "The Art and Science of Reading WPA Slave Narratives," in *The Slave Narratives*, ed. Charles T. Davis and Henry Louis Gates Jr. (New York: Oxford University Press, 1985), 41.

42. Aunt Margaret Bryant in *The American Slave*, pt. 1, 147; Henry Brown, ibid., 124; Sabe Rutlege, ibid., pt. 4, 67, 68. Such stories of slave life (usually without Rutlege's embellishments) are often used to present the harshest side of slavery. The absence of any discussion as to why or for whom the slaves were working results in an incomplete representation of their working life. We need to be sure that the Rutlege family members were working for themselves and whether their nocturnal activities did indeed reflect a high level of family industry, enterprise, and education, or only the more common picture of gross exploitation. These busy times constituted a major part of the slaves' "offtimes" and were used to cement family relations and to socialize as well as train young children, effecting the "transmission of cultural patterns from generation to generation." See Joyner, *Down by the Riverside*, 50–57 and 128.

43. Gramling would easily qualify for inclusion in Jayne Morris-Crowther's sample of substantial slaveholders. See her "Economic Study of the Substantial Slaveholders of Orangeburg County," 296–97.

44. Morgan, "Ownership of Property by Slaves," 401.

45. Gramling Plantation Journal, entry for April 22, 1842.

46. Ibid., March 1846.

47. See Negro cotton accounts for the relevant years, ibid.

48. The few references to the slaves' food allowance suggest that the Gramling

slaves were fairly well looked after in this respect. Distributed among thirty slaves on November 5, 1847, were fourteen bushels of corn, which constituted "half allowance till November 15." Gramling had the "other half [of] corn and just about 15 or 20 bushels in the potato house for the children" (Gramling Plantation Journal, entry for Friday, November 5, 1847). See Chapter 3 below for further discussion of slave allowances. See also Loren Schweninger, "Slave Independence and Enterprise in South Carolina, 1780–1865," *South Carolina Historical Magazine* 93 (1992): 101–25.

49. Nehemiah Adams may have overstated the position of women on antebellum plantations when he referred to the "annihilation . . . of the father in the domestic relations of slaves" (quoted in Willie Lee Rose, *Rehearsal for Reconstruction: The Port Royal Experiment* [New York: Vintage Books, 1964], 137). Closer to the mark may have been the "complementarity of roles" position favored by Deborah White in *"Ar'n't I a Woman?"*, 158.

50. Gramling Plantation Journal, entries for November 8, 1847, April 27, 1848, October 6, 1847, March 30, 1851.

51. James D. Trezevant Plantation Diary, 1845–58, SCL. See entry for March 9, 1846.

52. The 1,206 farms in Beaufort District in 1850 held an average of 34 head of sheep. Figures are from 1850 Census of the United States. See also Trezevant Plantation Diary, May 5, 1849.

53. In 1860, Trezevant's slave force totaled thirty-nine slaves. See the 1860 Slave Schedules in the 1860 Census for the United States.

54. Trezevant Plantation Diary. See Listing of Hands for January 1851 and Slave Earnings, no date.

55. Catherine Clinton, *The Plantation Mistress: Woman's World in the Old South* (New York: Pantheon Books, 1982), 40 and passim; Anne Firor Scott, *The Southern Lady: From Pedestal to Politics, 1830–1930* (Chicago: University of Chicago Press, 1970), esp. chap. 1. See also White, *"Ar'n't I a Woman?"*, 158, on complementary roles. Slave masters sometimes imposed their own notions of patriarchy and male dominance on their slaves. See Genovese, *Roll, Jordan, Roll*, 489–93.

56. Connors Plantation Journal, entry for July 16, 1841.

57. Ibid., entries for July 27, August 10, 11, and 12, 1841. Some low-country slaves completed two tasks in one day and had the next day as a holiday. This practice was used on the Connors plantation. See also Joyner, *Down by the Riverside*, 51.

58. Connors Plantation Journal, entries for August 4 and 18, 1842.

59. Ibid., September 6, 10, 29, and October 2, 1842.

60. Witherspoon Family Plantation Record Book, 1839–54, SCL, entry for November 1852.

61. Joyner, *Down by the Riverside*, 51.

62. Ball, *Fifty Years in Chains*, 212, 217.

63. See List of Cotton picked in the Witherspoon Family Plantation Record Book; Jessie Williams in *The American Slave*, pt. 4, 202.

64. T. C. Means Cotton Book for 1858 and Slave Accounts for 1860 in the Mary Hart Means Papers, SCL.

65. For an extensive discussion of the efforts made by slaves in Louisiana to organize into families, their "intense familial attachments," and the "persistent urge within a fragmented slave community to reunite or rebuild despite the pain associated with such efforts and adjustments," see Malone, *Sweet Chariot*, quotes from pages 2–3.

Chapter Three. In Sickness and in Health: Disease, Death, and Family Disruption

1. The impact of sales, gifts, and estate division on family stability will be discussed in Chapter 4.

2. Cheryll Ann Cody, "Slave Demography and Family Formation: A Community Study of the Ball Plantations, 1720–1896" (Ph.D. diss., University of Minnesota, 1982), 241–42.

3. Amos Gadsden in *The American Slave*, pt. 2, 91–92; Maria Jenkins, ibid., pt. 3, 27.

4. Louisa Gause, ibid., pt. 2, 107–9.

5. Dolly Haynes, ibid., 29. See the discussion below of the difficult process slaves had to undergo if they were to find suitable marriage partners.

6. See Cody, "Slave Demography and Family Formation."

7. Elias Dawkins in *The American Slave*, pt. 1, 315; Bill McNeil, ibid., pt. 3, 164.

8. Paul D. Escott, *Slavery Remembered: A Record of Twentieth-Century Slave Narratives* (Chapel Hill: University of North Carolina Press, 1979), 48.

9. Jacob Rhett Motte Letters and Papers, 1743–1902, Duke University Library, Durham, North Carolina. Exeter was similar to frontier plantations in that it was in what Herbert Gutman termed the first phase of settlement; the owner was likely to be young, and his primary aim was to construct a labor force through gift, purchase, or marriage. As Gutman pointed out, the effect on slaves was likely to be traumatic because it most certainly meant the destruction of earlier kin networks. The second phase was characterized by stabilization and reproduction of the labor force and the third phase by the death of the owner and dispersal of the labor force. See Gutman, *Black Family*, 138. Ann Patton Malone, in *Sweet Chariot*, uses this

framework as a starting point in her investigation of the part played by Louisiana slaves in the process of organizing and reorganizing themselves into families, households, and communities.

10. Elizabeth Hyde Botume, *First Days Amongst the Contrabands* (1893; rpt. New York: Arno Press and the New York Times, 1968), 155. For additional examples of slaves marrying for utilitarian reasons see White, *"Ar'n't I a Woman?"*, 150–51, and Chapter 4 below.

11. Botume, *First Days Amongst the Contrabands*, 155.

12. Motte plantation records for the 1840s and 1850s.

13. For information on the importance of the extra nutrients required during pregnancy, the importance for the future general health of children, and extras needed during illness, see Richard H. Steckel, "A Peculiar Population: The Nutrition, Health and Mortality of American Slaves from Childhood to Maturity," *Journal of Economic History* 46 (1986): 721–41.

14. Willson Plantation Book.

15. Fripp Slave Record, 1804–1860, in John Edwin Fripp Family Papers, SHC, entry for July 7, 1857.

16. Ibid., McMillen, *Motherhood in the Old South*, 34–36, 106.

17. Fripp Slave Record, entries for April 23, 1857, and January 11–16, 1858.

18. Antebellum medical wisdom tended toward the practice of keeping pregnant women as active as possible. The committee report from the Louisiana State Medical Society, for example, concluded that "those females who take most exercise . . . produce the most vigorous and healthy children" (quoted in McMillen, *Motherhood in the Old South*, 36). See also Leslie Howard Owens, *This Species of Property: Slave Life and Culture in the Old South* (New York: Oxford University Press, 1978), 40; see also the brief account of Dr. Turnipseed by Henry Jenkins in *The American Slave*, pt. 3, 24.

19. Fripp Slave Record, entries for April 22 and February 22, 1858.

20. Women whose workloads were lightened were more likely to have surviving infants, but, as one scholar calculates, "the infants with the best chance of surviving were those whose mothers were older, [and who] experienced a substantial lessening of their work in the field during the first trimester" (John Campbell, "Work, Pregnancy, and Infant Mortality Among Southern Slaves," *Journal of Interdisciplinary History* 14 [1984]: 808, 809).

21. Fripp Slave Record, entries for April 10, July 7, 1858.

22. See Campbell, "Work, Pregnancy, and Infant Mortality Among Southern Slaves," 806.

23. Susan Hamlin in *The American Slave*, pt. 2, 236.

24. Owens, *This Species of Property*, 32.

25. Henry Jenkins in *The American Slave*, pt. 3, 24; Andrew Flinn, "Rules for the Plantation, 1840," in Flinn Plantation Records, SCL.

26. Owens, *This Species of Property*, 40–41.

27. Ryer Emmanuel in *The American Slave*, pt. 2, 12–13; Gracie Gibson, ibid., 213–14.

28. Adeline Jackson, ibid., pt. 3, 3; Connors Plantation Journal, entry for August 30, 1841.

29. Fripp Slave Record, entries for May 16, June 9, December 11, 29, 1857.

30. Todd L. Savitt, *Medicine and Slavery: The Diseases and Health Care of Blacks in Antebellum Virginia* (Urbana: University of Illinois Press, 1978), chap. 1. McMillen writes: "In the ... South, the ambitious approach of the physicians was no safer, no less painful, and no more sensible than the ways of the midwives. Parturient women who used midwives may even have had a better survival rate, because attendants who did not examine their patients and who shrank from intrusions upon the natural process were less likely to expose women to infection" (*Motherhood in the Old South*, 93). This is not to say that slaves in general and parturient slave women were safe from the practices of the slave midwives whose sanitary techniques were not always sound. For example, one "vicious practice ... was the use of cobwebs on the stump of the umbilical cord just after it had been cut." The cobwebs were used to stop the flow of blood from the cut area, but the tetanus germ could be introduced from the cobwebs (usually collected from stable walls) into the navel, causing convulsions after about nine days—popularly known as the "nine-day fit." See Vennie Deas-Moore, "Medical Adaptions of a Culture Relocated from Africa to the Sea Islands of South Carolina," *The World & I* 2 (1987): 482. See below for further discussion of slaves' control of their own health.

31. Richard Brockington and Mary H. Brockington Slave Journal, in P. S. Bacot Family Papers, SCL. Subsequent quotations and figures are from this source.

32. Law Papers, Account Book, 1830–79.

33. Gramling Plantation Journal, entries for March 30, 1851, and October 14, 1847. As one scholar points out, "Despite the availability ... of an easy preventive [smallpox flared up occasionally among slaves and planters]. Following such an occurrence, planters winced a bit and usually vowed anew to have every member of their household, black and white, vaccinated, but they rarely did" (Owens, *This Species of Property*, 32–33, 37).

34. Gramling Plantation Journal, entries for October 31, November 27, 1850, January 21, 1851, January 2, 1852.

35. Connors Plantation Journal, entries for July 14, August 26, 28, 10, 12, September 13, 21, 1841.

36. Owens, *This Species of Property*, 40–41.

37. Ibid., 32–33, on the benefit of rest and on slaves being rushed back to work.

38. George Washington to General Alex Spotswood, Epigraph, ibid. The fewer slaves masters owned, the larger a proportion of the masters' capital each would constitute. At one extreme, masters with a large number of slaves might have tended toward disinterest or indifference regarding their slaves' health, which would have rebounded badly on the slave, whereas poorer masters who had all their capital invested in a slave or two might be more determined to recover their costs quickly and make a profit, which again could have rebounded badly on the slave.

39. David Gavin Diary, 1855–73, SHC.

40. Phillips, *American Negro Slavery*, 301.

41. "Because of the scarcity of doctors, planters relied increasingly on themselves and on any number of medically oriented bondsmen" (Owens, *This Species of Property*, 34).

42. Joe Rutherford in *The American Slave*, pt. 4, 56; Sam Polite, ibid., pt. 3, 273.

43. Deas-Moore, "Medical Adaptions," 482.

44. Joyner, *Down by the Riverside*, 205–6; Peter H. Wood, *Black Majority: Negroes in Colonial South Carolina from 1640 Through to the Stono Rebellion* (New York: Norton, 1974), 131–66; Margaret Washington Creel, *"A Peculiar People": Slave Religion and Community Among the Gullahs* (New York: New York University Press, 1988), chap. 1.

45. Joyner, *Down by the Riverside*, 148.

46. The newborn was regarded as not being of this world until nine days had passed. A slave midwife told Matthew Lewis, "Oh massa, till nine days over, me no hope for them." See entry for January 13, 1816, in M. G. Lewis, *Journal of a West Indian Proprietor, 1815–17* (1845; rpt. New York: Houghton Mifflin, 1929), 87. In her account of the Ga people Margaret J. Field found that if the child died before nine days, "it is considered as having never been born and has no name" (*Religion and Medicine of the Ga People* [London: Oxford University Press, 1937], 173). Thus, as Edward Brathwaite points out, this slave custom has a living connection with rituals of birth in West Africa (*Folk Culture of the Slaves in Jamaica* [London: New Beacon Books, 1970], 5).

47. Gracie Gibson in *The American Slave*, pt. 2, 213–14. Long after slavery Deas-Moore's mother had her wear "as a precaution . . . little sacks of 'asphitti' around our necks in the belief [handed down from her great-grandmother] that inhaling the odor would prevent our catching a cold" ("Medical Adaptions," 481).

48. For one notable exception see Gramling Plantation Journal, entry for March 30, 1851; see also Owens, *This Species of Property*, 32–33.

49. Margaret Hughes in *The American Slave*, pt. 2, 329; Henry Ryan, ibid., pt. 4, 73.

50. Victoria Adams in *The American Slave*, pt. 1, 12.

51. In 1823, John Lance and William Ellerbe, two doctors in the up-country district of Chesterfield, announced that they had opened a hospital in Cheraw for sick Negroes. Noting that in many cases on plantations the distance from a physician was prohibitive, they offered to provide nursing care and a proper diet for one dollar per day with an additional fee for operations (*Cheraw Intelligencer and Southern Register*, quoted in Suzanne C. Linder, "Pioneer Physicians in Marlboro County, 1760–1824," *South Carolina Historical Magazine* 81 [1980]: 242).

52. Millie Barber in *The American Slave*, pt. 1, 38–39; Susan Hamlin, ibid., pt. 2, 236.

53. McMillen, *Motherhood in the Old South*, 28.

54. George Fleming in *The American Slave*, Supplement 11, 130.

55. Owens, *This Species of Property*, 35; Deas-Moore, "Medical Adaptions," 482; Fripp Slave Record, entries for April 22, 1857, January 16, 1858, November 25, 1857.

56. Gus Feaster in *The American Slave*, pt. 2, 55.

57. Solomon Caldwell, ibid., pt. 1, 171; Lucinda Miller, ibid., pt. 3, 191–92.

58. Granny Cain, ibid., pt. 1, 167.

59. The experience of house and field slaves differed markedly, contends John Blassingame, the position of house servant being "rejected by all blacks who had not been trained for it since childhood" because such servants were "taught by the planter that they were superior to other blacks," ("Status and Social Structure," 139).

60. Lila Rutherford in *The American Slave*, pt. 4, 57–58; Granny Cain, ibid., pt. 1, 168. See William Ballard's account of his master's son, who was a physician, ibid., pt. 1, 26–27.

61. Ellen Swindler, ibid., pt. 4, 82; Mary Veals, ibid., pt. 4, 156; Mary Johnson, ibid., pt. 3, 57; Emoline Wilson, ibid., pt. 4, 213.

62. Milton Marshall, ibid., pt. 3, 172–75; Wallace Davis, ibid., pt. 1, 305; John Davenport, ibid., 241.

63. George Briggs, ibid., pt. 1, 81.

64. Two students of slave medicine suggest that because "many bondsmen had little faith in white doctors but much in black practitioners, they were likely to be more effective . . . much of the faith derived from the comfort given a slave by one of his fellows as opposed to a too austere aloof white, convinced not only of his own superiority but of black inferiority as well." They also point out that "even if few slave remedies actually cured, they did not kill, which is better than sometimes

can be said for heroic white medicine" (Kenneth F. Kiple and Virginia Himmel-steib King, *Another Dimension to the Black Diaspora: Diet, Disease, and Racism* [Cambridge: Cambridge University Press, 1981], 170). A good example of the practice of spirit or faith healing is captured in the following account by Thomas B. Chaplin, a Beaufort District planter. Chaplin had a severe distrust and intense dislike for "an old Negro doctor and fortune teller." In 1845, he assisted in the prosecution of Old Cuffy before a Magistrates and Freeholders Court in the hope that Cuffy would be sentenced to leave the parish; his fellow magistrates, however, decided otherwise. For the beating of another slave, Old Sancho, Cuffy was sentenced to receive thirty-five lashes, "which he took without a murmur." It seems that both Cuffy and Sancho were Negro doctors, which might have been the cause of the altercation between them. In February 1846, one Billy (who may have been white) came over from the mainland to bring his sister Nancey "to my old man Sancho to see if he, as a negro doctor can do anything for her. She is deranged" (Thomas B. Chaplin, Plantation Journal, South Carolina Historical Society, Charleston, South Carolina, entries for January 18, 1845, and February 1846).

65. See Kiple and King, *Another Dimension to the Black Diaspora*, 170.

66. David Golightly Harris Journal, in Harris Papers, SHC, entry for October 20, 1860.

67. Of course, the high costs of medicine may have proved prohibitive for some masters while others simply lacked faith in the medical profession and convinced themselves that they could do better.

68. Savitt, *Medicine and Slavery*, 69.

69. Ibid., 70; on young slaves' retarded development, see Steckel, "Peculiar Population," 725.

70. For discussions on the nutritional value of slave allowances see Genovese, *Roll, Jordan, Roll*, 62–63 and 603–5; Robert William Fogel and Stanley L. Engerman, *Time on the Cross* (Boston: Little, Brown, 1974), 1:109–15, who suggest that the "average daily diet of slaves was quite substantial" (113); Richard Sutch, "The Treatment Received by American Slaves: A Critical Review of the Evidence Presented in *Time on the Cross*," *Explorations in Economic History* 12 (1975): 335–438; Kenneth F. Kiple and Virginia H. Kiple, "Slave Child Mortality: Some Nutritional Answers to a Perennial Puzzle," *Journal of Social History* 10 (1977): 284–309; Owens, *This Species of Property*, chap. 3.

71. Kiple and Kiple, "Slave Child Mortality," 287, suggest that during the prenatal period the fetus will do its best to satisfy its own needs for minerals, even if the mother is deficient, by drawing on her skeletal stores.

72. Savitt, *Medicine and Slavery*, 91 and passim.

73. Sam Mitchell in *The American Slave*, pt. 3, 200.

74. Sam Polite, ibid., 272; John Campbell, "'My Constant Companion': Slaves and Their Dogs in the Antebellum South," in *Working Toward Freedom: Slave Society and Domestic Economy in the American South*, ed. Larry E. Hudson Jr. (Rochester: University of Rochester Press, 1994), 53–76.

75. Daphney Wright, ibid., pt. 4, 266–69.

76. Henry Brown, ibid., pt. 1, 119, 124.

77. Thomas Goodwater, ibid., pt. 2, 116–18.

78. Joe Rutherford, ibid., pt. 4, 55; Prince Smith, ibid., 117–8.

79. For an alternative interpretation see Jones, *Born a Child of Freedom*, chap. 3.

80. Several accounts among the claims before the Southern Claims Commission present pictures of slaves operating almost entirely independent of their masters and acquiring considerable property. See Claim 17033 wherein Mack Duff Williams of Charleston claimed goods in the value of $200; George Hollow, SCC Claim 15645, for which he was allowed $284; and F. Alonzo Jackson, SCC Claim 15646, who was allowed $250.

81. William Oliver in *The American Slave*, pt. 3, 218.

82. Peggy Grigsby, ibid., pt. 2, 215. See the discussion of fence laws in Steven Hahn, *The Roots of Southern Populism: Yeoman Farmers and the Transformation of the Georgia Upcountry, 1850–1890* (New York: Oxford University Press, 1983).

83. Henry Ryan in *The American Slave*, pt. 4, 71.

84. Mom Sara Brown, ibid., pt. 1, 138.

85. Sylvia Cannon, ibid., pt. 1, 180–85.

86. Washington Dozier, ibid., 330–31.

87. Charlie Grant, ibid., pt. 2, 171–72.

88. Peter Clifton, ibid., pt. 1, 205.

89. See Owens, *This Species of Property*, 55–56; Joyner, *Down by the Riverside*, chap. 3; Genovese, *Roll, Jordan, Roll*, 540–45.

90. Walter Long in *The American Slave*, pt. 3, 118. For differing opinions among masters on food preparation see Breeden, ed., *Advice Among Masters*, 92, 107.

91. Sam Rawls in *The American Slave*, pt. 4, 5.

92. Hester Hunter, ibid., pt. 2, 339; Genovese, *Roll, Jordan, Roll*, 544–45; Louisa Collier in *The American Slave*, pt. 1, 218–20.

93. Hector Godbold in *The American Slave*, pt. 2, 143; Hester Hunter, ibid., 342; Genia Woodberry, ibid., pt. 4, 221.

94. Harmon in Breeden, ed., *Advice Among Masters*, 92.

95. A South Carolina planter writing in 1857, in Breeden, ed., *Advice Among Masters*, 107.

96. Hector Smith in *The American Slave*, pt. 4, 101–2.

97. Margaret Hughes, ibid., pt. 2, 327.

98. Dave White, ibid., pt. 4, 191–92.

99. Jane Johnson, ibid., pt. 3, 48–49.

100. Henry Jenkins, ibid., pt. 3, 23–25.

101. Jake McLeod, ibid., 157–58.

102. Genovese, *Roll, Jordan, Roll*, 623–25.

103. Benjamin Russell in *The American Slave*, pt. 4, 51.

104. William Ballard, ibid., pt. 1, 26–27. In contrast to the more arduous work required in growing sugar cane, rice, and cotton, the production of wheat as a staple (more usually associated with free white families in northern America) probably allowed the up-country slaves a physically less demanding work routine. For a discussion of the relationship between cotton and wheat production, see James R. Irwin, "Exploring the Affinity of Wheat and Slavery in the Virginia Piedmont," *Explorations in Economic History* 25 (1988): 295–322.

105. Millie Barber in *The American Slave*, pt. 1, 39; D. Cunningham, ibid., 235.

106. Caleb Craig, ibid., 229–30; Phillip Evans, ibid., pt. 2, 34–37; Andy Marion, ibid., pt. 3, 168.

107. Sena Moore, ibid., pt. 3, 209–10.

108. Gordon Bluford, ibid., pt. 1, 62; George Fleming, ibid., Supplement, Vol. 2, 129–34.

109. Milton Marshall, ibid., pt. 3, 172–74.

110. Victoria Perry, ibid., 260. For a case of a master being punished by the court for not adequately providing for his slaves, see State v. Bowen, May 1849, Strobart, 573, in Catterall, ed., *Judicial Cases Concerning American Slavery*, 2:573. On feeding slaves, see Fogel and Engerman, *Time on the Cross*, 109–15.

111. Madison Griffin in *The American Slave*, pt. 2, 212–13.

112. Lucinda Miller, ibid., pt. 3, 191–92.

113. Bouregard Corry in *The American Slave*, pt. 1, 227–28. Kiple and Kiple suggest that because of the high frequency of lactose intolerance—"occasioned by the absence of the lactose enzyme (an autosomal recessive trait) which metabolizes milk sugars into absorbable monosaccharides"—among black Americans of West African origin, most African Americans "discover sometime after infancy (all infants are lactose tolerant obviously, else none would live) that if they drink milk they can expect gastro intestinal complaints within thirty to ninety minutes; continued use brings on severe abdominal cramps, bloating and diarrhea." One obvious result would be that these slaves would have derived little calcium from milk. See "Slave Child Mortality," 284–309.

114. Gus Feaster in *The American Slave*, pt. 2, 43–56.

115. Breeden, ed., *Advice Among Masters*, 89.

116. Fripp Slave Record, entries for November 1857 and April 1858. A drum is a large river-bottom fish popular in the South.

117. The reasons why planters kept journals probably varied; it seems, however, that, like Thomas B. Chaplin, they all wanted a record of their "thoughts and observations, also any little occurrences that may take place . . . whether concerning the family or the plantation." This may have been Chaplin's initial intention, but within a few years the exercise had become far more self-conscious, moving from the opening "mirror-of-life phase" to a time when he thought he was "writing for his children as well as for future readers, an heirloom." See Rosengarten, *Tombee*, 190. Another planter, Dr. J. B. Witherspoon of Lancaster, stated in his journal that he proposed "to record the general occurrence of the plantation, the different kinds of work the Negroes are engaged at and such." The exercise would be self-indulgent: "I think," he wrote, "by keeping such a book it will make me more diligent in Business and I will perhaps learn more accuracy and punctuality besides this such a journal will be useful as a reference in after years." Witherspoon also hoped to maintain an "exact account of all expenditures of money." He concluded in the journal's opening paragraph, "This year I want to be exact, altruistic, diligent and industrious." The journal was begun on January 1, 1852, with clear, daily accounts of life on the plantation, but by January 20 daily accounts had ceased. An entry for January 20 and 21 began, "Same routine as yesterday," and the next was a brief summary of the previous three days. The tedium experienced by Dr. Witherspoon is all too clear; he concluded the journal with an entry for April 9 and 10, which read, "Hoe hands Ploughs & men engaged at the same work as yesterday." Only the most meticulous (or vain) planters would spend the time and energy to record one of the more routine plantation activities. See Witherspoon Family Plantation Record Book, 1839–54.

118. William E. Sparkman Plantation Diary, SHC, entries for March 1844 to February 1845.

119. John Berkeley Grimball Journal, in Grimball Papers, SHC, entries for March 1834 and April 1834.

120. Gavin Diary, entries for November 1855, April 1858, December 1860, and Gavin's record book. The term *self-esteem* describes the "self-view that a person has most of the time." See Darlene Powell Hopson and Dereck S. Hopson, *Different and Wonderful: Raising Black Children in a Race-Conscious Society* (New York: Prentice Hall, 1990), 34. For Michelle Moody-Adams self-respect—"due respect for ones' own worth"—has two fundamental components. The first involves the conviction that "one best affirms one's own value by using one's abilities and talents to contribute to one's survival." The second component "is a willingness to do what-

ever is in one's power to enhance or develop one's abilities and talents." Self-esteem, distinct from a sense of one's own worth or value, is the "confidence in one's life plan." See "Race, Class and the Social Construction of Self-Respect," *Philosophical Forum* 24 (1992): 252, 253.

121. Gramling Plantation Journal, entries for November 5, 1847, and April 1852.

122. Letters to William Winningham, February 8, March 22, and May 13, 1855, Harriott Pinckney Letters.

123. Brevard Diary, entries for December 1860, January 3, 1861.

124. Hammond, "Notes to Overseer," 24, Hammond Papers.

125. For a record of meat killed see J. D. Ashmore Plantation Journal, January 1854, Duke University Library, Durham, North Carolina.

126. On the slave owner's lack of attention to details regarding slave allowances, see Fogel and Engerman, *Time on the Cross*, 110.

Chapter Four. To Love and to Cherish: The Slave Family

1. Virginia Heyer Young describes "American Negro culture as an entity expressing itself in childrearing and family forms." See "Family and Childhood in a Southern Negro Community," *American Anthropologist* 72 (1970): 286.

2. See figures collected from the U.S. Census in Wallace, *South Carolina*, 708–9.

3. "Eligible" here refers to women aged between sixteen and forty and men aged between eighteen and fifty who wished to marry or remarry, have children, and live as a family group. Men or women already married and living in a family group are not eliminated from the sample. Nor does consanguinity disqualify them because all that is required is a guide to the maximum number of potential eligibles to be found in a given slave population.

4. Andy Marion in *The American Slave*, pt. 3, 167; and A. Broome, ibid., pt. 1, 104.

5. Sam Mitchell, in *The American Slave*, pt. 3, 201–2; *Southern Agriculturalist* 6 (June 1833), quoted in Breeden, ed., *Advice Among Masters*, 240.

6. Sam Polite in *The American Slave*, pt. 3, 271. See Escott, *Slavery Remembered*, 50–51. Unless there were some concrete advantages, it is doubtful that slaves would have willingly chosen to have two masters in their lives. Only 27.5 percent of the former slaves who reported marriages to the Works Progress Administration interviewers had married people who lived on different plantations. Sometimes there were benefits to be enjoyed by a slave whose spouse lived on a nearby plantation, in which case the slave could choose which plantation would constitute "home." Frank Davis, for example, who hired out as a carpenter, chose the comfort

of his wife's plantation and "made her house my home" (Testimony of Frank Davis, SCC Claim 10088, for which he was allowed $166). See also Moore, "South Carolina and the Southern Claims Commission."

7. George C. Rogers, *The History of Georgetown County, South Carolina* (Columbia: University of South Carolina Press, 1970).

8. R. F. W. Allston Family Papers, True Blue Plantation Journal, South Carolina Historical Society, Charleston; Lucinda Miller in *The American Slave*, pt. 3, 191–92; Rogers, *History of Georgetown County*, 265.

9. John W. Blassingame, *The Slave Community: Plantation Life in the Antebellum South* (New York: Oxford University Press, 1979), 164; Escott, *Slavery Remembered*, 50–51. A more recent study on the slave family in Louisiana is more circumspect on the troubling matter of "choice." See Malone, *Sweet Chariot*, 221–22; White, *"Ar'n't I a Woman?"*, 110; Carole Elaine Merritt, "Slave Family and Household Arrangements in Piedmont Georgia" (Ph.D. diss., Emory University, 1986), 131.

10. Some 19 percent of owners held more than one hundred slaves, and some 25 percent owned from ten to ninety-nine slaves. According to the 1850 census, there were some 382 owners of between 101 and 199 slaves (Wallace, *South Carolina*, 708).

11. Willson Plantation Book. Of course, the primary consideration for slaves enjoying any choice as to whom they married and where was available partners.

12. On the significance of naming practices and family structure see Cody, "Naming, Kinship and Estate Dispersal," 192–211; Gutman, *Black Family*, chap. 5.

13. The three phases parallel Herbert Gutman's cycle of slave family network destruction, construction, and dispersal. See Gutman, *Black Family*. For a recent discussion of this model see Cheryl Ann Cody, "Sale and Separation: Four Crises for Enslaved Women on the Ball Family Plantations, 1764–1865," in *Working Toward Freedom: Slave Society and Domestic Economy in the American South*, ed. Larry E. Hudson Jr. (Rochester: University of Rochester Press, 1994), 119–42.

14. Gutman suggested that the slaves on the South Carolina Good Hope plantation displayed the "strength and pervasiveness of slave exogamous beliefs." Although the evidence supporting any general commitment to this practice is weak, its existence would have further reduced the choice of partners available to eligibles in the second and particularly in the third stage of settlement. See Gutman, *Black Family*, 138, 88–95. The strongest support for the existence of this practice is probably Judge René Beauregard, who was quoted as saying: "Some planters strictly prohibited the marriage of cousins. Planters themselves would marry cousins but their negroes were too valuable to be permitted to degenerate" (V. Alton Moody, *Slavery on Louisiana Sugar Plantations* [1928; rpt. New York: AMS Press,

1976], 94ff.). Ann Patton Malone studied statistical information for Louisiana in her discussion of the slave family, household, and community structure. See *Sweet Chariot*, chap. 3. On the Good Hope plantation in 1835–56, twenty-eight percent of the slaves were related by blood. See Charles Wetherell, "Slave Kinship: A Case Study of the South Carolina Good Hope Plantation, 1835–1856," *Journal of Family History* 6 (1981): 294–308.

15. See Escott, *Slavery Remembered*, 50–51.

16. See, for example, the discussion in Blassingame, "Status and Social Structure," 137–51.

17. Susan Diane Toliver, in "The Black Family in Slavery, the Foundation of Afro-American Culture: Its Importance to Members of the Slave Community" (Ph.D. diss., University of California, Berkeley, 1982), divided families into the following groupings: simple nuclear: husband, wife, and children; incipient nuclear: husband and wife; attenuated nuclear: single parent and children; simple extended: husband, wife, children, and other relatives (101).

18. The Guignard slave list also provides the opportunity to assess the age at first birth for both mothers and fathers. Because ages are given rather than dates of birth and there is no information on slaves sold away, the calculation can serve only as a general guide. Modal age at first birth for this sample of slave women was twenty-two; men typically fathered their first child at age twenty-five. See Guignard Plantation Records, South Carolina Historical Society, Charleston.

19. Their names were linked in one of the slave accounts.

20. Based on his study of South Carolina Good Hope plantation records, Gutman concludes that "most children lived with two parents, and most adults lived in long-lasting marriages" (*Black Family*, 45). Another study found that on plantations in the Georgia piedmont "two parent households were not characteristic of small and moderate size slave holdings." And on holdings with twenty or fewer slaves, most children lived in single-parent households and the father was generally on a separate slaveholding (Merritt, "Slave Family," 6).

21. The recollections of up-country slaves such as Mary Johnson and her fellows reveal the contours of a part of the state where farms and small plantations rather than large plantations predominated. Farther removed from the dominating influence of large plantations and planters, slaveholding in the hinterland was less uniform than in the plantation belt. Indeed, over 80 percent of rural whites and over 45 percent of all slaves in the up-country lived on small or medium-sized farms rather than on plantations. Roughly 20 percent of these farms were operated by slaveholders who owned more than five but fewer than twenty slaves. See the discussion of the influence of Black Belt planters in Hahn, *Roots of Southern Populism*, chap. 1; also Lacey K. Ford, *Origins of Southern Radicalism: The*

South Carolina Upcountry, 1800–1860 (New York: Oxford University Press, 1988), chap. 2.

22. Frank Adamson in *The American Slave*, pt. 1, 14.

23. Louisa Davis, ibid., 300.

24. George Fleming, ibid., pt. 2, 127–36. Not all slaves would have welcomed the frequent frolics on or off the plantation for as Albert J. Raboteau writes, "To religious slaves, fiddling, dancing, and secular music were the devil's work" (*Slave Religion: The "Invisible Institution" in the Antebellum South* [New York: Oxford University Press, 1978], 222).

25. Caroline Farrow in *The American Slave*, pt. 2, 39. The practice was to wear a stiff white shirt bosom over the shirt and held up around the neck. When no shirt was worn, the bosom, worn alone, gave the appearance of a shirt and bosom.

26. This matter is linked with the work and garden system and the ability of slaves to earn cash from their efforts and is discussed by Hudson, "'All That Cash.'"

27. Elijah Green in *The American Slave*, pt. 2, 83; Gus Feaster, ibid., 47.

28. Gus Feaster, ibid., 61. E. Franklin Frazier argued that the slaves were stripped of their own culture but soon "learnt to reflect the social values which the white master class exemplified in their behavior" to support his claim that the structure of the slave family was influenced by their close proximity to white families. See "The Negro Slave Family," *Journal of Negro History* 15 (1930): 209.

29. Gabe Lockier in *The American Slave*, pt. 3, 115. The games played by young men and women during courtship were probably not dissimilar in Europe, Africa, and the United States. Gutman and Genovese both point out that slave courting rituals employed folk beliefs including popular riddles and language, as well as what might be considered conventional practices. See Genovese, *Roll, Jordan, Roll*, 470–72, on courting; Gutman, *Black Family*, 73–74, on slave as opposed to white courting practices. For a fuller discussion of the place of cornshucking in the slaves' world, see Roger D. Abrahams, *Singing the Master: The Emergence of African American Culture in the Plantation South* (New York: Pantheon Books, 1992), chaps. 1–2.

30. Gus Feaster in *The American Slave*, pt. 2, 51. The implication that the virtue of young slave women might have been compromised through the payment of small sums of money is all too clear.

31. Govan Littlejohn, ibid., pt. 3, 106. Joyner writes: "While other streams of African religion either converged or co-existed with Christianity, belief in magical shamanism—called voodoo or hoodoo in the New World—continued an underground existence outside of the Christian tradition." Conjuration, practiced in secret, was a part of this African religious legacy that informed the slaves' religious

practices. The conjurer or shaman "could be relied upon by their patrons both for protection and the relief from spells and for laying spells on their enemies." Thus "through sorcery" the conjurer could "cure an illness, kill an enemy, or secure someone's love" (*Down by the Riverside*, 142–50, quotes on pages 144 and 146). Raboteau suggests that "a rich tradition of folk belief and practices, including conjuring . . . flourished in the slave quarters." Many slaves "and whites as well, knew the world of conjure to be real because they had experienced its power" (*Slave Religion*, 275–76).

32. Gus Feaster in *The American Slave*, pt. 2, 47–52.

33. See George Frederick Holmes, Review of *Uncle Tom's Cabin*, in Eric L. McKitrick, ed., *Slavery Defended: The Views of the Old South* (Englewood Cliffs, N.J.: Prentice-Hall, 1963), 107 (Holmes's article was originally published in the *Southern Literary Messenger* 18 [December 1852]).

34. Jane Johnson in *The American Slave*, pt. 3, 49; Ben Horry, ibid., pt. 2, 304.

35. In some instances, conceded E. Franklin Frazier, "a sort of public opinion in the slave community had some effect on the significance of marriage bonds" (*Negro Family*, 30).

36. Benjamin Russell in *The American Slave*, pt. 4, 51.

37. Frazier, "Negro Slave Family," 220–21. Jumping the broom may have been the final act of a proper ceremony, as well as a ceremony in itself. Raboteau, *Slave Religion*, suggests that occasionally the broomstick ceremony was combined with the regular marriage rite at the slaves' request so that "they felt more married" (228–30). This part of the wedding ceremony may have proved the most memorable and therefore most frequently recalled by those who were children under slavery.

38. Faust, *James Henry Hammond*, 85.

39. Margaret Hughes in *The American Slave*, pt. 2, 329.

40. Testimony of Will Cook, SCC Claim 591.

41. Paul Escott writes, "In most cases it seems that the separation involved in marrying abroad only heightened the joy of those times spent together" (*Slavery Remembered*, 52).

42. Testimony of Priscilla Prince, SCC Claim 268.

43. Imagine the pleasure and joy felt by Lucinda Miller, her siblings, and her mother when the only "luxuries" they enjoyed under slavery were occasioned by her father's twice-weekly visits. Imagine her father's satisfaction in being able to bring such joy to his family. See Lucinda Miller in *The American Slave*, pt. 3, 192.

44. Caleb Craig in *The American Slave*, pt. 1, 231.

45. U.S. Census for 1850.

46. Louisa Davis in *The American Slave*, pt. 1, 300.

47. Millie Barber, ibid., 39.

48. Morgan Scurry, ibid., pt. 4, 89; Mary Veals, ibid., pt. 4, 167–68; Emoline Wilson, ibid., 214; Nellie Loyd, ibid., pt. 3, 128; Albert Means, ibid., 183–84.

49. See Gutman, *Black Family*, 290–92; and Genovese, *Roll, Jordan, Roll*, 472–73.

50. Proceedings of a Military Commission in the case of Moses "colored man," July 29–August 15, 1862, MM-2734, Court Martial Case Files, Ser. 15, RG 153, Freedmen and Society Project Papers, University of Maryland, College Park. Subsequent material on the trial is from this source.

51. James Henry Hammond was one planter who would have punished Maria and June for their infidelity. Hammond "acted as a family court judge and meted out whippings to those whose sexual infidelity had become disruptive to plantation order." Indeed, he recorded having "flogged Tom Kollock. . . . Gave him 30 with my own hand [for] interfering with Maggy Campbell, Sullivan's wife" (Faust, *James Henry Hammond*, 85).

52. The slaves' desperate need for family support, trust, and mutual sharing is the most cogent explanation for why slaves, as Malone points out, displayed "a persistent urge within a fragmented slave community to reunite or rebuild despite the pain associated with such efforts and adjustments." It also explains why the slaves Gutman studied were so keen to have their families around them following emancipation and why they rushed to have their slave unions (as legal to them as they could possibly be) legalized in the public world of their former masters within which they were now obliged to function. See Malone, *Sweet Chariot*, 2–3; Gutman, *Black Family*.

53. Some slaveholders argued that weak affectional ties between slave mothers and their children reduced the former's sense of loss when children were sold away, and even some objective commentators have expressed similar ideas. "There is less family feeling and attachment to each other than among the ignorant Irish," wrote one visitor to the Sea Islands in 1862. "Though I don't know how much allowance to make for their being so much less demonstrative in their emotions, and more inured to suffering," the writer conceded (Pearson, ed., *Letters from Port Royal*, 15). As Frederic Bancroft astutely pointed out, however, "Interested persons easily satisfied themselves that slaves were almost indifferent to separations" despite the "thousands of advertisements telling that runaways were supposed to have returned to their old homes or gone to kindred from whom they had been parted" (*Slave Trading in the Old South* [Baltimore: J. H. Furst, 1931], 206). E. Franklin Frazier, in concluding his chapter "Motherhood in Bondage," stated that "pregnancy and childbirth often meant only suffering for the slave mother who, because of her limited contacts with her young, never developed that attachment which grows out of physiological and emotional responses to its needs" (*Negro Family*, 49). More re-

cently, Bobby Frank Jones took a similar position in "A Cultural Middle Passage: Slave Marriage and the Family in the Antebellum South" (Ph.D. diss., University of North Carolina, Chapel Hill, 1965).

54. Charlie Davis in *The American Slave*, pt. 1, 252; John Collins, ibid., 225.

55. Henry Gladney, ibid., pt. 2, 129; Tom Rosoboro, ibid., pt. 4, 43–44.

56. Emanuel Elmore, ibid., pt. 2, 6–9.

57. For a discussion of slave owners' use of the threat of sale as a weapon in their war against the slaves, see Jones, *Born a Child of Freedom*, chap. 2 and passim. The exact number of marriages that were broken through sale is not known. Robert Fogel and Stanley Engerman suggest that no more than 13 percent of interregional slave sales resulted in marriage breakups (*Time on the Cross*, 49). Michael Tadman, in a more recent work that examines the impact of the interregional trade on slave marriages, writes that "when slaves married, most would not be separated by sale" and that the trade would have prematurely broken about 20 percent of upper South marriages. Families in the lower South, the region less affected by the trade because it was the net recipient of slaves, "could expect longer marriages and fewer forced interruptions. . . . Here, the risk of separation was about one third that faced by Upper South slaves" (*Speculators and Slaves: Masters, Traders, and Slaves in the Old South* [Madison: University of Wisconsin Press, 1989], 174). Throughout the slave South the marriage institution was normal and an expected rite of passage. Nevertheless, forced separations were sufficiently widespread that deep distrust of those who were primarily responsible for marriage breakup was endemic.

58. Susan Hamlin in *The American Slave*, pt. 2, 231–36; Sylvia Cannon, ibid., pt. 1, 180–84; Sylvia Chisholm, ibid., 199.

59. Peter Clifton, ibid., pt. 1, 206–7; Lizzie Davies, ibid., 293; Silva Durant, ibid., 339.

60. Samuel Boulware, ibid., 67.

61. George Fleming, ibid., pt. 2, 132; Isaiah Butler, ibid., pt. 1, 158.

62. Malone, *Sweet Chariot*, 2.

63. Motte Plantation Journal, 1845–65.

64. Chaplin Plantation Journal, entry for May 3, 1845; see also Rosengarten, *Tombee*.

65. Gracie Gibson in *The American Slave*, pt. 2, 113.

66. Jake McLeod, ibid., pt. 3, 157.

67. Isiah Jefferies, ibid., 17.

68. Millie Barber, ibid., pt. 1, 140; Caleb Craig, ibid., 230.

69. Savilla Burrell, ibid., 150.

70. Sena Moore, ibid., pt. 3, 209.

71. Bancroft, *Slave Trading in the Old South*, 78. Although "market forces, rather

than sentiment for family, were . . . always likely to predominate with slaveholders," as Michael Tadman suggests, sentiment as well as economic benefits could combine to encourage masters and traders alike to sell slaves in family groups, including the old, the very young, and the disabled as well as prime hands. Of course, traders working in areas where small slaveholders predominated would find it more difficult to trade slaves in family groups. See Tadman, *Speculators and Slaves*, 136–40.

72. Susan Hamlin recalled Clory, a washerwoman, who was afraid that she would fight with her mistress again and, not wanting to kill her mistress, "she begged to be sold." For her first attack she was whipped—"de worst I ebber see a human bein' got," Hamlin recalled. She recovered from the beating but "didn't get any better but meaner until our master [who "ain't nebber want to sell his slaves"] decide it was bes' to rent her out" (*The American Slave*, pt. 2, 234–35).

73. The term *household* is used to describe "a basic social unit in which people, whether voluntarily or under compulsion, pool their income and resources. As such, it has no necessary relation to family, although members of households may (and probably were in the case of the slaves) coterminous with family membership. In this sense, Charles Ball was a member of the household when he found himself living with a family of slaves. This usage of the term is particularly useful for the slave family because frequently 'strangers' were taken in and became members of what was necessarily "a unit with extensions." See Elizabeth Fox-Genovese, *Within the Plantation Household: Black and White Women in the South* (Chapel Hill: University of North Carolina Press, 1988), 31; Ball, *Fifty Years in Chains*; Owens, *This Species of Property*, 210.

74. Nancey Washington had to overcome obstacles to win her heart's desire. Her experiences as a slave in Marion District were a little out of the ordinary. Her master, Giles Evanson, "ne'er hab nuttin' but women colored peoples . . . say he ain' wan' no man colored peoples." When Nancey married at the age of about sixteen, "right there in my massa yard," she was an exception. She had married a man "offen uh rich man plantation" even though the Evansons "n'er wan me to marry." Both Nancey and Evanson might have been influenced because the slave in question was from a "rich man plantation"—a fact likely to dissolve a master's opposition to his slave marrying off the home place (Nancey Washington in *The American Slave*, pt. 4, 184).

Conclusion: To Have and to Hold

1. Magistrates and Freeholders Court Papers for Anderson District, Case 129, May 4, 1842, State Archives, Columbia, South Carolina.

2. Ibid. See Deborah Gray White's discussion of conjugal role relations in *"Ar'n't I a Woman?,"* 158.

3. In 1860 there were some 1,210 farms in the up-country districts with an average of 142 acres of improved land and 242 acres of unimproved land. In low-country Beaufort, there were 931 farms with 294 improved acres and 957 unimproved acres. See Smith, *Economic Readjustment of an Old Cotton State*, 81; Mary Jane Kelly in *The American Slave*, pt. 3, 89.

4. As Sharon Ann Holt writes, "Enslaved people must have struggled continually to separate doing for their loved ones from contributing to the profits of their oppressors" ("Symbol, Memory, and Service: Resistance and Family Formation in Nineteenth-Century African America," in *Working Toward Freedom: Slave Society and Domestic Economy in the American South*, Larry E. Hudson Jr., ed. [Rochester: University of Rochester Press, 1994], 204).

5. For a fuller discussion see Hudson, "'All That Cash,'" 192–210.

6. Even E. Franklin Frazier could concede that where husband and wife were permitted to cultivate patches as a means of supplying themselves with extra food or better clothing, cooperation for these common ends helped to strengthen the bonds between them. See Frazier, *Negro Family*, 30.

7. See discussion in Chapter 1.

8. Better-organized families probably contained a member or two who had the respect of the black as well as the white community. Masters hesitated "to punish respected slaves who could foment resistance among other slaves." If slaveholders were indeed able to prevent the law from "insulating slaves from their master's will," only well-organized and "economically sound" slave families could seriously hope "to provide that insulation themselves." See Edward L. Ayers, *Vengeance and Justice: Crime and Punishment in the Nineteenth-Century American South* (New York: Oxford University Press, 1984), 133, 135.

9. Frazier, *Negro Family*, 30. Because the marriage of one African affects his or her descent group so profoundly, the group is likely to take a much greater interest in the choice of a spouse and to exercise much more control and limitation upon the choice of a partner. These factors render African marriage much more group-oriented, than is Western marriage. As slave families became economically distinct, they may have reflected additional features of traditional African behavior. For example, the choice of a marriage partner became the subject of the economic and political needs of the group as poorer families sought to make kinship alliances with stronger and more economically powerful families. See William G. Blum, *Forms of Marriage: Monogamy Reconsidered* (Elaoret, Kenya: AMECEA Publications, 1989), 21.

10. See Tadman, *Speculators and Slaves*, 133–78. Slave traders were increasingly obliged to give at least lip service to slave owners who insisted that their slaves be kept in family units. As Kenneth M. Stampp writes, "They often purchased slaves in family groups and promised not to divide them. . . . They made these promises to win good will or to quiet the consciences of the sellers." See Stampp, *Peculiar Institution*. See also Anne Loveland, *Southern Evangelicals and the Social Order, 1800–1860* (Baton Rouge: Louisiana State University Press, 1980), 186–218.

Bibliography

Primary Sources

MANUSCRIPT COLLECTIONS

Duke University, William R. Perkins Library, Durham, North Carolina
J. D. Ashmore Plantation Journal, 1853–54.
Daniel W. Jordan Papers.
Jacob Rhett Motte Letters and Papers.

University of Maryland, College Park, Maryland
Proceedings of a Military Commission in the case of Moses "colored man," July 29–August 15, 1862, MM-2734, Court Martial Case Files, Ser. 15 RG 153, Freedmen and Society Project Papers.

National Archives, Washington, D.C.
Slave Schedules. In the Seventh and Eighth Censuses of the United States, 1850 and 1860.
Records of the Southern Claims Commission. Record Group 217 (General Accounting Office, Third Auditors Office), Boxes 236 to 244.

South Carolina Historical Society, Charleston, South Carolina
R. F. W. Allston and Family Papers, True Blue Plantation Journal.
Ball Family Papers.
Thomas B. Chaplin Plantation Journal.
Cheves Middleton Papers.

South Carolina State Department of Archives and History, Columbia, South Carolina
John Hammond Moore. "South Carolina and the Southern Claims Commission, 1871–1880.
Magistrates and Freeholders Court Trial Papers.

219

University of North Carolina, Southern Historical Collection, Chapel Hill, North Carolina
John DeSaussure Plantation Book.
John Edwin Fripp Family Papers.
David Gavin Diary.
John Berkeley Grimball Papers.
David Golightly Harris Papers.
Alexander J. Lawton Plantation Diary.
Manigault Family Papers.
Ben Sparkman Plantation Records.
William E. Sparkman Plantation Diary.

University of South Carolina, South Caroliniana Library, Columbia, South Carolina.
Brockington Slave Journal in P. S. Bacot Family Papers.
Keziah Goodwyn Hopkins Brevard Diary.
William J. Connors Plantation Journal.
Andrew Flinn, "Rules for the Plantation," in A. Flinn Plantation Records.
Michael Gramling Plantation Journal.
James Henry Hammond Plantation Journal.
Thomas Cassels Law Papers.
Guignard Family Records.
Mary Hart Means Papers.
Miller-Furman-Dabbs Family Papers.
Harriott Pinckney Letters.
James D. Trezevant Plantation Diary.
J. O. Willson Plantation Book.
Witherspoon Family Plantation Record Book in Witherspoon Family Papers.

PUBLISHED SOURCES

Ball, Charles. *Fifty Years in Chains*. 1837. Reprint. New York: Dover, 1970.
Berlin, Ira, Barbara J. Fields, Steven F. Miller, Joseph P. Reidy, and Leslie S. Rowland, eds. *Free at Last: A Documentary History of Slavery, Freedom, and the Civil War*. New York: New Press, 1992.
Berlin, Ira, Barbara J. Fields, Thavolia Glymph, Joseph P. Reidy, and Leslie S. Rowland, eds. *Freedom: A Documentary History of Emancipation, 1861–1867*, Ser. 1, Vols. 1, 111. Cambridge: Cambridge University Press, 1985, 1990.
Blassingame, John W., ed. *Slave Testimony: Two Centuries of Letters, Speeches, Interviews, and Autobiographies*. Baton Rouge: Louisiana State University Press, 1977.

Bibliography

Botkin, B. A. *Lay My Burden Down: A Folk History of Slavery*. Athens: University of Georgia Press, 1989.

Botume, Elizabeth Hyde. *First Days Amongst the Contrabands*. 1893. Reprint. New York: Arno Press and the New York Times, 1968.

Breeden, James O., ed. *Advice Among Masters: The Ideal in Slave Management in the Old South*. Westport, Conn.: Greenwood Press, 1980.

Catterall, Helen Tunnicliff, ed. *Judicial Cases Concerning American Slavery and the Negro*. Vol. 2. Washington, D.C.: Carnegie Institute of Washington, 1929.

De Bow, J. D. B. *The Statistical View of the United States: Compendium of the Seventh Census*. Washington, D.C.: Beverly Tucker, 1854.

Easterby, J. H., ed. *The South Carolina Rice Plantation as Revealed in the Papers of Robert F. W. Allston*. Chicago: University of Chicago Press, 1945.

Kemble, Frances Anne. *Journal of a Residence on a Georgian Plantation in 1838–1839*. 1863. Reprint. Athens: University of Georgia Press, 1984.

Kennedy, Joseph C. G. *Population of the United States, Compiled from the Original Return of the Eighth Census*. Washington, D.C.: U.S. Government Printing Office, 1864.

McKitrick, Eric L., ed. *Slavery Defended: The Views of the Old South*. Englewood Cliffs, N.J.: Prentice-Hall, 1963.

Moore, John Hammond, ed. *A Plantation Mistress on the Eve of the Civil War: The Diary of Keziah Goodwyn Hopkins Brevard, 1860–1861*. Columbia: University of South Carolina Press, 1993.

Olmsted, Frederick Law. *The Cotton Kingdom: A Traveller's Observations on Cotton and Slavery in the American Slave States*. 1861. Reprint. New York: Modern Library, 1984.

Pearson, Elizabeth Ware, ed. *Letters from Port Royal: Written at the Time of the Civil War*. Boston: W. B. Clarke, 1906.

Rawick, George P., ed. *The American Slave: A Composite Autobiography*. 19 vols. Westport, Conn.: Greenwood Press, 1972.

———. *The American Slave: A Composite Autobiography*. Supplement. Ser. 1, 12 vols. Westport, Conn.: Greenwood Press, 1977.

Secondary Sources

BOOKS

Abbot, Martin. *The Freedmen's Bureau in South Carolina, 1865–1875*. Chapel Hill: University of North Carolina Press, 1967.

Abrahams, Roger D. *Singing the Master: The Emergence of African American Culture in the Plantation South.* New York: Pantheon Books, 1992.

Albanase, Anthony G. *The Plantation as a School.* New York: Vantage Press, 1976.

Ayers, Edward L. *Vengeance and Justice: Crime and Punishment in the Nineteenth-Century American South.* New York: Oxford University Press, 1984.

Bancroft, Frederic. *Slave Trading in the Old South.* Baltimore: J. H. Furst, 1931.

Barnwell, John G. *"Love of Order": The Origins and Resolution of South Carolina's First Secession.* Chapel Hill: University of North Carolina Press, 1979.

Berlin, Ira. *Slaves Without Masters: The Free Negro in the Antebellum South.* New York: Vintage Books, 1976.

Berlin, Ira, and Ronald Hoffman, eds. *Slavery and Freedom in the Age of the Revolution.* Charlottesville: University Press of Virginia, 1985.

Berlin, Ira, and Philip D. Morgan, eds. *Cultivation and Culture: Labor and the Shaping of Slave Life in the Americas.* Charlottesville: University Press of Virginia, 1993.

————. *The Slaves' Economy: Independent Production by Slaves in the Americas.* London: Frank Cass, 1991.

Blassingame, John W. *The Slave Community: Plantation Life in the Antebellum South.* Oxford: Oxford University Press, 1979.

Blum, William G. *Forms of Marriage: Monogamy Reconsidered.* Elaovet, Kenya: AMECEA Publications, 1989.

Boles, John B. *Black Southerners, 1619–1869.* Lexington: University Press of Kentucky, 1983.

Brathwaite, Edward. *Folk Culture of the Slaves in Jamaica.* London: New Beacon Books, 1970.

Christensen, A. M. *Afro-American Folk-Lore Told Round Cabin Fires on the Sea Islands of South Carolina.* Boston: J. G. Cupples, 1892.

Clinton, Catherine. *The Plantation Mistress: Woman's World in the Old South.* New York: Pantheon Books, 1982.

Collins, Bruce. *White Society in the Antebellum South.* New York: Longman, 1985.

Creel, Margaret Washington. *"A Peculiar People": Slave Religion and Community Among the Gullahs.* New York: New York University Press, 1988.

Crum, Mason. *Gullah: Negro Life in the Carolina Sea Islands.* Durham: Duke University Press, 1940.

David, Charles T., and Henry Louis Gates Jr., eds. *The Slave's Narrative.* New York: Oxford University Press, 1985.

Davis, Paul A., Herbert G. Gutman, Richard Sutch, Peter Temin, and Gavin Wright. *Reckoning with Slavery: A Critical Study in the Quantitative History of American Negro Slavery.* New York: Oxford University Press, 1976.

Dew, Charles B. *Bond of Iron: Master and Slave at Buffalo Forge*. New York: Norton, 1994.

Du Bois, W. E. B. *The Negro American Family*. 1908. Reprint. New York: Negro Universities Press, 1969.

Dusinberre, William. *"Them Dark Days": Slavery in the American Rice Swamps*. New York: Oxford University Press, 1995.

Edwards, Bryan. *The History, Civil and Commercial, of the British West Indies*. 5 vols. 1819. Reprint. London: AMS Press, 1966.

Elkins, Stanley M. *Slavery: A Problem in American Institutional and Intellectual Life*. Chicago: University of Chicago Press, 1959.

Escott, Paul D. *Slavery Remembered: A Record of Twentieth-Century Slave Narratives*. Chapel Hill: University of North Carolina Press, 1979.

Faust, Drew Gilpin. *James Henry Hammond and the Old South: A Design for Mastery*. Baton Rouge: Louisiana State University Press, 1982.

Field, Margaret J. *Religion and Medicine of the Ga People*. London: Oxford University Press, 1937.

Fogel, Robert William. *Without Consent or Contract: The Rise and Fall of American Slavery*. New York: Norton, 1989.

Fogel, Robert William, and Stanley L. Engerman. *Time on the Cross: The Economics of American Negro Slavery*. Boston: Little, Brown, 1974.

Ford, Lacey K. *Origins of Southern Radicalism: The South Carolina Upcountry, 1800–1860*. New York: Oxford University Press, 1988.

Fox-Genovese, Elizabeth. *Within the Plantation Household: Black and White Women in the South*. Chapel Hill: University of North Carolina Press, 1988.

Fox-Genovese, Elizabeth, and Eugene Genovese. *Fruits of Merchant Capital: Slavery and Bourgeois Property in the Rise and the Expansion of Capitalism*. New York: Oxford University Press, 1983.

Franklin, John Hope. *The Free Negro in North Carolina, 1790–1860*. Chapel Hill: University of North Carolina Press, 1943.

Fraser, Walter J. Jr., R. Frank Saunders Jr., and Jon L. Wakelyn, eds. *The Web of Southern Social Relations: Women, Family, and Education*. Athens: University of Georgia Press, 1985.

Frazier, E. Franklin. *The Negro Family in the United States*. 1939. Reprint. Chicago: University of Chicago Press, 1966.

Freehling, William W. *Prelude to Civil War: The Nullification Crisis in South Carolina, 1816–1836*. New York: Harper & Row, 1965.

Genovese, Eugene. *From Rebellion to Revolution: Afro-American Slave Revolts in the Making of the New World*. New York: Vintage Books, 1981.

————. *The Political Economy of Slavery: Studies in the Economy and Society of the Slave South*. New York: Vintage Books, 1967.

————. *Roll, Jordan, Roll: The World the Slaves Made*. New York: Pantheon Books, 1974.

————. *The World the Slaveholders Made: Two Essays in Interpretation*. New York: Pantheon Books, 1969.

Goldin, Claudia Dale. *Urban Slavery in the American South, 1820–1860: A Quantitative History*. Chicago: University of Chicago Press, 1976.

Gray, Lewis Cecil. *History of Agriculture in the Southern United States to 1860*, Vol. 1. Washington, D.C.: Carnegie Institution, 1933.

Gutman, Herbert G. *The Black Family in Slavery and Freedom, 1750–1925*. New York: Pantheon Books, 1976.

————. *Slavery and the Numbers Game: A Critique of "Time on the Cross."* Urbana: University of Illinois Press, 1975.

Hahn, Steven. *The Roots of Southern Populism: Yeoman Farmers and the Transformation of the Georgia Upcountry, 1850–1890*. New York: Oxford University Press, 1983.

Harris, J. William. *Plain Folk and Gentry in a Slave Society: White Liberty and Black Slavery in Augusta's Hinterland*. Middletown, Conn.: Wesleyan University Press, 1985.

Henry, H. M. *The Police Control of the Slave in South Carolina*. 1914. Reprint. New York: Negro Universities Press, 1968.

Herd, E. Don Jr. *The South Carolina UpCountry, 1540–1980: Historical and Biographical Sketches*. Vol. 2. Greenwood, S.C.: Attic Press, 1982.

Herskovits, M. J. *The Myth of the Negro Past*. New York: Harper & Brothers, 1941.

Hopson, Darlene Powell, and Dereck S. Hopson. *Different and Wonderful: Raising Black Children in a Race-Conscious Society*. New York: Prentice-Hall, 1990.

Hudson, Larry E. Jr., ed. *Working Toward Freedom: Slave Society and Domestic Economy in the American South*. Rochester: University of Rochester Press, 1994.

Hurd, Geoffrey. *Human Societies: An Introduction to Sociology*. London: Routledge & Kegan Paul, 1977.

Johnson, Guy B. *Folk Culture on St. Helena Island, South Carolina*. Chapel Hill: University of North Carolina Press, 1930.

Jones, Jacqueline. *Labor of Love, Labor of Sorrow: Black Women, Work and the Family from Slavery to the Present*. New York: Basic Books, 1985.

Jones, Norrece T. Jr. *Born a Child of Freedom Yet a Slave: Mechanisms of Control and Strategies of Resistance in Antebellum South Carolina*. Hanover: Wesleyan University Press, 1990.

Joyner, Charles. *Down by the Riverside: A South Carolina Slave Community*. Urbana: University of Illinois Press, 1984.

Bibliography

Karasch, Mary C. *Slave Life in Rio de Janeiro, 1808–1850*. Princeton: Princeton University Press, 1987.

Kiple, Kenneth F., and Virginia Himmelsteib King. *Another Dimension to the Black Diaspora: Diet, Disease, and Racism*. Cambridge: Cambridge University Press, 1981.

Kolchin, Peter. *Unfree Labor: American Slaves and Russian Serfs*. Cambridge, Mass.: Belknap Press of Harvard University Press, 1987.

Kulikoff, Allan. *Tobacco and Slaves: The Development of Southern Cultures in the Chesapeake, 1680–1800*. Chapel Hill: University of North Carolina Press, 1986.

Levine, Lawrence W. *Black Culture and Black Consciousness: Afro-American Folk Thought from Slavery to Freedom*. Oxford: Oxford University Press, 1977.

Lewis, M. G. *Journal of a West Indian Proprietor, 1815–17*. 1845. Reprint. New York: Houghton Mifflin, 1929.

Littlefield, Daniel C. *Rice and Slaves: Ethnicity and the Slave Trade in Colonial South Carolina*. Baton Rouge: Louisiana State University Press, 1981.

Loveland, Anne. *Southern Evangelicals and the Social Order, 1800–1860*. Baton Rouge: Louisiana State University Press, 1980.

Malone, Ann Patton. *Sweet Chariot: Slave Family and Household Structure in Nineteenth-Century Louisiana*. Chapel Hill: University of North Carolina, 1992.

Martin, Elmer, and Joanne Martin. *The Black Extended Family*. Chicago: University of Chicago Press, 1978.

Matthews, Donald G. *Slave Religion in the Old South*. Chicago: University of Chicago Press, 1977.

Mbiti, John S. *African Religion and Philosophy*. New York: Doubleday, 1970.

McDonald, Roderick A. *The Economy and Material Culture of Slaves: Goods and Chattels on the Sugar Plantations of Jamaica and Louisiana*. Baton Rouge: Louisiana State University Press, 1993.

McMillen, Sally. *Motherhood in the Old South: Pregnancy, Childbirth, and Infant Rearing*. Baton Rouge: Louisiana State University Press, 1990.

Miers, Suzanne, and Igor Kopytoff, eds. *Slavery in Africa: Historical and Anthropological Perspectives*. Madison: University of Wisconsin Press, 1977.

Mintz, Sidney W. *Caribbean Transformations*. Chicago: Aldine, 1974.

Moody, V. Alton. *Slavery on Louisiana Sugar Plantations*. 1928. Reprint. New York: AMS Press, 1976.

Mullin, Michael. *Africa in America: Slave Acculturation in the American South and the British Caribbean, 1736–1831*. Urbana: University of Illinois Press, 1993.

Oakes, James. *The Ruling Race: An Interpretation of the Old South*. New York: Knopf, 1982.

Owens, Leslie Howard. *This Species of Property: Slave Life and Culture in the Old South*. New York: Oxford University Press, 1978.

Parsons, Elsie Clews. *Folk-Lore of the Sea Islands of South Carolina*. Cambridge, Mass.: American Folk-Lore Society, 1923.

Patterson, Orlando. *The Sociology of Slavery: An Analysis of the Origins, Development and Structure of Negro Slave Society in Jamaica*. London: McGibbon & Kee, 1967.

Phillips, Ulrich B. *American Negro Slavery: A Survey of the Supply, Employment and Control of Negro Labor as Determined by the Plantation Regime*. New York: D. Appleton-Century, 1918.

———. *Life and Labor in the Old South*. Boston: Little, Brown, 1929.

Pope, Thomas. *The History of Newberry County, South Carolina*. Vol. 1: 1749–1860. Columbia: University of South Carolina Press, 1973.

Postell, William D. *The Health of Slaves on Southern Plantations*. Baton Rouge: Louisiana State University Press, 1951.

Raboteau, Albert J. *Slave Religion: The "Invisible Institution" in the Antebellum South*. New York: Oxford University Press, 1978.

Reidy, Joseph P. *From Slavery to Agrarian Capitalism in the Cotton Plantation South: Central Georgia, 1800–1880*. Chapel Hill: University of North Carolina Press, 1992.

Roark, James L. *Masters Without Slaves: Southern Planters in the Civil War and Reconstruction*. New York: Norton, 1977.

Rogers, George C. *The History of Georgetown County, South Carolina*. Columbia: University of South Carolina Press, 1970.

Rose, Willie Lee. *Rehearsal for Reconstruction: The Port Royal Experiment*. New York: Vintage Books, 1964.

Rosengarten, Theodore. *All God's Children: The Life of Nate Shaw*. London: Jonathan Cape, 1975.

———. *Tombee: Portrait of a Cotton Planter*. New York: William Morrow, 1986.

Saville, Julie. *The Work of Reconstruction: From Slave to Wage Laborer in South Carolina, 1860–1870*. Cambridge: Cambridge University Press, 1994.

Savitt, Todd. *Medicine and Slavery: The Diseases and Health Care of Blacks in Antebellum Virginia*. Urbana: University of Illinois Press, 1978.

Scott, Anne Firor. *The Southern Lady: From Pedestal to Politics, 1830–1930*. Chicago: University of Chicago Press, 1970.

Shorter, Edward. *The Making of the Modern Family*. London: Collins, 1970.

Smith, Alfred G. *Economic Readjustment of an Old Cotton State: South Carolina, 1820–1860*. Columbia: University of South Carolina Press, 1958.

Smith, Julia Floyd. *Slavery and Rice Culture in Low Country Georgia, 1750–1860*. Knoxville: University of Tennessee Press, 1985.

Sobel, Mechal. *Trabelin' On: The Slave Journey to an Afro-Baptist Faith*. Westport, Conn.: Greenwood Press, 1979.

———. *The World They Made Together: Black and White Values in Eighteenth-Century Virginia*. Princeton: Princeton University Press, 1987.

Stampp, Kenneth M. *The Peculiar Institution: Slavery in the Antebellum South*. New York: Vintage Books, 1956.

Staples, Robert. *The Black Family: Essays and Studies*. Belmont, Calif.: Wadsworth, 1978.

Stuckey, Sterling. *Slave Culture: Nationalist Theory and the Foundations of Black America*. New York: Oxford University Press, 1987.

Tadman, Michael. *Speculators and Slaves: Masters, Traders, and Slaves in the Old South*. Madison: University of Wisconsin Press, 1989.

Taylor, Rosser H. *Antebellum South Carolina: A Social and Cultural History*. Chapel Hill: University of North Carolina Press, 1942.

Tushnet, Mark. *The American Law of Slavery, 1810–1860*. Princeton: Princeton University Press, 1981.

Van Deburg, William L. *The Slavedrivers: Black Agricultural Labor Supervisors in the Antebellum South*. Westport, Conn.: Greenwood Press, 1979.

Vandiver, Louise Ayer. *Traditions and History of Anderson County*. Atlanta: Ruralist Press, 1928.

Wallace, David Duncan. *South Carolina: A Short History*. Chapel Hill: University of North Carolina Press, 1951.

Webber, Thomas. *Deep Like the Rivers: Education in the Slave Quarter Community, 1831–1865*. New York: Norton, 1978.

White, Deborah Gray. *"Ar'n't I a Woman?": Female Slaves in the Plantation South*. New York: Norton, 1985.

Willie, Charles V. *A New Look at Black Families*. Bayside, N.Y.: General Hall, 1981.

Wood, Betty. *Women's Work, Men's Work: The Informal Slave Economies of Lowcountry Georgia*. Athens: University of Georgia Press, 1995.

Wood, Peter H. *Black Majority: Negroes in Colonial South Carolina from 1640 Through to the Stono Rebellion*. New York: Norton, 1974.

ARTICLES

Arney, William Ray. "Maternal-Infant Bonding: The Politics of Falling in Love with Your Child." *Feminist Studies* 6 (1980): 547–70.

Bailey, Kenneth K. "Protestantism and Afro-Americans in the South: Another Look." *Journal of Southern History* 41 (1975): 451–72.

Bauman, Herman. "The Division of Work According to Sex in African Hoe

Culture." *Journal of the International Institute of African Languages and Culture* 1 (July 1928): 289–319.

Blassingame, John W. "Status and Social Structure in the Slave Community: Evidence from New Sources." In *Perspectives and Irony in American Slavery*, edited by Harry P. Owens, 137–51. Jackson: University Press of Mississippi, 1976.

———. "Using the Testimony of Ex-Slaves: Approaches and Problems." In *The Slave Narratives*, edited by Charles T. Davis and Henry Louis Gates Jr., 78–98. New York: Oxford University Press, 1985.

Campbell, John. "As 'A Kind of Freeman'?: Slaves' Market-Related Activities in the South Carolina Upcountry, 1800–1860." In *The Slaves' Economy: Independent Production by Slaves in the Americas*, edited by Ira Berlin and Philip D. Morgan, 131–69. London: Frank Cass, 1991.

———. "Work, Pregnancy, and Infant Mortality Among Southern Slaves." *Journal of Interdisciplinary History* 14 (1984): 153–67.

Cassity, Michael J. "Slaves, Families and 'Living Space': A Note on Evidence and Historical Context." *Southern Studies* 17, pt. 2 (1978): 209–15.

Clifton, James M. "The Antebellum Rice Planter as Revealed in the Letterbook of Charles Manigault, 1846–1848." *Southern Historical Magazine* 74 (1973): 119–27.

———. "The Rice Driver: His Role in Slave Management." *South Carolina Historical Magazine* 82 (1981): 331–53.

Cody, Cheryll Ann. "Naming, Kinship and Estate Dispersal: Notes on Slave Family Life on a South Carolina Plantation, 1786–1833." *William and Mary Quarterly* 39 (1982): 192–211.

———. "Sale and Separation: Four Crises for Enslaved Women on the Ball Family Plantations, 1764–1865." In *Working Toward Freedom: Slave Society and Domestic Economy in the American South*, edited by Larry E. Hudson Jr., 119–42. Rochester: University of Rochester Press, 1994.

Craton, Michael. "Changing Patterns of Slave Families in the British West Indies." *Journal of Interdisciplinary History* 1 (1979): 1–36.

Deas-Moore, Vennie. "Medical Adaptions of a Culture Relocated from Africa to the Sea Islands of South Carolina." *The World & I* 2 (1987): 474–85.

Durden, Robert F. "The Establishment of Calvary Protestant Episcopal Church for Negroes in Charleston." *South Carolina Historical Magazine* 65 (1964): 63–84.

Escott, Paul D. "The Art and Science of Reading WPA Slave Narratives." In *The Slave Narratives*, edited by Charles T. Davis and Henry Louis Gates Jr., 40–48. New York: Oxford University Press, 1985.

Frazier, E. Franklin. "The Negro Slave Family." *Journal of Negro History* 15 (1930): 198–259.

Faust, Drew Gilpin. "Culture, Conflict, and Community: The Meaning of Power on an Antebellum Plantation." *Journal of Social History* 14 (1980): 83–97.

Ford, Lacey K. "Self-Sufficiency, Cotton and Economic Development in the South Carolina Up Country, 1800–1860." *Journal of Economic History* 45 (1985): 261–67.

Green, Mary Fulton. "A Profile of Columbia in 1850." *South Carolina Historical Magazine* 70 (1969): 104–21.

Greenberg, Kenneth S. "Representation and the Isolation of South Carolina, 1776–1860." *Journal of American History* 64 (1977): 727–43.

Griffin, Jean Thomas. "West African and Black American Women: Historical Comparisons." *Journal of Black Psychology* 8 (1982): 55–73.

Grinde, Donald A. Jr. "Building the South Carolina Railroad." *South Carolina Historical Magazine* 77 (1976): 84–96.

Gutman, Herbert G. "Persistent Myths About the Afro-American Family." *Journal of Interdisciplinary History* 6 (1975): 181–210.

Hackney, Sheldon. "Southern Violence." *American Historical Review* 74 (1969): 907–25.

Higman, Barry. "The Slave Family and Household in the British West Indies, 1800–1834." *Journal of Interdisciplinary History* 6 (1975): 261–87.

Hindus, Michael S. "Black Justice Under White Law: Criminal Persecutions of Blacks in Antebellum South Carolina." *Journal of American History* 63 (1976): 579–99.

Holt, Sharon Ann. "Symbol, Memory, and Service: Resistance and Family Formation in Nineteenth-Century African America." In *Working Toward Freedom: Slave Society and Domestic Economy in the American South*, edited by Larry E. Hudson Jr., 192–210. Rochester: University of Rochester Press, 1994.

Hudson, Larry E. "'All That Cash': Work and Status in the Slave Quarters." In *Working Toward Freedom: Slave Society and Domestic Economy in the American South*, edited by Larry E. Hudson Jr., 77–94. Rochester: University of Rochester Press, 1994.

Irwin, James R. "Exploring the Affinity of Wheat and Slavery in the Virginia Piedmont." *Explorations in Economic History* 25 (1988): 295–322.

Jackson, Luther P. "Religious Instructions of Negroes, 1830 to 1860, with Special Reference to South Carolina." *Journal of Negro History* 15 (1930): 72–114.

January, Alan F. "The South Carolina Association: An Agency for Race Control in Antebellum Charleston." *South Carolina Historical Magazine* 78 (1977): 191–201.

Johnson, Michael P. "Runaway Slaves and Slave Communities in South Carolina, 1799–1830." *William and Mary Quarterly* 38 (1981): 418–41.

King, G. Wayne. "The Emergence of Florence County, South Carolina, 1853–1890." *South Carolina Historical Magazine* 82 (1981): 197–209.

King, James R. "African Survivals in the Black American Family." *Journal of Afro-American Issues* 4 (Spring 1976): 153–67.

Kiple, Kenneth F., and Virginia H. Kiple. "Slave Child Mortality: Some Nutritional Answers to a Perennial Puzzle." *Journal of Social History* 10 (1977): 284–309.

Kolchin, Peter. "Re-Evaluating the Antebellum Slave Community: A Comparative Perspective." *Journal of American History* 70 (1983): 579–601.

Labinjoh, Justin. "The Sexual Life of the Oppressed: An Examination of the Family Life of Antebellum Slaves." *Phylon* 35 (1974): 375–97.

Lantz, Herman R. "Family and Kin as Revealed in the Narratives of Ex-Slaves." *Social Science Quarterly* 60 (1980): 667–75.

Lees, William B. "The Historical Development of Limerick Plantation: A Tidewater Rice Plantation in Berkeley County, South Carolina, 1683–1945." *South Carolina Historical Magazine* 82 (1981): 44–62.

Linder, Suzanne C. "Pioneer Physicians in Marlboro County, 1760–1824." *South Carolina Historical Magazine* 81 (1980): 232–44.

MacDonald, J. S., and L. MacDonald. "The Black Family in the Americas: A Review of the Literature." *Sage Race Relations Abstracts* 3 (February 1978): 1–42.

McDonald, Roderick A. "Independent Economic Production by Slaves on Antebellum Louisiana Sugar Plantations." In *The Slaves' Economy: Independent Production by Slaves in the Americas*, edited by Ira Berlin and Philip D. Morgan, 182–208. London: Frank Cass, 1991.

McDonnell, Lawrence T. "Money Knows No Master: Market Relations and the American Slave Community." In *Developing Dixie: Modernization in a Traditional Society*, edited by Winfred B. Moore Jr., Joseph F. Tripp, and Lyon G. Tyler Jr., 31–44. Westport, Conn: Greenwood Press, 1988.

Menard, Russell R. "The Maryland Slave Population, 1658 to 1730: A Demographic Profile of Blacks in Four Counties." *William and Mary Quarterly* 32 (1975): 29–54.

Mercer, P. M. "Tapping the Slave Narrative Collection for the Responses of Black South Carolinians to Emancipation and Reconstruction." *Australian Journal of Politics and History* 25 (1979): 358–74.

Moody-Adams, Michelle. "Race, Class and the Social Construction of Self-Respect." *Philosophical Forum* 24 (Winter 1992): 251–66.

Moore, John Hammond. "Getting Uncle Sam's Dollars: South Carolinians and the Southern Claims Commission, 1871–1880." *South Carolina Historical Magazine* 82 (1981): 248–62.

Morgan, Philip D. "Black Society in the Lowcountry, 1760–1810." In *Slavery and Freedom in the Age of the Revolution*, edited by Ira Berlin and Ronald Hoffman, 83–141. Charlottesville: University Press of Virginia, 1983.

———. "The Ownership of Property by Slaves in the Mid-Nineteenth Century Low Country." *Journal of Southern History* 49 (1983): 399–420.

———. "Work and Culture: The Task System and the World of Low Country Blacks, 1700 to 1860." *William and Mary Quarterly* 39 (1982): 563–99.

Morris-Crowther, Jayne. "An Economic Study of the Substantial Slaveholders of Orangeburg County, 1860–1880." *South Carolina Historical Magazine* 86 (1985): 296–314.

Moynihan, Daniel P. "The Negro Family: A Case for National Action." In *The Moynihan Report and the Politics of Controversy*, edited by Lee Rainwater and William L. Yancey, 38–124. Cambridge, Mass.: MIT Press, 1967.

Olwell, Robert. "Loose, Idle and Disorderly: Slave Women in the Eighteenth-Century Charleston Marketplace." In *More than Chattel: Black Women and Slavery in the Americas*, edited by David Barry Gaspar and Darlene Clark Hine. Bloomington: Indiana University Press, 1996.

Racine, Philip N. "The Spartanburg District Magistrates and Freeholders Court, 1824–1865." *South Carolina Historical Magazine* 87 (1986): 197–212.

Richards, Sherman R., and George M. Blackburn. "A Demographic History of Slavery: Georgetown County, South Carolina, 1850." *South Carolina Historical Magazine* 75 (1974): 215–24.

Schweninger, Loren. "Slave Independence and Enterprise in South Carolina, 1780–1865." *South Carolina Historical Magazine* 93 (1992): 101–25.

Senese, Donald J. "The Free Negro and the South Carolina Courts, 1790–1860." *South Carolina Historical Magazine* 68 (1967): 140–53.

Shlomowitz, Ralph. "The Origins of Southern Sharecropping." *Agricultural History* 55 (1979): 557–75.

Starobin, Robert S. "Privileged Bondsmen and the Process of Accommodation: The Role of House Servants and Drivers as Seen in Their Own Letters." *Journal of Social History* 15 (1971): 46–70.

Steckel, Richard H. "The Fertility of American Slaves." *Research in Economic History* 7 (1982): 239–86.

———. "A Peculiar Population: The Nutrition, Health and Mortality of American Slaves from Childhood to Maturity." *Journal of Economic History* 46 (1986): 721–41.

———. "Slave Mortality: Analysis and Evidence from Plantation Records." *Social Science History* 3 (1979): 86–114.

Sutch, Richard. "The Treatment Received by American Slaves: A Critical Review of the Evidence Presented in *Time on the Cross.*" *Explorations in Economic History* 12 (1975): 335–438.

Wetherell, Charles. "Slave Kinship: A Case Study of the South Carolina Good Hope Plantation, 1835–1856." *Journal of Family History* 16 (1981): 294–308.

Whitten, David O. "Medical Care of Slaves: Louisiana Sugar Region and South Carolina Rice District." *Southern Studies* 16 (1977): 153–80.

Wiggins, David K. "The Play of Slave Children in the Plantation Communities of the Old South, 1820–1860." *Journal of Sport History* 7 (1980): 21–39.

Young, Virginia Heyer. "Family and Childhood in a Southern Negro Community." *American Anthropologist* 72 (1970): 269–88.

Unpublished Papers, Theses, and Dissertations

Cody, Cheryll Ann. "Slave Demography and Family Formation: A Community Study of the Ball Plantations, 1720–1896." Ph.D. diss., University of Minnesota, 1982.

Dean, Deola F. "The Antebellum Slave Woman, 1830–1865: A General Survey." Ph.D. diss., Atlanta University, 1975.

Dunn, Richard S. "The Black Family Under Slavery." Paper presented at the colloquium Minorities in American History, Institute of United States Studies, London, May 4, 1988.

Fieldstein, Stanley. "The Slave's View of Slavery." Ph.D. diss., New York University, 1969.

Henderson, William C. "Spartan Slaves: A Documentary Account of Blacks on Trial in Spartanburg, South Carolina." Ph.D. diss., Northwestern University, 1978.

Hindus, Michael Stephen. "Prison and Plantation: Criminal Justice in Nineteenth-Century Massachusetts and South Carolina." Ph.D. diss., University of California, Berkeley, 1975.

Jones, Bobby Frank. "A Cultural Middle Passage: Slave Marriage and Family in the Antebellum South." Ph.D. diss., University of North Carolina, Chapel Hill, 1965.

Mendenhall, Marjorie Stratfford. "A History of Agriculture in South Carolina, 1790–1860: An Economic History." Ph.D. diss., University of North Carolina, Chapel Hill, 1940.

Merritt, Carole Elaine. "Slave Family and Household Arrangement in Piedmont Georgia." Ph.D. diss., Emory University, 1986.

Morgan, Philip D. "The Development of Slave Culture in the Eighteenth Century Plantation America." Ph.D. diss., University College, London, 1977.

Smith, Caroline Amanda. "An Analysis of Direct and Violent Methods of Control of Plantation Field Slaves in the Antebellum South." M.A. thesis, University of Warwick, 1980.

Toliver, Susan Diane. "The Black Family in Slavery, the Foundation of Afro-American Culture: Its Importance to Members of the Slave Community." Ph.D. diss., University of California, Berkeley, 1982.

Index

Adams, Victoria, 8, 109
Adamson, Frank, 154
African traditions: in family forms, 61,
 187 (n. 3); in marriage, 217 (n. 9); in
 medicine, 108; in notions of "free-
 dom," 197 (n. 35); in religion, 213
 (n. 31)
Alexander, Bob, 134, 143
Alexander, Nat, 111, 134, 143
Allman, Jacob, 27
Alston, J. P., 143, 181
Andrew (Duckworth), 177–79
Ashmore, J. D., 139

Bailey, Osland, 120
Ball, Charles, 34, 37, 40, 52, 55
Ball slaves, 79
Ballard, William, 130
Barber, Millie, 109, 110, 130, 161, 174
Barrel making, 104
Bass, Emily, 33
Bass, William, 28
Black, Martha, 109
Black, Samuel, 109
Bluford, Gordon, 132
Bostick, Oliver P., 11, 21
Bothume, Elizabeth, 86
Boulware, Samuel, 170
Breeden, James O., 135
Brevard, Keziah Goodwyn Hopkins,
 59–61, 139
Brevard slaves: Dick, 59, 60, 61; Frank,

61, 139; Harry, 60; Jim, 60; John, 61,
 139; Ned, 59, 60
Briggs, George, 114
Broad wives, 142, 144, 149, 160, 213
 (n. 41)
Brockington, Mary H., 98, 99
Brockington slaves, 99, 100, 101;
 Annemarie, 98; Anney, 99; Dianer,
 98; Eliza, 100; Elizabeth, 99;
 George, 98; Hennder, 100; Judy, 99;
 Kittey, 98; Lizer, 98, 99; Lurindar,
 99, 100; Milly, 100; Murtilla, 99;
 Nancey, 99; Old Betty, 100; Old
 Daphne, 100; Peter, 98; Rian, 99;
 Silvey, 98
Brown, Edward, 42
Brown, Henry, 12, 65, 119
Brown, Mom Sarah, 122
Bryant, Aunt Margaret, 65
Bryant, Robert, 24
Burrell, Savilla, 174
Butler, Judge Pickens, 29, 109

Cain, Granny, 112
Caldwell, Suella, 111
Candy (Oliver), 177–78
Cannon, Sylvia, 6, 30, 33, 123, 169
Chaplin, John, 12, 64
Chaplin, Thomas, 172–73
Chisholm, Sylvia, 169
Clifton, Peter, 124, 170
Clothing allowance, 118, 132

Willson plantation, 47, 55, 144, 151, 153
Willson slave quarters, 149, 150, 151
Wilson, Emoline, 113, 162
Winning, Lias, 119, 120
Winningham, William, 54, 138
Witherspoon, J. B., 75
Witherspoon slaves, 77; Anthony, 76; Dilsey, 76; George, 76; Jacob, 76; Peggy, 76; William, 76
Women: and birth control, 196 (n. 28); compromised virtue of, 212 (n. 30); earnings of, 73; incentives to have children, 59; pregnancy and additional health risks, 81; supplementary family income, 59; work and

pregnancy, 59, 71, 93–94, 95, 96. *See also* Single women
Woodberry, Genia, 13, 125
Woodberry, Celia, 80
Work: of aged slaves, 195 (n. 3); of children, 197 (n. 29); positive incentives to, 75; of pregnant women, 59, 71, 93–94, 95, 96; and productivity of female slaves, 69,
Work and garden system, xix, xxii, 11, 12, 13, 14, 15, 16, 17, 18, 32, 34, 40, 46, 59, 66, 67, 71, 73, 98, 104, 129, 143, 158, 176, 179, 180, 212 (n. 26)
Wright, Daphney, 119

Zimmerman, John, 6